First World War
and Army of Occupation
War Diary
France, Belgium and Germany

31 DIVISION
94 Infantry Brigade,
Brigade Machine Gun Company
15 May 1916 - 28 February 1918

WO95/2366/5

The Naval & Military Press Ltd
www.nmarchive.com
Published in association with The National Archives

Published by

The Naval & Military Press Ltd

Unit 10 Ridgewood Industrial Park,

Uckfield, East Sussex,

TN22 5QE England

Tel: +44 (0) 1825 749494

www.naval-military-press.com

www.nmarchive.com

This diary has been reprinted in facsimile from the original. Any imperfections are inevitably reproduced and the quality may fall short of modern type and cartographic standards.

© Crown Copyright
Images reproduced by permission of The National Archives, London, England, 2015.

Contents

Document type	Place/Title	Date From	Date To
Heading	WO95/2366-5 Brigade Machine Gun Company		
Heading	31st Division 94th Infy Bde 94th Machine Gun Coy. May 1916-Feb 1918		
War Diary		15/05/1916	30/05/1916
Miscellaneous	121/9020 (A.G.I.)	31/05/1917	31/05/1917
Heading	R War Diary of 94 M Gun Co June 1916		
War Diary		22/06/1916	30/06/1916
Miscellaneous	D.A.G. G.H.Q. 3rd Echelon	16/08/1916	16/08/1916
Miscellaneous	94 M.G.C. War Diary for June 1916	14/08/1916	14/08/1916
Miscellaneous	D.A.G. G.H.Q. 3rd Echelon	08/07/1917	08/07/1917
Heading	H. Qrs. 31st. Division.	31/07/1917	31/07/1917
Miscellaneous	94. M.G. Coy's War Diary For June 1916	05/07/1917	05/07/1917
Miscellaneous	Head-Quarters, Thirty-First Division	24/06/1917	24/06/1917
Miscellaneous	H.Q. 94 Inf. Bde.	28/06/1917	28/06/1917
Heading	94th Bde. 31st Div. War Diary 94th Brigade Machine Gun Company. 1st to 31st July 1916		
Heading	War Diary 94th Machine Gun Coy 1st July to 31st July 1916 Vol 3		
War Diary		01/07/1916	31/07/1916
Miscellaneous	From: O.C. No. 94 M.G. Coy. To: D.A.G. 3rd Echelon	01/09/1916	01/09/1916
War Diary	In the Field	01/08/1916	31/08/1916
Heading	War Diary 94 Machine Gun Coy 31st Division September 1916 Vol 5		
War Diary	In The Field	01/09/1916	30/09/1916
Heading	War Diary 94 Machine Gun Coy. 31st Division October 1916 Volume 6		
War Diary	In the Field	01/10/1916	31/10/1916
Heading	War Diary No 94 Machine Gun Coy. 31st Division November 1916 Volume 7		
War Diary	In the Field	01/11/1916	30/11/1916
Operation(al) Order(s)	94th Machine Gun Company Operation Order No. 2	03/11/1916	03/11/1916
Operation(al) Order(s)	94th Machine Gun Company Operation Order No. 3	06/11/1916	06/11/1916
Operation(al) Order(s)	94th Machine Gun Company Operation Order No. 4		
Operation(al) Order(s)	94th Machine Gun Company Operation Order No. 5	17/11/1916	17/11/1916
Operation(al) Order(s)	94th Machine Gun Company Operation Order No. 6		
Operation(al) Order(s)	94th Machine Gun Company Operation Order No. 7		
Heading	War Diary 94 Machine Gun Coy. 31st Division December 1916 Vol 8		
War Diary	In the Field	01/12/1916	31/12/1916
Miscellaneous	94th Machine Gun Company Trench Standing Orders.	11/11/1916	11/11/1916
Miscellaneous	94th Machine Gun Company additions to Trench Standing Orders	16/12/1916	16/12/1916
Operation(al) Order(s)	94th Machine Gun Company Operation Order No. 8		
Operation(al) Order(s)	94th Machine Gun Company Operation Order No. 9	02/12/1916	02/12/1916
Operation(al) Order(s)	94th Machine Gun Company Operation Order No. 10	06/12/1916	06/12/1916
Operation(al) Order(s)	94th Machine Gun Company Operation Order No. 11	10/12/1916	10/12/1916
Operation(al) Order(s)	94th Machine Gun Company Operation Order No. 12	16/12/1916	16/12/1916
Operation(al) Order(s)	94th Machine Gun Company Operation Order No. 13	22/12/1916	22/12/1916
Operation(al) Order(s)	94th Machine Gun Company Operation Order No. 14	28/12/1916	28/12/1916

Type	Description	From	To
Miscellaneous	94 Machine Gun Company Operation Order No Appendix II	29/10/1916	29/10/1916
Miscellaneous	94th Machine Gun Company alterations in Trench Standing Orders.		
Miscellaneous			
Heading	War Diary 94th Machine Gun Company From:-1st January 1917 to 31st January 1917 (Volume XIII)		
War Diary	In the Field	01/01/1917	31/01/1917
Operation(al) Order(s)	94th Machine Gun Company Operation Order No. 1 Appendix No. 1	02/01/1917	02/01/1917
Operation(al) Order(s)	94th Machine Gun Company Operation Order No. 2 Appendix No. 2		
Miscellaneous	94th Infantry Brigade Order No. 155. Appendix No. 3	28/01/1917	28/01/1917
Miscellaneous	Company Orders. By: Captain F.B. Cowan. 94th Machine Gun Company. Appendix II		
Heading	War Diary 94th Machine Gun Company From:- 1st February 1917 to 28th February 1917 Volume XIV		
War Diary	In the Field	01/02/1917	28/02/1917
Heading	War Diary 94th Machine Gun Company From 1.3.17 to 31.3.17 Volume XV		
War Diary	In the Field	01/03/1917	31/03/1917
Operation(al) Order(s)	94th Machine Gun Company Haming Order No. 3 Appendix I	15/03/1917	15/03/1917
Heading	War Diary (Original) Of 94th Machine Gun Company From:- 1st April 1917 To 30th April 1917 (Volume XVI)		
War Diary	In the Field	01/04/1917	30/04/1917
Operation(al) Order(s)	94th Machine Gun Company. Operation Order No. 8 Appendix I		
Operation(al) Order(s)	94th Machine Gun Company Operation Order No. 9 Appendix II		
Operation(al) Order(s)	94th Machine Gun Company Operation Order No. 10 Appendix III	22/04/1917	22/04/1917
Miscellaneous	G.S., 2nd Division. Appendix IV		
Operation(al) Order(s)	94th Machine Gun Company Operation Order No. 11 Appendix V	27/04/1917	27/04/1917
Operation(al) Order(s)	94th Machine Gun Company. Operation Order No. 12 Appendix VI	30/04/1917	30/04/1917
Heading	War Diary 94th Machine Gun Company 31st Division May 1917 Volume XVII		
War Diary	In the Field	01/05/1917	31/05/1917
Operation(al) Order(s)	94th Machine Gun Company-Operation Order No. 13 Appendix I	02/05/1917	02/05/1917
Operation(al) Order(s)	94th Machine Gun Company. Operation Order No. 14 Appendix II	04/05/1917	04/05/1917
Operation(al) Order(s)	94th Machine Gun Company-Operation Order No. 15 Appendix III	07/05/1917	07/05/1917
Operation(al) Order(s)	94th Machine Gun Company-Operation Order No. 16 Appendix No IV	08/05/1917	08/05/1917
Operation(al) Order(s)	94th Machine Gun Company. Operation Order No. 17 Appendix No V	09/05/1917	09/05/1917
Operation(al) Order(s)	94th Machine Gun Company. Operation Order No. 18 Appendix No VI	17/05/1917	17/05/1917
Miscellaneous	Appendix I. to Operation Order No. 18	17/05/1917	17/05/1917
Operation(al) Order(s)	94th Machine Gun Company-Operation Order No. 19 Appendix VII	20/05/1917	20/05/1917

Type	Description	Start	End
Heading	War Diary 94th Machine Gun Coy. 31st Division June 1917 Vol 14		
War Diary	In the Field	01/06/1917	30/06/1917
Heading	Appendix I to Operation Order No. 24		
Operation(al) Order(s)	94th Machine Gun Company. Operation Order No. 20 (Appendix I)	10/06/1917	10/06/1917
Miscellaneous	94th Machine Gun Company Relief Table with Operation Order No. 20	09/06/1917	09/06/1917
Operation(al) Order(s)	94th Machine Gun Company Operation Order No. 21 (Appendix II)	14/06/1917	14/06/1917
Operation(al) Order(s)	94th Machine Gun Coy Instructions Connected with Operation Order No 21		
Operation(al) Order(s)	94th Machine Gun Company-Operation Order No. 22 (Appendix III)	19/06/1917	19/06/1917
Miscellaneous	94th Machine Gun Company Relief Table in Connection with Operation Order No. 22	19/06/1917	19/06/1917
Operation(al) Order(s)	94th Machine Gun Coy. Operation Order No 23. (Appendix IV)	26/06/1917	26/06/1917
Operation(al) Order(s)	94th Machine Gun Coy. Operation Order No. 24. (Appendix V)	26/06/1917	26/06/1917
Operation(al) Order(s)	94th Machine Gun Company. Operation Order No. 25. (Appendix VI)	29/06/1917	29/06/1917
Heading	War Diary 94 Machine Gun Company 31st Division July 1917 Vol 15		
War Diary	In the Field	01/07/1917	31/07/1917
Operation(al) Order(s)	94th Machine Gun Company, Operation Order No. 26 Appendix I		
Operation(al) Order(s)	94th Machine Gun Company, Operation Order No. 27 Appendix II	12/07/1917	12/07/1917
Operation(al) Order(s)	Operation Order No. 28 Appendix III	20/07/1917	20/07/1917
Heading	War Diary 94th Machine Gun Company 31st Division August 1917 Vol 16		
War Diary	In the Field	01/08/1917	31/08/1917
Operation(al) Order(s)	94th Machine Gun Company, Operation Order No. 29 Appendix I		
Operation(al) Order(s)	94th M.G. Coy. Operation Order 30 Appendix II	08/08/1917	08/08/1917
Operation(al) Order(s)	94th M.G. Coy. Operation Order No. 31 Appendix III	13/08/1917	13/08/1917
Operation(al) Order(s)	No. 94 M.G. Coy. Operation Order No. 32 Appendix IV		
Operation(al) Order(s)	94th Machine Gun Company, Operation Order No. 33 Appendix V	28/08/1917	28/08/1917
Heading	War Diary 94th Machine Gun Company 31st Division September 1917 Vol 17		
War Diary	In the Field	01/09/1917	30/09/1917
Operation(al) Order(s)	The 94th Machine Gun Company-Operation Order No. 34. Appendix I		
Operation(al) Order(s)	The 94th Machine Gun Company. Operation Order No. 35. Appendix II		
Operation(al) Order(s)	94th M.G. Coy. Operation Order No. 36 Appendix III	09/09/1917	09/09/1917
Miscellaneous	Fire Direction Table		
Operation(al) Order(s)	94th M.G. Coy. Operation Order No. 37 Appendix IV		
Operation(al) Order(s)	94th Machine Gun Company, Operation Order No. 38 Appendix IV		
Heading	War Diary 94 Machine Gun Coy. 31st Division October 1917 Vol 18		
War Diary	In the Field	01/10/1917	31/10/1917

Type	Description	Start	End
Operation(al) Order(s)	94th M.G. Coy Operation Order No. 39 Appendix I	02/10/1917	02/10/1917
Operation(al) Order(s)	94 M.G. Coy Operation Order No.	03/10/1917	03/10/1917
Operation(al) Order(s)	94th M.G. Coy Operation Order No. 40 Appendix II	07/10/1917	07/10/1917
Operation(al) Order(s)	94th Machine Gun Company. Operation Order No. 41 Appendix III		
Heading	War Diary 94th Machine Gun Company. 31st Division November 1917 Vol 19		
War Diary	In the Field	01/11/1917	30/11/1917
Operation(al) Order(s)	94th Machine Gun Company Operation Order No. 42 Appendix I		
Operation(al) Order(s)	Operation Order No. 43 94th Machine Gun Company. Appendix II	05/11/1917	05/11/1917
Operation(al) Order(s)	94th Machine Gun Company. Operation Order No. 44 Appendix III	13/11/1917	13/11/1917
Heading	War Diary Of 94th Machine Gun Coy. From 1st Dec 1917 To 31st Dec 1917 Vol 20		
War Diary	In the Field Oppy Sector	01/12/1917	04/12/1917
War Diary	In the Field	05/12/1917	07/12/1917
War Diary	Mount St. Eloi	07/12/1917	10/12/1917
War Diary	In the Field	11/12/1917	14/12/1917
War Diary	St, Catherine Area	14/12/1917	16/12/1917
War Diary	In the Field	17/12/1917	18/12/1917
War Diary	Acheville Sector	18/12/1917	22/12/1917
War Diary	In the Field	22/12/1917	29/12/1917
War Diary	Qcurie Area	30/12/1917	31/12/1917
Operation(al) Order(s)	Operation Order No. 45 94th Machine Gun Company (Orders by Capt. R.L. Bailey M.C.) Appendix I	13/12/1917	13/12/1917
Operation(al) Order(s)	94th Machine Gun Company. Operation Order No. 46 Appendix II		
Operation(al) Order(s)	94th Machine Gun Company. Operation Order No. 47 Appendix III	28/12/1917	28/12/1917
Heading	War Diary Of 94th Machine Gun Company From 1st Jan 1918 To 31st Jan 1918 Volume XXV		
War Diary	In the Field	01/01/1918	31/01/1918
Operation(al) Order(s)	94th Machine Gun Company. Operation Order No. 48 Appendix I		
Operation(al) Order(s)	94th Machine Gun Company. Operation Order No. 49 Appendix II		
Operation(al) Order(s)	94th Machine Gun Company. Operation Order No. 50 Appendix III		
Heading	War Diary (Original) Of 94th Machine Gun Company From 1st February 1918 To 28th February 1918 Volume 26		
War Diary	In the Field	01/02/1918	28/02/1918
Operation(al) Order(s)	Operation Orders by Lieut J.S. Wilson M.C. Commanding 94th M.G. Coy. Operation Order No. 51 Appen I		
Operation(al) Order(s)	Operation Order No. 52		
Operation(al) Order(s)	94th Machine Gun Company Operation Order No. 53		
Miscellaneous	Movement Order By:- Lieut. J.S. Wilson M.C. Commanding 94th M.G. Coy.	28/02/1918	28/02/1918

WO/95/2366/5

94 Brigade Machine Gun Company.

31ST DIVISION
94TH INFY BDE

94TH MACHINE GUN COY.
MAY 1916 - FEB 1918

Army Form C. 2118.

Vol 1

9th Machine Gun Coy.

WAR DIARY
or
INTELLIGENCE SUMMARY XXXI

(Erase heading not required.)

Instructions regarding War Diaries and Intelligence Summaries are contained in F. S. Regs., Part II. and the Staff Manual respectively. Title Pages will be prepared in manuscript.

Place	Date	Hour	Summary of Events and Information	Remarks and references to Appendices
	15.5.16		Left GRANTHAM en-route for B.E.F. France.	May 16 / Feb. 8
	17.5.16		Arrived at HAVRE.	
	21.5.16		" COURCELLES. Friday. (Sunday.)	
			MONDAY. 22.5.16.	
			No I. Section under Lieut Williams & Saunders proceeded to the trenches & took over PARADISE, CHICHESTER, MONT, & TROSSACHS. M. G. Emplacements.	
			TUESDAY. 23.5.16.	
			Report from Lieut Williams that we had opened fire on an enemy working party with considerable effect. A few shells came near CHICHESTER but no damage was done. The remainder of the Company were exercised in Physical Drill & Gun Drill during the day.	

Army Form C. 2118.

WAR DIARY
or
INTELLIGENCE SUMMARY
(Erase heading not required.)

9th Larkins Gun Coy.

WEDNESDAY 24.5.16.

I visited the trenches, noting the Emplacement, & then visited the front line trench, but could find no place for Emplacement along the whole front. Everything was quiet during day & night.

THURSDAY. 25.5.16.

During night 24-25 everything very quiet, but Lt Williams harassed about 200ft of the Enemy line, resulting in retaliation by the Bosch, who developed his Emplacement but did no water damage. (TROSSACHS.)

Lieut Saunders report that he observed a number of German parties on left front, but having no track but could not give any definite information.

Night of 25-26 passed off very quietly.

Army Form C. 2118.

WAR DIARY
or
INTELLIGENCE SUMMARY

(Erase heading not required.)

9th Machine Gun Coy.

Place	Date	Hour	Summary of Events and Information	Remarks and references to Appendices
			FRIDAY. 26.6.16. Everything quiet during the day, gave orders not to fire from damaged Emplacement (TROSSACHS). 77 m.m. guns fairly active from K.29.B.2.2. during evening. No.1. Section relieved during afternoon by No.2. Section under 2Lt Hill & Steward. Everything fairly quiet during night 26-27. SATURDAY. 27.6.16. Heavy German Artillery fire on ROB ROY Trench. H.E. & WHIZ-BANGS between 9 p.m. & 4 p.m. Luting further to report from Trenches. I visited the trenches during the afternoon & found the men keen & interested in their work. Every day during the week by exercised in Gun Drill, Elementary & Advanced.	

Army Form C. 2118.

WAR DIARY
or
INTELLIGENCE SUMMARY
(Erase heading not required.)

94. Machine Gun Coy.

Place	Date	Hour	Summary of Events and Information	Remarks and references to Appendices
			SUNDAY. 28.5.16.	
			Nothing of importance to report during the day. Voluntary Church Parade, 40% volunteered. During night heavy Bombardment both sides, no material damage done to portion of sector held by 94. M.G. Coy.	
			MONDAY. 29.5.16.	
			Nothing to report from trenches. Coy at Gun Drill. Sent an officer to D.A.D.O.S. Turnerley, result :- 40 Shrapnel Helmets for men, although previously applied for twice. Moral. If you want anything fetch it, don't ask for it. During day only an occasional T.M. going off. One of Corporals. (HARKINSON) saw Enemy Gun Pit, reported to Artillery, who shelled it. Enemy T.M. Emplacement suspected by another Corporal (JACKSON), who is watching it. No positions given, but will ascertain as soon as possible.	

Army Form C. 2118.

WAR DIARY
or
INTELLIGENCE SUMMARY
(Erase heading not required.)

94 Machine Gun Coy.

Place	Date	Hour	Summary of Events and Information	Remarks and references to Appendices
			TUESDAY. 30.5.16. Nothing to report from trenches, everything being quite quiet. No. 3. Section under Lt Walsh & Lt Tate returned to No 2. Section which relieved to Courcelles correctly & looking quite fit.	

F. Hurnd Capt
94 m.b. Coy

C O P Y.

121/9020 (A.G.1.)  31st. May, 1917.

Sir,

I am directed to inform you that War Diaries from the units shown on the attached list have not been received for the periods shown against each unit, and I am to request that you will be good enough to cause these War Diaries to be furnished without delay.

I am,

Sir,

Your obedient Servant,

(Sgnd.) I. L. B. Vesey, Lt.Col.,
A. A. G.,
for Director of Organization.

D. A. G.,
3rd. Echelon.
G. H. Q.
France.

Rev Wm Beauf. of.
9th M Genis Co
June 1916

Previous Diary ended on
June 21-7-16

Army Form C. 2118.

WAR DIARY
or
INTELLIGENCE SUMMARY
(Erase heading not required.)

VOL. 2

JUNE

Place	Date	Hour	Summary of Events and Information	Remarks and references to Appendices
			22nd June 1916.	
			Day spent in Salving & Cleaning after the line. A Party of 1 Officer & 30 N.C.O. & men proceeded on fatigue to the trenches.	
			23rd, 24th & 25th June 1916.	
			Whole Coy. on fatigue to Trenches, Ammunition carrying.	
			26th, 27th & 28th June. 1916	
			Whole Coy. on fatigue to trenches, water and ammunition carrying. On evening of 27th the # Officers & 9 gun teams chosen to take part in the attack proceeded to join the units of the Brigade, with which they were to co-operate & go forward in the attack.	
			29th June 1916.	
			Cleaning & preparing for attack, & Coy. fatigue packing limbered wagon.	
			30th June. 1916.	
			I proceeded to the trenches with the Remainder of my Coy, leaving the Transport under Lieut Lascoe (Transport Officer) at Warnimont Wood.	

[signature] Capt.
O.C. No. 94 M.G. COY.

II

D.A.G.
G.H.Q.
3rd Echelon.

Secret

HEADQUARTERS
31st DIVISION.
No. 485A
Date 16-8-16

  Forwarded. The War Diary for period 1st to 21st June was destroyed by fire which occurred at H.Q. 94th Machine Gun Company on 21st.

D.H.Q.
16.8.16.

J. Annesley Lt. Col.
G.S. & L.J.
for Major. General.
Commanding 31st Division

Subject:- 94. M.G. Co. War Diary for June 1916

SECRET.

HEADQUARTERS, 94th INFANTRY BRIGADE.
No. I.(S) 28
Date 14.8.16

37 DIVISION.
14.8.16

37. DIV.

Reference your 485 A dated 10-8-16
the M.G. Coy. reports that their War Diary for the period 22nd to 30th June, (after the fire at AUTHIE) was not forwarded.

Original copy of the War Diary for the above period is now forwarded herewith.

Brigadier-General,
Commanding 94. Infantry Brigade.

94. Inf. Bde. H.Q.
14 - 8 - 16.

D. A. G.
G. H. Q.
3rd Echelon.

Not attached.

Please see preceding minute.

The War Diary of 94th M.G.Co. for period 22nd to 30th June was forwarded to you on 16.8.16, under this office No.485A (Your No.140/452a of 31.7.17.)

H.D. Annesley Lt. Colonel
for
Brigadier General
Commanding 31st Division.

A.G's OFFICE AT THE BASE
CENTRAL REGISTRY
11 JUL 1917
C. R. No.

H. Qrs.,
31st. Division.

Please attach the remainder of this correspondence.

G. H. Qrs.,   Captain,
3rd. Echelon.   D. A. A. G.,
27th. July, 1917.   for D. A. G.

D. A G.
  G. H. Q. 3rd Echelon.

Herewith.

140/2122.

E D Melville Captain
D.A.A.G
for Major General,
Commanding 31st Division.

31.7.17.

SUBJECT:-
94. M.G.COY'S WAR DIARY FOR JUNE 1916,
Loss of,

> HEADQUARTERS,
> 94th
> INFANTRY BRIGADE.
> No. I.28/1.
> Date 5.7.17.

Headquarters,
31. Division.

> No. 186
> Date 6-7-17

With reference to attached the O.C. 94. Machine Gun Coy. reported on August 9th. 1916, that all his company records including the War Diary for June 1916 had been destroyed by fire at AUTHIE-ST-LEGER.

Subsequently a war diary for the period June 22nd. to June 30th. was compiled and forwarded to Divisional H.Q. on August 14th. 1916 under this office No. I.s.28.

No other records are available.

[signature]

Brigadier-General,
Commanding 94th. Infantry Brigade.

B.H.Q.
5.7.17.

Head-quarters,

    Thirty-first Division.

        Reference to the attached copy of War Office letter please cause the undermentioned War Diaries to be forwarded without delay:-

    94th. Machine Gun Co..........June, 1916.

G. H. Qrs.,
3rd. Echelon.
24th. June, 1917.

                      Captain,
                      D. A.A.G.
                      for D. A. G.

H.Q.
94 Inf. Bde:

HEADQUARTERS No. 485/200 A 28 JUN 1917 31st DIVISION

For information and necessary action.

Please report when the War Diary for the period mentioned has been despatched.

G.H. Melville
Captain
D.A.A.G. 31st Divn

D.A.G.
28/6/17

94th Bde.
31st Div.

WAR DIARY

94th BRIGADE

MACHINE GUN COMPANY.

1st to 31st JULY 1916.

Confidential Vol ~~2~~ 3

War Diary

94th Machine Gun Coy

1st July to 31st July

1916

Army Form C. 2118.

WAR DIARY or INTELLIGENCE SUMMARY

(Erase heading not required.)

94 Machine Gun Coy.

Place	Date	Hour	Summary of Events and Information	Remarks and references to Appendices
			SATURDAY. 1.7.16	

9 Gun teams were sent into action with the Regiments of the Bde. in the following manner. 3 Gun teams with 11th East Lancashires, 2 with 12th Yorks & Lancs., 2 with 13th Yorks & Lancs. & 2 with 14th Yorks & Lancs. making a total of 14 Officers & 63 men. Of these only 1 officer & 22 men returned uninjured, of the remainder 2 Officers were wounded, one missing, 4 and suffered from shock & 5 men reported killed, 19 wounded, & 14 reported missing. Among the remaining gun teams, there was only one casualty, one man being killed in the trenches while standing to his gun.

2nd & 3rd July. 1916

Nothing to report, except that guns were kept in front line trenches day & night. No further Casualties.

4th July. 1916.

During day everything quiet; received orders to prepare for relieving. This occurred at 11.40 p.m, the company being relieved by 114 M.G. Coy.

Army Form C. 2118.

WAR DIARY
or
INTELLIGENCE SUMMARY
(Erase heading not required.)

94 Machine Gun Coy.

Place	Date	Hour	Summary of Events and Information	Remarks and references to Appendices
			5th July 1916 After long & wearisome wandering in trenches, with water & mud over the boots & in some places nearly to the knee, I arrived with the remnant of my company at Colincamps, where I found limbers & chargers waiting. I loaded up my limbers with what remained of my paraphernalia & marched off to billets, arriving at 4 a.m. 5.7.16, where the men received a hot breakfast, prepared for them by the Transport, & then slept for a few hours. **6th July 1916.** Paraded at 10 a.m, & proceeded to Bezaincourt, a distance of 12 miles, & had just settled down, when I was told I would have to move again the next day. During day men rested. **7th July 1916.** Removed to Billet 2½ miles away & settled down, and was eventually told I should have to leave again shortly; Coy. repacking limbers, & started clearing up.	

Army Form C. 2118.

WAR DIARY
or
INTELLIGENCE SUMMARY
(Erase heading not required.)

94 Machine Gun Coy.

Place	Date	Hour	Summary of Events and Information	Remarks and references to Appendices
			8th July 1916.	
			Orders to proceed on 8-7-16, to another billet by train; Coy. broken up into 4 parties which proceeded at different times during the day, & eventually arrived at destination on morning of 9-7-16.	
			9th, 10th & 11th July 1916.	
			Carried on with cleaning of accoutrements & limbers, & had an order that I should proceed at some near date to Calonne so as to be in the 1st E. area, which I accordingly did on:-	
			12th July 1916.	
			and got into billet, & the Coy. rested for the day. The Officers listened to an address given by the 11th Army Corps Commander. The Officers	
			13th July 1916	
			Coy. at Gun Drill during the morning & proceeded for a bath in the afternoon. Parade for Gun Drill was carried on from 5 to 6.30 p.m.	
			14th July 1916.	
			Coy. had orders to hold itself in readiness to proceed to Vielle Chapelle, leaving at 11 p.m. & arriving at 1-30 a.m on 18th inst.	

Army Form C. 2118.

WAR DIARY
or
INTELLIGENCE SUMMARY
(Erase heading not required.)

94 Machine Gun Coy.

Place	Date	Hour	Summary of Events and Information	Remarks and references to Appendices
			15th July, 1916. Nos. 1 & 2 Sections, under Lieuts. Howard & Williams, proceeded to the trenches and took over 8 Emplacements from 182nd M.G. Coy, the other 2 sections resting.	
			16th July, 1916. Nothing doing. I visited the trenches & Emplacements & found everything correct, men comfortable.	
			17th & 18th July. 2 Section cleaning gear. Nothing to report.	
			19th July, 1916. ½ Coy out of trenches at Drill with rifles, as the Tripods lost on 2nd July were not yet replaced. During the morning the Brigadier of 94 Infy. Bde. visited the Billet & inspected the men at Drill & in their personal effects & expressed himself on the whole satisfied.	
			20th July, 1916. ½ Coy. at Rifle Drill & Lecture from 6.30 a.m. to 6.15 p.m.	

Army Form C. 2118.

WAR DIARY
or
INTELLIGENCE SUMMARY
(Erase heading not required.)

9th M. Gun Coy.

Place	Date	Hour	Summary of Events and Information	Remarks and references to Appendices
			21st July. 1916. ½ Coy in trenches relieved by the 2 Sections from Billets under the 2nd in command Lieut. Hill & Lieut. Durrant.	
			22nd July. 1916. 1 & 2 Sections at Coy Drill from 6.30 a.m. to 6 p.m. A man (Pte Devonshire) reported hit slightly in the hand & evacuated from the trenches by Doctor in 1st Aid Post. Nothing of any great importance to report.	
			23rd July. 1916. In morning, Church parade for Sections out of trenches, following by Coy. Drill in afternoon. Nothing of any importance to report from the trenches. Orders received for 1 Section to be relieved from the trenches as the section front is lessened.	
			24th July. 1916. Order received for 6 Gun teams to proceed to trenches to take over 6 new emplacements from 116 M.G. Coy. Accordingly the morning was spent in preparation & at 12.30 the 6 Gun teams under Lieuts. Seward & Williams proceeded to the trenches. 4 Gun teams under Lieut. Hill were relieved by another M.G. Coy.	

WAR DIARY or INTELLIGENCE SUMMARY

Army Form C. 2118.

93rd Machine Gun Coy.

Place	Date	Hour	Summary of Events and Information	Remarks and references to Appendices
			25th July. 1916. Men not in trenches employed during morning by belt-filling; in the afternoon the majority were away to the trenches, ration-carrying. Lieut. Hill return from trenches. Nothing of importance to report.	
			26th July. 1916. In the morning, men not in trenches were repacking limbers, & in afternoon ration carrying to gun teams. I visited trenches, accompanied by the O.C. & a "Relief" of 93 M.G. Coy, & L/Cpl Blood. While in the trenches a heavy trench mortar shell, bursting in the trench, wounded the O.C. of 93 M.G. Coy & killed L/Cpl Blood. Nothing of importance to report from gun teams in the trenches.	
			27th July. 1916. Received orders to move into the billets occupied by 93 M.G. Coy. Accordingly, morning was spent in shifting, while in the afternoon & evening, Gun Teams arrived from the trenches, having been relieved by 93 M.G. Coy.	
			28th July. 1916. Whole day spent in cleaning up kit after return from trenches.	

Army Form C. 2118.

WAR DIARY
or
INTELLIGENCE SUMMARY
(Erase heading not required.)

94th Machine Gun Coy.

Place	Date	Hour	Summary of Events and Information	Remarks and references to Appendices
	29th July 1916.		In the morning the whole Company paraded for Gun Drill (Elementary) This was also carried on during the afternoon & in the evening the men paraded for a Lecture.	
	30th July 1916.		School parade in the morning for C.Os at Vielle Chapelle & for R.Os at Croix Barbé. In the afternoon rifle inspection & Drill. In the evening two new officers:- Lieuts E.S. Rees, 8th Wilts, & A.M.G. Cavt. 13th H.L.I., joined the company.	
	31st July 1916.		The day was spent in Elementary & Advanced Machine Gun Drill, with a Lecture in the evening.	

B. Funnel Capt.
Comdg. 94 M.G. Coy.

No. 94 M.G. COY.
1 SEP 1916
MACHINE GUN CORPS.

From: O.C. NO. 94 M. G. COY.
To: D.A.G. 3rd Echelon.

Herewith original of my "War Diary" for the month of August. 1916.

D. Dunn Captn.
O.C. NO. 94 M. G. COY.

WAR DIARY or INTELLIGENCE SUMMARY

Army Form C. 2118.

Place	Date	Hour	Summary of Events and Information	Remarks and references to Appendices
In the field	1st August 1916.		The day was spent in Elementary and advanced Gun Drill, with a lecture in the evening.	
	2nd August 1916.		Morning and afternoon were spent in Elementary & Advanced Gun Drill, followed in the evening by a lecture on "Gas." During the day the officers proceeded to the trenches to reconnoitre certain roads in the Brigade sector	
	3rd August 1916.		Part of the morning (9.a.m - 10 a.m.) was spent in Company Drill (Artillery formation); the remainder of the morning being devoted to Gun Drill (varied). In the afternoon all Guns, Spare Parts, &c, were thoroughly overhauled & cleaned, - (preparation for proceeding to the trenches) - this being followed in the evening by a lecture. Received Orders for 10 of my Gun teams to relieve 93 M.G. Coy. in the trenches on 4/8/16, & also for me to take over the Headquarters of 93 M.G. Coy. on same date.	
	4th August 1916.		Took over Hdqrs. of 93 M.G. Coy during day, while at 10.45 a.m, 10 of my Gun teams left for trenches to relieve 93 M.G. Coy. The teams were under 2/Lieuts Howard, Williams, Durrant, Rex & Cant. Subsequently reports were received from these officers to the effect that the reliefs had been safely accomplished	

WAR DIARY or INTELLIGENCE SUMMARY

Army Form C. 2118.

No. 94 M.G. COY.
MACHINE GUN CORPS

5th August. 1916.

The few men not in the trenches spent the day in cleaning up the roads & circles in & around the billet. 2nd Lieut Williams reports that Guns in 9 & 10 Emplacements were not fired during the night owing to our wiring parties & patrols being out. At No. 9 Emplacement the men are employed in preparation for construction of an alternative Emp: for night firing. He also reports refusal of Inf: Officer i/c round No. 10 Emp: to supply 2 bombers for flanks of Emp: owing to shellhandedness. Lt Durrant reports quiet afternoon. Taight-ing gun did not fire. Nothing of further importance to report. Except for a little J.M. activity front line gun fired on grp at S.11.A.5.3. Remain.

6th August. 1916.

As yesterday, the few men left behind occupied the morning in thoroughly cleaning billet & environs, & in the afternoon were ration carrying to the trenches. Q.M.S.M. O'Meara proceeded to trenches with ration party & returned in the morning of the

7th August. 1916.

reporting enemy activity in use of rifle grenades on the night of the 6th inst. Men in billet employed in general fatigues in morning & ration carrying in the afternoon. Nothing further of importance to report from the trenches.

8th August. 1916.

Men in billet employed as yesterday. I received an order to meet the Brigadier General gun.4/13 de at Euston, to accompany him on a tour of the trenches in the sector held by 94 Inf. Bde. but owing to my being indisposed, my place was taken by Lieut. Hill, 2nd in Command of Coy. Nothing of importance to report from Trenches.

WAR DIARY or INTELLIGENCE SUMMARY

(Erase heading not required.)

Army Form C. 2118.

Summary of Events and Information

9th August. 1916.

Report received from Lt Durant embodying request that an extra gun should be sent to take up position in front line in front of Copse Keep, to co-operate with our patrols during night; to be kept in Copse Keep during day; as gun in Copse Keep cannot give direct fire on L.G. trench line. Infy. Bde. Commander offered to loan 1 or 2 gunners if necessary, to help with this extra gun.

Received orders that 4 Guns in Left Sector under Lt. Williams & Rex would be relieved by 182 M.G. Coy on 10/8/16 & that 2 additional guns were to be sent to Right Sector under Efo. Howard. Durrant T. Cant.

10th August. 1916.

In the morning, the two teams for the Right Sector left for the trenches, while the 4 teams on the left were relieved by 182 M.G. Coy, & returned in billet in the evening. Nothing to report from Gun teams remaining in trenches.

11th August 1916.

Men in billet spent day in cleaning up after return from trenches. 36 men arrived during morning, viz; 1 M.C. & 8 men detached from each of, 11th Bath. E. Lancs. Regt, 12th, 13th, & 14th Bath. Lancs. Regt, to be permanently attached to Coy, & trained in duties of a machine gunner. 1 man also arrived from Base, additional to War Establt as trained waterman.

WAR DIARY or INTELLIGENCE SUMMARY

Army Form C. 2118.

12th August 1916.

½ Coy. out of the trenches was occupied in cleaning guns, etc.: Men attached to Coy. from 9th Battalion:- N.C.O's under L.S.M. O'Meara, & men, in squads, under Sgts. Ward, Hetcher & Blair, & Cpl. Jackson respectively, were instructed in Elementary Machine Gun Drill & Mechanism, followed by a "General Topics" lecture by C.S.M. Nothing to report from trenches.

13th August 1916.

Church parade in morning for N.C.O's & C/E. In afternoon, Gun Drill for attached N.C.O's & Men. Lieut. Still proceeded to trenches with Officer of 183 M.G. Coy. to point out the various emplacements & positions at present occupied by Gun teams of my Company.

14th August 1916.

Attached N.C.O's & men, under respective instructors, instructed during day in Elementary Gun Drill & Mechanism with a lecture on the "Care & Cleaning of the Gun." 6 Gun teams under Lieut. Williams & Rea proceeded to trenches during morning, to relieve 6 of the Gun teams under Lieuts. Stewart, Durrant & Gant, while the 2 additional Gun teams, in Right Sector, which took up positions on 10.8.16, remain in Trenches. Relief being safely & effectually accomplished, the relieved Gun teams, with Officers, arrived in billet during afternoon & early evening. Two new officers, Lieuts. Lands, O.G. (13th Warwicks) & Sykes, J. (4th D.L.I), arrived from M.G. Base to fill the vacancies in the Coy.

WAR DIARY
or
INTELLIGENCE SUMMARY

Army Form C. 2118.

15th August. 1916.
Attached N.C.Os & men, under respective instructors, occupied by Elementary Gun Drill, Mechanism of Gun & a second lecture on Care & Cleaning. The Gun Teams from the trenches spent the day in cleaning up all guns & gear. Nothing special to report from the trenches.

16th August. 1916.
Attached N.C.Os & men instructed as usual in Machine Gunnery. Two extra Gun Teams for the Right Sector under Lieut. Hands, proceeded to trenches at 1 p.m. & took up defensive positions.

17th August. 1916.
Attached N.C.Os & 4 men paraded as usual for instruction in Machine gunnery. The few men of the Coy. not in trenches were employed in cleaning up billet. Nothing of importance to report from the trenches.

18th August. 1916.
Acting on Orders, Coy. moved in morning to reserve billet (in Béthune reserve area) & old billet was taken over by 183 M.G. Coy. Ten gun teams in the trenches were relieved by teams of 183 Coy, & relieved teams arrived safely in billet during afternoon & evening.

19th August. 1916.
Attached N.C.Os & men instructed in Machine gunnery as usual. Coy. spent the day in cleaning up all gear & equipment after return from the trenches.

WAR DIARY or INTELLIGENCE SUMMARY

20th August. 1916.

Church parade in morning (R.C's & C. of E's), for Coy and attached O.R. Afternoon spent in cleaning all guns. Received notice that the Brigadier will inspect company in full marching order & Transport with mules, looked in on Tuesday 22nd August.

21st August 1916.

Morning spent in repacking limbers ready for Brigadier's Inspection tomorrow; afternoon occupied by Coy. in telegraph rifles & equipment for same purpose, and at 5.30 p.m. paraded in full marching order to ensure that everything was correct.

22nd August 1916.

Inspection at 10 a.m. by Brig-General Comdg. 94 Infy. Bde., of Coy & Transport. In the afternoon, Coy. & attached men were at Coy. & Rifle Drill.

23rd August 1916.

Coy. & attached men were at Coy. & Rifle Drill during the morning & Elementary Gun Drill in the afternoon.

24th August 1916.

Attached O.R. at Gun Drill during the day. Coy. paraded for Bay. & Rifle Drill during the morning, while in the afternoon, Nos 1 & 2 on each gun were instructed in use of revolvers.

WAR DIARY or INTELLIGENCE SUMMARY

Army Form C. 2118.

NO. 94 M.G. COY. MACHINE GUN CORPS

25th August 1916.
Received orders that teams of my Coy. were to relieve gun teams of 183 M.G. Coy. in the trenches on 26-8-16. Accordingly the 8 teams required spent the day in preparation. Remainder of Coy. at Gun Drill.

26th August 1916.
8 Gun teams, under Lieut. Howard, Williams, Rea & Hards, proceeded to the trenches to take over the positions occupied by 183 M.G. Coy. Subsequently, reports were received to say that the relief had been safely & effectively accomplished. I took over the Headquarters & billets of 183 M.G. Coy during the morning.

27th August 1916.
Coy. & attached paraded for Church in the morning. Men not on this fatigue were detailed for ration carrying to the gun teams in the trenches.

28th August 1916.
In the morning Gun Drill for Coy. & attached, while in the afternoon a party was detailed for ration carrying. Men not on this fatigue were employed by cleaning guns. This was followed by a lecture on "Musketry" by Lieut. Cont. Lieut. Sykes proceeded to the trenches to assist other officers.

Army Form C. 2118.

WAR DIARY
or
INTELLIGENCE SUMMARY
(Erase heading not required.)

Place	Date	Hour	Summary of Events and Information	Remarks and references to Appendices
			29th August 1916. In the morning, Gun Drill, (Advanced), for Coy. + attached, followed in afternoon by full marching order + kit inspection at 2.15 p.m. + a lecture from 3.30 p.m. to 4.30 p.m. Also a party was ration-carrying to Gun Teams in the trenches. Nothing to report from trenches.	
			30th August 1916. Same as yesterday. At 6.30 p.m, 10 men arrived from M.G. Base as reinforcement to Coy.	
			31st August 1916. Men were employed on cleaning up the roads + ditches in environs of Millets, + in the afternoon were ration carrying to the trenches. 8 Gun Teams were picked ready for the relief, on 1/9/16 of Gun Teams in trenches.	
				Signed .... Capt. O.C. NO. 94 M. G. COY.

1 SEP 1916

Confidential

Vol. 5

War Diary.

94. Machine Gun Coy.

31st Division

September 1916.

WAR DIARY
or
INTELLIGENCE SUMMARY
(Erase heading not required.)

Army Form C. 2118.

Vol V

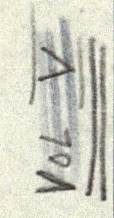

No. 94 M.G. COY. MACHINE GUN CORPS

Place	Date	Hour	Summary of Events and Information	Remarks and references to Appendices
In the Field	1-9-16	—	Gun teams under 2nd Lieut. Lant & Sykes proceeded at 9 a.m. to the trenches to relieve those away this Howard, Williams, Rees & Hinds. Subsequently during the afternoon, the relieved teams arrived safely in billet & a report was received to the effect that the relief had been safely & successfully accomplished. I received an order that on 3/9/16, 4 more Gun teams are to go to take up positions in the trenches.	X
"	2-9-16	—	Coy was occupied during the day in cleaning up all guns & gear after return from the trenches in preparation for the relief of 4 teams tomorrow.	X
"	3-9-16	—	At 1.a.m. 4 Gun teams, under 2nd Lt. Williams & Rees, proceeded with all guns & gear necessary to take over positions in the trenches; while remainder of Coy. in billet accompanied the teams as a fatigue party. In the afternoon a party was detailed to carry rations. A casualty was reported from the team under L/Sgt. Parrish, being No.890 Pte. H. Stubbs, who was accidentally wounded on the bridge of the nose by something which flew from a pit in which he was burning rubbish found in the dug out at Lorette Post. It's mind only slight. Lt Durrant reports that fighting patrols all along the line on night of 2/3/9/16 were forced to retire owing to enemy wire being good & front line strongly held. Also reports inspected enemy M.G. Emplacent at S.M. 15.a.9.4. in front of enemy wire. Has been reported & is being further investigated.	X
"	4-9-16	—	A fatigue party under Mr. Howard was away carrying ammunition, stores & from C.O. Bombing School to the trenches (Chateau Rd.), from which post some was to be carried to front line Emplacement (left sector). In the afternoon— rations carrying to the trenches. Nothing to report from trenches.	X
"	5-9-16	—	Men at Coy. H.Q. & 7 am Drill in the morning & ration carrying to trenches in afternoon. No report from trenches.	X
"	6-9-16	—	As yesterday, men in billet at Coy. Drill etc. during the morning & ration carrying to trenches in the afternoon. I paid a visit to the trenches in the left of the sector. Chapelle sector & found everything satisfactory & correct. Nothing of importance to report. We will left billet for 4 Days' Rest at Bray on 8.9.16.	X

WAR DIARY or INTELLIGENCE SUMMARY

Army Form C. 2118.

NO. 94 M.G. COY.
MACHINE GUN CORPS

Place	Date	Hour	Summary of Events and Information	Remarks and references to Appendices
In the Field	7-9-16	—	Men again at Coy. Drill during the morning & in the afternoon ordinary ration carrying to the trenches & another fatigue preparing to make winter standings for the mules & horses. A party of 6 men & 1 N.C.O. (Pte. Jackson) was also employed during the morning on repairing a M.G. Emplact. in Sandbag Alley. I again visited the trenches & arranged with my Section Officers for the continuance of co-operation with the infantry in the matter of indirect & overhead fire. Nothing further to report.	✗
"	8-9-16	—	Men employed on the new winter standings during the day, while in the afternoon a party was carrying to the trenches. In the morning Mr Hanks paid a visit to the trenches, accompanied by C.S.M. & Sgt. Bickford. Nothing to report. Sgt. Ward later reports Brigadier's satisfaction at the way in which the men of his gun team are employed during the day. Nothing further to report.	✗
"	9-9-16	—	As yesterday, men on fatigue in construction of winter standings, with a ration party in the afternoon. Nothing to report from trenches.	✗
"	10-9-16	—	Church parade in morning for R.Cs. + C of E & in the afternoon ration carrying to the trenches. Pte Williams reported 2 casualties. A gun was placed for giving indirect fire over L.F.39 dots at M.36.c.2.8. at 10 p.m. Enemy sent over a salvo of shrapnel, killing Pte Murphy A.W.J. & Lapps.95th 94 M.G. Coys. T.M. & Highfield PTE. Morton was slightly grazed on the arm by another salvo of shrapnel. Received orders that tomorrow 11-9-16, 93rd M.G. Coy. will relieve my gun teams in trenches, & my Coy. will go, with Bde. into Army Reserve.	✗
"	11-9-16	—	12 Gun teams arrived from trenches during day, having been relieved by 93 M.G. Coy. During the rest of the day the men were resting.	✗
"	12-9-16	—	Men, from the trenches spent the day in cleaning up all gear & equipment. T.R.C.O.'s 70 men were on fatigue 95th J.C.B. This fatigue to be daily until further orders. I received an order that the 15 Bugler Coys of 94 Infy Bde. will report the 172 letters on Thursday 14-9-16 at 10 a.m., when Coy G be in full marching order & limbers to be packed according to the Mobilisation Table for a Machine Gun Company.	✗
"	13-9-16	—	Men on fatigue, preparing for general inspection during morning & in the afternoon Nos 172 letters packed up, limbers for same. At 9 a.m., 8 men (Surplus to Establishment) left me to report to R.Q.6 L.O. 9449. Wt. W.14957/Ag.9 750,000 10/15 J.B.C. & A. Forms/C.2118/12 74 to 96 F M.G. Coys, 32nd Division.	✗

WAR DIARY or INTELLIGENCE SUMMARY

Army Form C. 2118.

(Erase heading not required.)

Instructions regarding War Diaries and Intelligence Summaries are contained in F. S. Regs., Part II. and the Staff Manual respectively. Title Pages will be prepared in manuscript.

Place	Date	Hour	Summary of Events and Information	Remarks and references to Appendices
In the Field	14-9-16	—	Nos. 3+4 sections paraded at 4 p.m. for stewart & Howard M.G.Drill. At 11 a.m. the Brigadier toured up Inf.Bde. inspected Nos. 1+2 sections in full marching order & with limbers packed according to Mob. Table for a M.G. Coy. In the afternoon most of the Officers + N.C.Os. attended a lecture on bayonet fighting, given by the Army Inspector of Gymnasia at Bde. H.Q. Men on General Fatigues.	☓
"	15-9-16	—	Received orders to take over the billets + Emplacements (in trenches of Foncbert Sector) of 90th M.G.Coy. on 16-9-16. Accordingly, with 8 other officers of my Coy., I visited the Emplacements, posts + billets to be taken over. Coy. on General Fatigues + preparations for movement during the day.	☓
"	16-9-16	—	I took over the H.Q. + Billets of 90th M.G.Coy. at Loisne (X.22.d.7,8) + 12 Gun teams under Lts. Howard, Williams, Rees + Hands, proceeded to trenches to relieve teams of 90 M.G. Coy. Everything satisfactorily accomplished 4 p.m.	☓
"	17-9-16	—	Men employed during day in cleaning up billets, which were left in dirty condition by 90 M.G. Coy. In the afternoon, a party was ration carrying to gun teams in the trenches. Sgt. Fletcher reports Brigadiers satisfaction at the clean state of his emplacements + dugouts. Nothing further to report from the trenches.	☓
"	18-9-16	—	The yesterday, men in billet were on fatigue, & cleaning up and repairing roofs of billets + stabling. A party was detailed for ration-carrying to the trenches. Nothing to report from the trenches.	☓
"	19-9-16	—	Same as yesterday.	☓
"	20-9-16	—	Same as yesterday. Relieved in order to accompany Brigadier, Q.M.Gen.F.Bde., on tour of my gun teams in trenches 21-9-16.	☓
"	21-9-16	—	Accordingly, I went with the Brigadier this morning + during the day, visited with him, all my gun teams in the trenches, finishing in the early evening. Men in billet were employed, during morning, on repairing of billets + in afternoon, on ration carrying.	☓
"	22-9-16	—	Men employed as yesterday. In the evening a report was received from Lt. Howard that he had had a complaint from an Infy. Officer in front line, that one of our guns was firing on our own front line. Accordingly, Lieut. Hill + 2nd Lt. Major proceeded to trenches at 10.30 p.m. to make investigations + arrived back at H.Qrs. in early morning of 23/9/16:—	☓

WAR DIARY or INTELLIGENCE SUMMARY

Army Form C. 2118.

(Erase heading not required.)

Instructions regarding War Diaries and Intelligence Summaries are contained in F.S. Regs., Part II. and the Staff Manual respectively. Title Pages will be prepared in manuscript.

Place	Date	Hour	Summary of Events and Information	Remarks and references to Appendices
In the Field	23-9-16	—	Reporting that there was no evidence to prove that it was one of my guns. Men employed in preparations for proceeding to trenches. (No 4 Section) to relieve gun teams under 2Lt. Williams & Fox. (No 1 Section). At 12.30p.m. the gun teams under 2Lt. Durrant, Grant & Sykes left for the trenches & after the relief had been satisfactorily accomplished the relieved gun teams arrived safely in billet.	
"	24-9-16	—	Church parade for men in billet in the morning. General fatigues & ration carrying in the afternoon. Nothing to report from the trenches.	
"	25-9-16	—	Men employed as yesterday during morning. After listening to a lecture on "Gas" by C.S.M. being instructed in gas orders issued by 31st Divn. Received orders that 6 men per Batt. of men attached to my Coy. are to report from gun team Batt. on 29th, owing to their being under strength. Also received orders that the men attached to my Coy. are to supply Bde. H.Q. guard until further orders. Nothing to report from trenches.	
"	26-9-16	—	Men in billet on General fatigues in morning, ration carrying in afternoon. With Lieut Hill, my 2nd in Command, I visited the trenches for the purpose of choosing alternative night-firing positions in COVERED TRENCH, pointed out as suitable by the Brigadier. Two men of No.1 Coy. proceeded in teams to U.K. this morning.	
"	27-9-16	—	Men in billet employed on repairing of shelters for horses & mules, & ration-carrying in the afternoon. According to orders received yesterday, 6 men per Batt. of the men attached to my Coy. returned to their units which are considerably under strength.	
"	28-9-16	—	Coy. in billet employed as yesterday. Nothing to report from the trenches.	
"	29-9-16	—	Coy. employed as yesterday. On return from baths at Vieille Chapelle in the afternoon, Officers & N.C.O.s of the Coy. proceeded to Vacant to attend a demonstration of the use of Flammenwerfer. Nothing to report from the trenches.	
"	30-9-16	—	4 Gun teams of No.1 Section, under 2Lts Williams & Fox, proceeded to trenches at 10.a.m. to relieve 4 teams of No.2 Section under 2Lts Howard & Hands. Relieved teams arrived safely in billet during the afternoon after a successfully accomplished relief.	

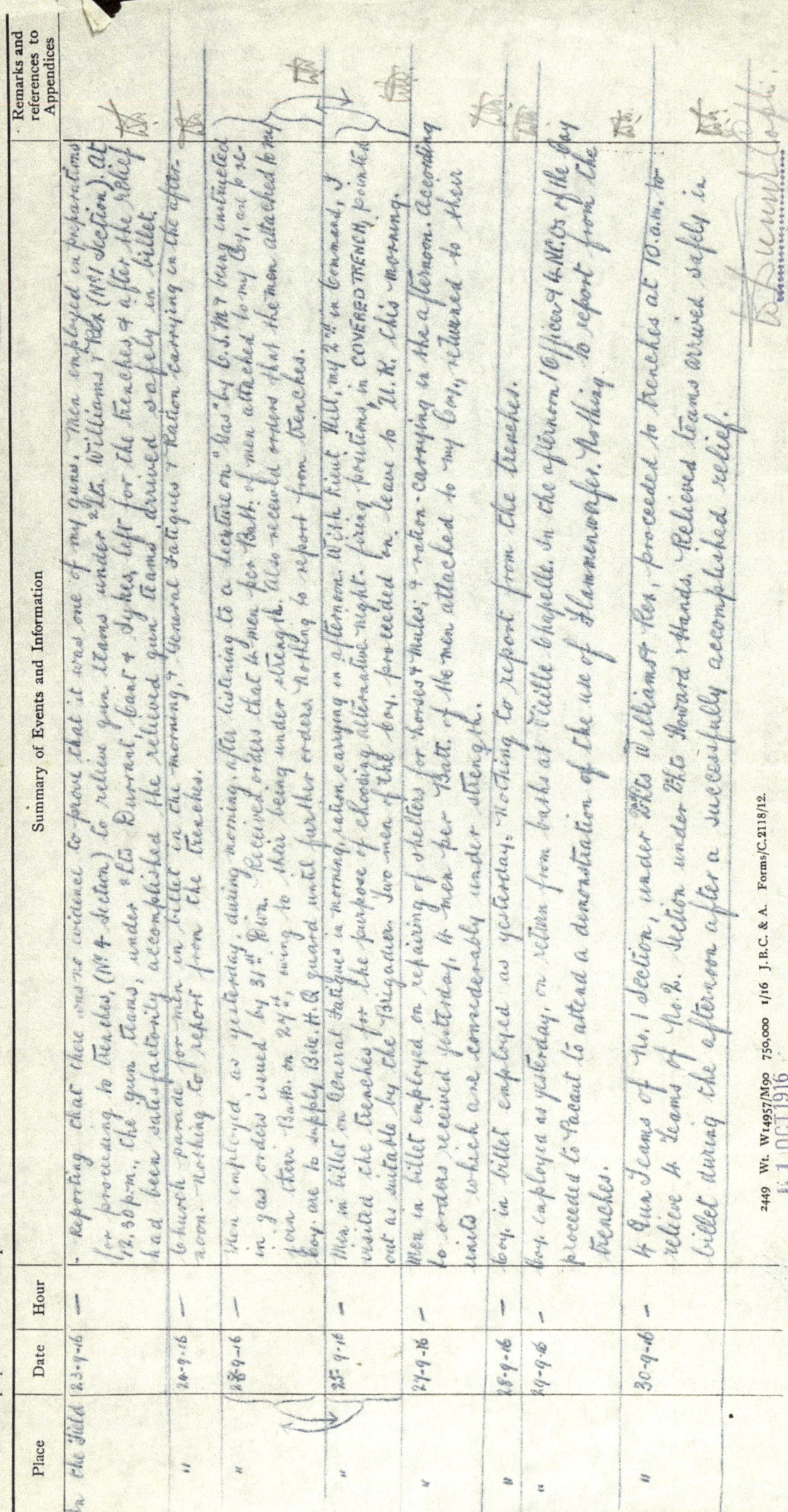

Confidential

Volume 6

War Diary.
94th Machine Gun Coy.
31st Division
October 1916.

WAR DIARY or **INTELLIGENCE SUMMARY**
(Erase heading not required.)

Army Form C. 2118.

No. 94 M.G. COY.
Vol N°10.

Place	Date	Hour	Summary of Events and Information	Remarks and references to Appendices
In the Field	1 OCT	11	Church parade for men out of trenches in morning. General fatigues & ration carrying during the afternoon.	M.C.
"	2 OCT	—	Received orders that my Coy. will be relieved tomorrow – 3/10/16, in the trenches by 13th M.G. Coy; who will take over my billets, while my Coy. proceeds to billets at ESSARS. O.C. & other officers of 13th M.G. Coy came over to inspect the billets, also the emplacements & posts in the trenches (Festubert sector).	M.C.
"	3 OCT	—	My billets taken over by 13th M.G. Coy, while men in billets proceeded to ESSARS where I took over the billets of 18th M.G. Coy. Meanwhile, 12 teams of 13th M.G. Coy. proceeded to the trenches to relieve my Gun teams, which arrived safely in billet during afternoon & evening.	M.C.
"	4 OCT	11	Coy. employed during the day, on overhauling the whole of the Company gear. - T all stores surplus to mobilisation equipment were despatched to Brigade Dump at No.5. Rue Marcellin, Berthelot, BETHUNE, while all unserviceable stores were sent to the Divnl. Salvage Dump. Received orders to move with the Division to ROBECQ on 5/10/16.	M.C.
"	5 OCT	—	Preparations were made for moving, during the morning & at 2.30.p.m. the Coy. moved off, marching to ROBECQ where billets were taken up at P.94.d.8.2. Lieut. F.B. Bowen arrived from 14th. M.G. Coy. to take over command of the 94th. M.G. Coy. from Capt. W. Dunn.	M.C.
"	6 OCT	—	At 9.a.m. Coy. was inspected by Lieut. Bowen. After this M.G. Training was carried out.	M.C.
"	7 OCT	—	Capt. W. Dunn left the Coy. to join the 2nd Batn. Welsh Regt. M.G. Training & preparations for moving off occupied the day. Coy. marched out of billets at 12. midnight 7 – 8th inst. proceeded to BERGUETTE station arriving there at 3.30.a.m. 8th inst.	D.C.
"	8 OCT	11	The Coy. entrained at BERGUETTE for DOULLENS (SOMME) at 6.40.a.m., & arrived at DOULLENS (H.18.a) at 4.10.p.m. marching, after detraining, to billets at SARTON.	M.C.

T.B.Bowen

Army Form C. 2118.

WAR DIARY
or
INTELLIGENCE SUMMARY
(Erase heading not required.)

Vol No 10

Place	Date	Hour	Summary of Events and Information	Remarks and references to Appendices
In the field	9 Oct	—	Day spent in cleaning up all guns & gun equipment:- M.G. training & Belt-filling.	DC
"	10 Oct	—	On each of these days, varied forms of M.G. training were carried out, including range practice for one section each day, & a lecture in the evenings at 5.15 p.m. to all Officers & N.C.Os.	DC
"	11 Oct	—		
"	12 Oct	—	A party of M.G. Officers & N.C.Os. left the Coy. each day to reconnoitre the frontage of the XIII Corps.	DC
"	13 Oct	—		
"	14 Oct	—		
"	15 Oct	—		
"	16 Oct	—	The Coy. took part during the morning, in a Brigade Scheme of attack. In the afternoon, M.G. training was carried out.	DC
"	17 Oct	—	The usual M.G. training was carried out.	DC
"	18 Oct	—	Received orders to move during the day, to WARNIMONT WOOD. Accordingly, all preparations were made, & the Coy. left billets at SARTON at 2.20 p.m., proceeding via THIEVRES & AUTHIE to WARNIMONT WOOD, arriving there at 4.45 p.m., & taking up huts at I.19.d.5,8 approx.	DC
"	19 Oct	—	Training was carried out in fields behind WARNIMONT WOOD about I.18.a.b.c.d.	DC
"	20 Oct	—		
"	21 Oct	—		
"	22 Oct	—	R.C. Church parade at 11 a.m. at 11th E. Lancs. Hd. Qrs. The usual M.G. training.	DC

M Cowin A

WAR DIARY
or
INTELLIGENCE SUMMARY

Army Form C. 2118.

Vol N° 10

Place	Date	Hour	Summary of Events and Information	Remarks and references to Appendices
In the field	23 OCT 24 OCT 25 OCT 26 OCT 27 OCT	—	On each of these days, M.G. training was carried out in the fields behind WARNIMONT WOOD. T.18.a.b.c.d.	T.C. T.C. T.C. T.C. T.C.
"	28 OCT	—	Received orders from 94th Infy. Bde. to be ready to take over the M.G. Emplacements in the trenches of the HEBUTERNE sector from the 93rd Infy. Bde. M.G. Coy.	T.C.
"	29 OCT	—	Received 94th Bde. Order No. 49 (extract- Appendix I). Issued Operation Order No.1. (Appendix II).	See appendices I & II.
"	30 OCT	—	A, B & C sections moved off from billets at WARNIMONT WOOD at 8.30 a.m. D section moved off at 9.30 a.m. & proceeded to SAILLY via ST LEGER & COIGNEUX. A, B & C sections took over gun positions from 93rd M.G. Coy. Relief complete at 2.15 p.m.	T.C.
"	31 OCT	—	3 sections in trenches. 1 section in billets at SAILLY, carrying on with M.G. training & providing ration parties to teams in the trenches. Situation normal. Considerable enemy shelling.	T.C.

APPENDIX I. (Extract).

94th Infantry Brigade Order No. 49.

(1) The 94th Infantry Brigade will relieve the 93rd Infy. Bde. in the line tomorrow, 30th inst.
(2) The relief of units will be carried out in accordance with attached table.

COPY NO 5.

Unit Relieving	Unit to be relieved	March off from Place & Hour	Route	Guides
94th M.G. Coy.	93rd M.G. Coy.	WARNIMONT WOOD. 8.30 a.m. 30.10.16	ST.LEGER- COIGNEUX- SAILLY.	To be at R.E. DUMP SAILLY-HEBUTERNE RD. 29-10-16. K.9.d.10 at 10 a.m.	Communication trenches In. JEAN BART, NAIRN & REVEL.

(Sd.) W. Leavitt. Captain.
Brigade Major.
94th Infantry Brigade.

Confidential

Volume ✕
Vol 7

War Diary.

No 94 Machine Gun Coy.   31st. Division

November 1916.

WAR DIARY or INTELLIGENCE SUMMARY

Army Form C. 2118.
Volume No. XI

No. 94 M.G. COY.
MACHINE GUN CORPS
Q1/24

Place	Date	Hour	Summary of Events and Information	Remarks and references to Appendices
A. M. Sud	1st Nov 1916		Coy. H.Q. at SAILLY 57d N.W. 21.B.31. Three sections in the trenches, one section in reserve at Coy H.Q. Situation normal.	J.B.C.
"	2nd Nov 1916		The situation in the trenches was normal. The enemy shelled SAILLY at intervals during the day.	J.B.C.
"	3rd Nov 1916		The enemy shelled SAILLY near Reserve Billet. One man wounded. Issued Operation Order No. 2.	appendix J.B.C.
"	4th Nov 1916		D. Section relieved 'A' Section in the trenches. Relief complete at 12.30 p.m. 'A' Section took over the reserve billets at SAILLY.	J.B.C.
"	5th Nov 1916		Situation normal. 2nd Lieut J. Edward and three other M.G. Os proceeded to CAMIERS to join M.G. School (on 35 course of M.G. Instruction. Lieut Howarth remained in the trenches	J.B.C.
"	6th Nov 1916		Orders received that the 94th Brigade was to be relieved by the 93rd Brigade on the 7th inst. Issued Operation Order No. 3. A Raid was carried out by the 13th & 14th Batts Y & L. Several of the guns of the company co-operated firing into enemy wire (not selected for attack) and support lines and also included bridge behind his trenches.	Attached II J.B.C.
"	7th Nov 1916		The 93rd Machine Gun Company relieved the 94th Machine Gun Company relief being complete at 1.30 p.m. Company marched to billets at COIGNEUX (57D.S.9.C.5.) recently occupied by 93rd Machine Gun Company on relieved.	J.B.C.

J.B.Cowell Capt.

WAR DIARY
or
INTELLIGENCE SUMMARY

(Erase heading not required.)

Army Form C. 2118.

Place	Date	Hour	Summary of Events and Information	Remarks and references to Appendices
In the Field	8th May 1916		Day devoted to cleaning of clothing. Inspection of huts and grounds.	MC
"	9th May 1916		Company paid. In huts at COIGNEUX. Day spent in cleaning of clothing, guns and also gun drill. A fatigue party were cleaning up the camp.	MC
"	10th May 1916		This morning were orders in MS. Brownrigg's name. Received orders from 9th Infantry Brigade to move out of huts at present occupied at COIGNEUX (Ref. map 57D Sq 2/5) and proceed to huts in WARNIMENT WOOD. Should move off in order verbally to all concerned. Packing of kubers was carried on until 2 pm. Company paraded in marching order ready to move off. Orders received from 9th Infantry Brigade that a polar tarp would accommodate one party [?] of 6 [?]. The kubers were already full. Asked huts a lot of [?] material and shelter in coats of sheep etc. Could not be [?].	MC
"	11th May 1916		In huts in WARNIMENT WOOD. Bayonet exercises in cleaning camp and clearing ammunition. A pocket of spare parts [?] was [?] to section.	MC
"	11th May 1916	2.30 pm	Received orders for 9th Infantry Brigade that in the event of operations on our front it would be arranged that on and from 13th inst. and that the 93rd Infantry Brigade being in the line would take over the duties of the 9th Infantry Brigade down for the 9th Infantry Brigade.	MC
"	12th May 1916		In huts in WARNIMENT WOOD. Morning spent on ordinary drill. Received orders from 9th Infantry Brigade that all huts would be taken over and that this boys O.M. were outside huts occupied by Brigade Staff at 1.30 pm and that two extra huts close by B.J. Room and Officers Quarters would have to be cleared. Required balance. Proceeded forthwith. Afternoon devoted to games. 4.30 pm orders from 9th Infantry Brigade to have an officer at advanced Brigade	MC

J. M. Crutchley

WAR DIARY or INTELLIGENCE SUMMARY

Army Form C. 2118.

(Erase heading not required.)

Instructions regarding War Diaries and Intelligence Summaries are contained in F. S. Regs., Part II. and the Staff Manual respectively. Title Pages will be prepared in manuscript.

Place	Date	Hour	Summary of Events and Information	Remarks and references to Appendices
3rd Aus M/G Coy (cont.)	12th Dec 1916		Adv Recce St LEGER at 10 p.m. to prepare of synchronise watches. Lieut Hill was detailed for this purpose. ZERO to be (for operations) fixed at 5.45 a.m.	WC
	13th Dec 1916		Attack by 92nd Infantry Brigade arrived on No Mans land from K23 a 8.1 to the hill K23c 05/15. Day of attack in vicinity of water being received to broadcast. Received orders that the 94th Infantry Brigade would relieve the 92nd and 93rd Infantry Brigades on the 8th/9th Jany on the night of the intent. And intended Brigade staff to be in to arrange for a motor lorry to be at the tram at 8/6 a.m. to move the Tour of the Bn stores etc. Ordered Russell to stand to breakfast 6.30 a.m. In the partion detailed for action from early in the morning.	WC
	14th 25.1.17	3.30 a.m. recd 94th Infantry Brigade Order No 88. 7 o.a.m Issued Operation order No.h. 8.15 a.m A, C.D. sections loaded and marched out. Guns detailed in Op Order left Appendix III proceeded direct to the trenches and were met there by the O.C. who had ridden on in Appendix IV advance in order to make arrangements for the relief with O.C. Coy 93 Machine Gun Company. B Section remained in camp to clear up and to let the Motor Company, when it arrived, and then proceeded to tram-pit lines at T 18 b 9. where tents were erected for the accommodation of that part of C section not in the line. 'D' section Q.M. stores and Orderly Room 1.30pm arrived at H a 8.a.m. on A.B. group in the line (K 18c 2/65) and met O.C. 93rd M.G. Coy and discussed details for the relief. Issued to allot Operation Order No 104 A.5 Pack guns in following positions (Reg Sgt) 37°NE 19°000) L KNOX ST K23a 6/25. 2 LAFAYETTE (Right) K22b 45/13 3 LAFAYETTE (Left) K22b 4/10	WC W Drew Capt

WAR DIARY or INTELLIGENCE SUMMARY

Army Form C. 2118.

Place	Date	Hour	Summary of Events and Information	Remarks and references to Appendices
Judah Redt Hebuterne (cont'd)			Ft MARIE LOUISE K.16.c 58/06, S. CEMETERY K.16.6 20/78 & PELISSIER K.16.9.90/49 & BATEUSE K.16.c 02/90. 8 FAITH ST K.16.b 30/75. With boy Sgt Bton at K.16.c. 25/65. Guides were arranged for from these positions. Also decided to keep one gun in reserve at boy Sgt Bton in order to be ready to proceed to JOHN COPSE in the event of orders being received to that effect. Applied to Brigade for instruction in the matter as JOHN COPSE in the attack by 92nd Infantry Brigade and 92nd Machine Gun Company had already made the provision.	W
		11.30 am	Sections detailed at 1st Draw No 4.	
			HEBUTERNE (K.16 60/33) and were met by an orderly who instructed 2nd Lieut Durrant and 2nd Lieut Lant that the 6. Occupied as them as boy Sgt Bton. Progressed 2nd Lieut Durrant and Lant arrived at boy Sgt Bton and were told the Am Dunteam. Orders were issued verbally for "A" Section to occupy 1 Knox St No 3 team, 2 LAFAYETTE No K.16. 3 LAFAYETTE No 16.2 team, 8 FAITH ST No 13 team, 8 FAITH ST 2 No 4 th team. MARIE LOUISE and "D" Section 5 CEMETERY No 10 team with the gun of "C" Section No 9 team in reserve at boy Sgt Bton 3 pm arrival of "D" section completes with exception of (A section) complete (Knox St) 3.30 pm Knox St 8 pm Knox St roadside fire	
	15th October 16		9 gun in bnt	
			1 gun in reserve.	
			O.C. "B" Section reconnoitred the HEBUTERNE defences.	W

J B Cowie C.V.

WAR DIARY or INTELLIGENCE SUMMARY

(Erase heading not required.)

Army Form C. 2118.

Place	Date	Hour	Summary of Events and Information	Remarks and references to Appendices
In the field (cont.)	15th Oct 1916	8.00 to 10.00	Situation in trenches normal. Casualties a.c. 1 man sh. Our alert On a recent bombardment met with German between 2.30 and 5 pm on our right ton 5pm. Received orders from O.C. 9th Infantry Brigade to place 2 O.R's in John Copse and night. (The gun in reserve at Bay Sd. Dev.) No 9 gun team under 12384 Bgh B Proud-foot instructed to proceed to take up position in JOHN COPSE and to vacate the position just before daylight. A draft of 1 O.R. joined the Coy from M.G. Corps Base Depot CAMIERS.	JC
"	16th Oct 1916	9 guns in line + reserve	Situation normal. Note no much enemy shelling up to 4 pm an extra HEBUTERNE shelled at intervals. No alteration in weather. Received orders by telephone from Brigade Major to attend at Bde Hd Qrs (J.14.b) at 9.30 am to interview the 2i/c 6 9th Infantry Brigade	JC
"	17th Oct 1916	9 guns in line + reserve	Issued Operation Orders No 5. 8.15am Proceeded to Bde Hd Qrs. 9.30am Interview Appendix V with Brigadier. Instruction received that Night Brigade would hold the line permanently from a point N. W. a peg of JENA STREET C7 to the right to be men of left boundary. Instructed that 8 machine guns of this Coy would be in this action. Ordered to reconnoitre 3 new positions and report on same to Bde Hd Qrs as early as possible. 11-30 am Orders received for an Officer to lie at left battalion Hd Qrs (K.16.c 2/2) in order to consult the CO Coine with the Coptn of M.G Officer 2nd about Barricading for them. He met the Corp M.G Officer and reconnoitred positions for that	JC

J.S. Cowan Lt

Army Form C. 2118.

WAR DIARY
or
INTELLIGENCE SUMMARY

(Erase heading not required.)

Instructions regarding War Diaries and Intelligence Summaries are contained in F.S. Regs., Part II. and the Staff Manual respectively. Title Pages will be prepared in manuscript.

Place	Date	Hour	Summary of Events and Information	Remarks and references to Appendices
	17th Nov 1916 (contd)		6 Machine Guns for the defence of HEBUTERNE village. Situation much quieter on the whole & very shortly to our right. Weather dull	MC
	18th 2/11/16		9 guns in line 7 " " in reserve. Carried out a thorough reconnaissance of the frontage to the held by the Brigade in accordance with instructions received from S.O.6 Bde yesterday. Sent in a report to 2nd Divn 91st Infantry Brigade on the reconnaissance. Recommended that 8 guns be put in the following position:- 1 Du GUASCLIN (K.16.a.30/40) Reserve line; 1 Fort MARIE LOUISE (K.10.c 55/6) already occupied 3 LABOUR TRENCH (K.16.a 80/15) to be put in reserve; to PASTEUR. Ct. (K.16.b 30/28) S. FAITH St right (K.10.c 40/30) Support line 6 PELISSIER K.10/48 Occupied. 1 BATEUSE K.16.69/70 Occupied. 8/FAITH ST.Lt K.16.658/80 Reserve line. Intersection relief carried out all guns except Knox St being clear by 12.15pm. Knox St relieved at 6.15pm. Exceptionally heavy enemy artillery barrage on the right Knox St when casualties Knox St shelled all day. Enemy M.Gs played on HEBUTERNE Casualties wounded slightly at duty 3502h t/ca L.J.5&GHT. S.S. Situation generally normal	RE
	19th Nov 1916		9 guns in line 7 " " reserve. Reconnoitred new position with Offr. Reg. OC left group of MgunsIncludes in a very bad state owing to very heavy rain yesterday afternoon	RE Blower Cpl

2449 Wt. W4957/M90 759,000 1/16 J.B.C. & A. Forms/C.2118/12

WAR DIARY or INTELLIGENCE SUMMARY

Army Form C. 2118.

(Erase heading not required.)

Place	Date	Hour	Summary of Events and Information	Remarks and references to Appendices
Inchton	19th Nov 1916	(contd)	front the two preceeding days. In many parts the parapets and trench walls had fallen away making progress along this line very difficult. Enemy artillery fire rather more active. Situation generally normal. Casualties nil.	
"	20th Nov 1916		9 guns in line 7 " " reserve Situation normal. Usual enemy artillery activity. Shells dropped in vicinity of Bay No 8a also near back section of Don Sd and intervallo b.ops. M.G. Officers regarding the HEADSTERNE defences. Casualties nil.	
"	21st Nov 1916		9 guns in line 7 " " reserve Received orders to attend at R.E.H.Q. this morning had interview with S.O.C. 92nd Infantry Brigade. Instructed to remove the gun from JOHN COPSE thus leaving only 8 gun in the line. Issued the necessary orders. Received B.M. Order No.9 graphic stated that 92nd Infantry Brigade Gun Coy would take over section of the B.M. Boston on 23-11-16. Gave orders to 6. B.M. Order No.92 cancelled and therefore certain sympathy attendant of Unit No 10 & cancelled B.M. Order No 93 received which stated that an Indian Battalion relief would take place on 22/11/16. Issued order to 1 Battalion in the kind normal generally. Casualties nil	Appendix VII
"	22nd Nov 1916		8 guns in line 8 " " reserve Inter-section relief turned out being completed at 2.30 p.m. Situation normal.	

T.P. Cruse Capt.

WAR DIARY or INTELLIGENCE SUMMARY

Army Form C. 2118.

Place	Date	Hour	Summary of Events and Information	Remarks and references to Appendices
South (sgd)	22nd Nov 1916 (contd)		2nd Lieut J.R. Bothwell M.G.C. joined from M.G.C. Base dept.	MC
"	23rd Nov 1916		8 guns in line 8 " reserve Officers quarters shifted to the DELL at present. Received instructions to attend at B.H.Q and interviewed S.O.E and Infantry Brigade. dead dog addition. 10pm 10in. Instructed to remove guns from Knox St. and place it in BRISOU SOUTH	MC
"	24th Nov 1916		8 guns in line 8 " reserve Reconnoitered BRISOUX trench with what I want O.C "D" Section. Decided best place for Vickers gun to be at about point K22 B84/75 just south of junction of BRISOUX TRENCH. Had interview with O.C right Batt in the L.F. and arranged known in connection with him the placing a Lewis gun at south end of BRISOUX trench with Vickers. Received orders to meet Capt M.G.C. at H4 216/93rd Infantry Brigade in order to reconnoiter the Northern culmination of trenches occupied by the 31st Division at 9.30am 25/11/16. Company handing started	MC
"	25th Nov 1916		8 guns in the line 8 " reserve Met Capts. A. S.O. as arranged and reconnoitered line with him, together with OC's 92 & 93 Machine Gun Companies	MC

W.B.Cowles Capt.

Army Form C. 2118.

WAR DIARY
or
INTELLIGENCE SUMMARY
(Erase heading not required.)

Place	Date	Hour	Summary of Events and Information	Remarks and references to Appendices
In the Field	25th Nov 1916		8 guns in line 8 " in reserve Issued Order No 8. Situation quiet generally.	J.C. Appendix VIII
	27th Nov 1916		Inter section relief effected by 2.30 p.m. Situation normal. Received instruction to meet Capt M.S.O. at H.Q. 2nd Infantry Brigade Staff at 9.30 am 28.11.16 in order to reconnoitre remainder of Divisional front & a view to placing machine guns definitely in the "RED LINE"	J.C.
	28th Nov 1916		8 guns in line 8 " reserve Went & ill reconnoitred the lines with Capt M.S.O. & provisional M.G. positions were decided upon. R.E. to make strong emplacements & dug out positions before these stations can be occupied. Casualties nil.	J.C.
	29th Nov 1916		8 guns in line 8 " reserve Situation normal. Casualties - sick to hospital 1	J.C.
	30th Nov 1916		Situation normal. Casualties, wounded slightly at duty - 1.	J.C.

T. Blank Captain
O.C. NO. 94 M. G. COY.

COPY No. 8.

94th MACHINE GUN COMPANY OPERATION ORDER. No. 2.

Ref. Map.] 57.D.N.E
1/20,000.

3.11.16.

1. "A" Section will be relieved in positions:- V.1, V.2 and LAFAYETTE (2 guns) by "D" Section on the morning of November 4th 1916.

2. O.C. "A" Section will leave a guide for each position at the Dump, HEBUTERNE at 9.15 a.m. 4/11/16.
   "D" Section will be at the dump at this time.

3. All S.A.A. in belts, tripods & all trench stores will be handed over by the N.C.Os at each position, receipts being taken.

4. On completion of relief "A" Section will be marched into billets at SAILLY by 2nd Lieut. A. M. Cant.
   Limbers will be at the dump at 12.30 p.m. to bring guns, etc. out.

5. 2nd Lieut Rex will remain in the line & assist 2nd Lieut Durrant.

6. Completion of relief to be reported to Company Headquarters.

Acknowledge.

Bowen, Captain.
O.C. NO. 94 M.G. COY.

Copy No. 1. 94th Infantry Brigade (for information).
"   "   2. C.O.
"   "   3. O.C. "A" Section.
"   "   4. O.C. "B"   "
"   "   5. O.C. "C"   "
"   "   6. O.C. "D"   "
"   "   7. O.C. Transport Section.
"   "   8. War Diary.
"   "   9. File.

COPY No. 8

94th Machine Gun Company Operation Order. No. 3.

Ref. Map 57D. NE.
1/20000

1. The 94th Machine Gun Company will be relieved in the positions at present held, by the 93rd Machine Gun Company, on November 7th 1916.

2. Section Officers will have a guide for each position, (except JOHN COPSE) at the Dump, HEBUTERNE, at 10.30 a.m. 7/11/16.

3. O.C. "D" Section will arrange for a guide for JOHN COPSE to remain behind at LAFAYETTE, who will take the relieving gun team to their position after dusk.

4. All trench stores etc. will be handed over by the N.C.O. at each position, who will obtain a receipt for same, also a certificate stating that the emplacements & dugouts are clean.

5. Limbers for guns, (except JOHN COPSE gun) to be at HEBUTERNE at the following times:-

   "C" Section. (4 guns) at 12 noon.
   "B" Section (4 ") " 12.30 p.m.
   "D" Section. (3 ") " 2.15 p.m.

   Only ½-limber will be up for each section.

6. Immediately after relief all gun teams, (except JOHN COPSE gun), will proceed to the Dump, HEBUTERNE, pack their limber ready for the Section Officer, who will march the section in COIGNEUX. A guide will be at the entrance to the village to show where the billets are.

7. The JOHN COPSE team (ie. the M.G. Officer's men) on relief will move to the position in the cemetery (K.26.c.17.35) where they will remain for the night. Their rations for the day (8/11/16) will be at their dugout there for them.

8. A half-limber will be at the dump HEBUTERNE at 10.0 a.m. 8/11/16 at which time the JOHN COPSE gun team will have their gun, spare parts, etc on the dump ready to pack. They will then proceed to billets in COIGNEUX.

9. Completion of relief to be reported to Company Headquarters.

   Acknowledge.

B. Cowen.
Captain
O.C. No. 94 M.G. COY.

Copy No. 1. - 94th Inf. Bde. (for information)
" " 2. O.C. M.G. Group.
" " 3. C. D.
" " 4. Lieut. Dick.
" " 5. 2Lt. Sykes.
" " 6. 2Lt. _____
" " 7. 2Lt. Gascoine.
" " 8. War Diary.
" " 9. File.

COPY No. 10   SECRET

94th Machine Gun Company Operation Order No. 4.

Ref. Map) 57 D.N.E.
) 1/20,000

1. The 94th Machine Gun Company will relieve the 92nd + 93rd Machine Gun Companies in the line today 14/11/16.

2. Dispositions of guns will be as follows.
   (a). 4 guns of "A" Section under 2Lt A. M. Cant in positions: V.1; V.2; LAFAYETTE + JOHN COPSE.
   (b). 4 guns of "D" Section under 2Lt. N. W. Durrant in positions: VERCINGETORIX; FORT MARIE LOUISE; CEMETERY; PELISSIER (V.12).
   (c). 1 gun of "C" Section in position: BATEUSE (V.13)
        (To come under command of 2Lt. Durrant.)
   (d). "B" section will be in reserve in SAILLY.
        O.C. "B" Section is responsible for reconnoitering the HEBUTERNE defences, which his guns will occupy in the event of an enemy attack.
   (e). The remainder of "C" Section will be in reserve in SAILLY.
   (f). The transport and Q.M. stores will be situated at Q.3.16.b.6.1.

3. Guides for each position will be at the dump HEBUTERNE at 9.30.a.m.

4. The unexpired portion of the today's rations, + to-morrow's rations will be carried by each team.

5. Trench stores will be taken over in the usual way. Lists of stores taken over to be sent to Company Hd. Qrs as early as possible.

6. Company Hd. Qrs. will be in the line at K.16.C.2.6.

7. Completion of relief to be reported to Company Hd. Qrs.

Acknowledge.

                                                JB Cowan
                                                Captain.
                                                O.C. 94th M.G. Coy

Copy No 1.   94th Infantry Brigade. (for information)
"   " 2.   O.C. 92nd M.G. Coy
"   " 3.   O.C. 93rd M.G. Coy
"   " 4.   C.O.
"   " 5.   O.C. "A" Section.
"   " 6.   "   "B"   "
"   " 7.   "   "C"   "
"   " 8.   "   "D"   "
"   " 9.   "   Transport
"   " 10.   "   War Diary.
"   " 11.   "   File

94th Machine Gun Company SECRET
Operation Order No 5

Ref. Map 57 DNE / 1/10000

1. The following inter section relief will take place on the morning of November 18th 1916:

   (a) "A" Section will be relieved in positions
      1. KNOX STREET
      2. LAFAYETTE (Right)
      3. LAFAYETTE (Left)
      4. FORT MARIE LOUISE
   by "C" Section, under 2/Lieut Sykes with Headquarters about K.2.d. 00/60 (MAISON PAS DEMIE)

   (b) "D" Section will be relieved in positions
      6. PELISSIER
      7. BATEUSE
      8. FAITH ST
   by "B" Section under 2/Lieut Rex with Headquarters about K.16.c. 75/80
   The gun of "D" Section in CEMETERY position will stand fast, and will come under command of 2/Lieut Rex when relief is complete.

   (c) The gun of "C" Section at present holding JOHN COPSE by night will be relieved by the fourth gun of "B" Section, which gun and team will proceed to bay Headquarters (K.16.c. 75/65) from the dump for guiding the team to the position in JOHN COPSE and remain there till dusk, when arrangements will be made.

2. "C" Section (3 guns) will parade at the transport field at 8.30am and "B" Section at 9.05am, on 18/11/16 and will proceed to the dump HEBUTERNE. Number 9 gun team at present holding JOHN COPSE by night will move into position at FORT MARIE LOUISE at 10.30am and will not require a guide.
   Rations for the day will be carried. O.C. "C" Section will arrange to take rations for his fourth gun team to be brought to bay H.Q.

3. Guides will be provided as follows to be at the dump HEBUTERNE at the times stated.
      3 guides from "D" Section at 9am for "C" Section
      "   "   "   "A"   "   " 9.45am for "B"   "

4. As it is impossible to relieve KNOX ST by daylight the team for this position will move to LAFAYETTE (Left) and remain there till dark. The team that is relieved will move to bay H.Q. on relief and remain there all night returning to Transport next day with empty ration limber.
   All mark III tripods, belt boxes and all trench stores will be handed over at each position. The special form issued to gun team commanders being used. Section officers will hand over all maps, barrage orders and any other useful information.

5. Limbers will be at the dump at the following times:
      For "D" Section ½ limber at 10.45 a.m.
      " "A"   "   ½   "   at 11.45 a.m.

6. After relief "D" Section will be responsible for the defence of the lines which have been occupied in the event of an enemy attack.

7. Lists of trench stores taken over will be sent to bay H.Q. as early as possible after relief.

8. Completion of relief to be reported.

Acknowledge.
                              6. 2/Lt Durrant (B Sect)
Copy to   1. O.C. 94 Infantry Brigade   7. 2/Lt Gascoyne (D.O.S.)
          2. O.C.   8. Lieut Hill
          3. 2/Lt Cork (A Sect)   9. Hqr. Diary
          4. 2/Lt Rex (B   ")   10. File
          5. 2/Lt Sykes (C ")

COPY No 10   94th Machine Gun Company.   SECRET.

Operation Order No. 6.

Ref. Map { 57° N.E.
          { 1/20000.

The following inter-section reliefs will take place on the morning of 22/11/16:—

(a) "C" Section will be relieved in positions,
    KNOX ST.
    LAFAYETTE (Right) } by "D" Section, & in position FORT MARIE LOUISE by that
        " (Left) } gun of "B" Section at present holding JOHN COPSE by
    night under 2nd Lieut Durrant.

(b) The gun of "B" Section holding JOHN COPSE by night will be relieved by a gun of "A" Section.

(c) The gun of "D" Section at present holding the cemetery position will be relieved by a gun of "A" Section under 2nd Lieut. A.M. Cant.

(d) The gun of "B" Section at present holding JOHN COPSE will proceed to FORT MARIE LOUISE immediately after relief.

"D" Section (3 guns), & two guns of "A" Section will parade at transport lines & move off at 9.a.m. 22/11/16, arriving at the dump HEBUTERNE at 10.a.m.
O.s.C. "B" & "C" Sections will have the necessary guides on the dump at this time.
O.C. "C" Section will have a guide for FORT MARIE LOUISE at the cemetery at 10.30 a.m.

3. Ingoing teams will draw gum boots at the gum boot store SAILLY on the way up. These boots will be put on after leaving the dump. Outgoing ones will take their gum boots out with them & leave them at the gum boot store SAILLY as they pass.

4. Rations for the day will be carried by all ranks. O.C. "D" Section will arrange for the rations for FORT MARIE LOUISE to be put on his limber. These will be met on the dump by a ration party.

5. All Tripods MK IV, belt boxes & trench stores will be handed over as usual, the special form issued to gun team commanders being used. Section Officers will hand over all maps, bearings & any useful information etc.

6. KNOX ST will be relieved by day if possible. If not possible, the team after relief at night will proceed to the CEMETERY returning to billets by the empty ration limber next day.

7. "C" Section & one gun of "D" Section will return to billets after relief. A Half-limber will be on the dump at 11.30 a.m.

8. The following reliefs will take place on the 23rd inst.
"D" Section will be relieved in positions,
    PELISSIER
    BATEUSE } by 3 guns of the 92nd Machine Gun Company.
    FAITH ST

9. O.C. "D" Section will have guides on the dump HEBUTERNE at 2 p.m. 23/11/16.

10. Trench stores will be handed over at each position in the usual way.

11. On relief all tripods MK IV & belt boxes will be taken to the CEMETERY & handed over to "A" Section.

12. The following moves will take place on the morning of 23/11/16.
2 guns of "A" Section will proceed to the CEMETERY arriving there at 12-noon & will be in mobile reserve there. Gum boots will be drawn from the gum boot store SAILLY on the way up. Tripods & belt boxes will be taken over from "B" Section later in the day.

13. Trench store lists will be sent to Coy. Hd. Qrs as early as possible after relief.

14. Completion of relief to be reported to Coy. Hd. Qrs.

Acknowledge.

                                                      B. Cowie, Captain.
                                                      O.C. 94th M.G. Coy.

COPY No 1. 94th Infy. Bde. (for information).
" " 2. O.C. 92nd M.G. Coy.
" " 3. C.O.
" " 4. Lieut Hill.
" " 5. O.C. "A" Section
" " 6. " "B" "
" " 7. " "C" "
" " 8. " "D" "
" " 9. " Transport
" " 10. War Diary.
" " 11. File.

COPY No 10.   SECRET.

94th Machine Gun Company.
Operation Order No 7.

Ref Map { 57D N.E.
         { 1/20,000.

1. Reference Operation Order No.6. of 21/11/16:-
The following paragraphs are cancelled, viz. 1(b), 1(c), 1(d), 2, 7, 8, 9, 10, 11, 12; and the following substituted:-

2. (a). "B" Section will be relieved in positions,-
   PELISSIER. }
   BATEUSE.   } by 3 guns of "A" Section on morning of 22/11/16.
   FAITH ST.   }
   (b). The gun of "D" Section holding the cemetery position will be relieved by the fourth gun of "A" Section on morning of 22/11/16.
   (c). The gun of "B" Section which recently held JOHN COPSE will move to position FORT MARIE LOUISE at 10.0 am. 22/11/16.

3. (a). "D" Section will parade at Transport lines & move off at 8.30 a.m., arriving at the dump HEBUTERNE at 9.30 a.m.
   (b). "A" Section will move off at 9.0 a.m. arriving at the dump HEBUTERNE at 10.0 a.m.
   (c). Gum Boots will be drawn en route. O.s.C. "B" & "C" Sections will arrange for guides to meet the relieving teams.

4. Gun Teams being relieved will march to billets after relief. A half limber for "B" Section will be at the dump at 11.0 a.m. A half limber for "C" Section will be at the dump at 12.30 p.m.

5. Paragraphs 1(a), 3, 4, 5, 6, 13 & 14 hold good.

    Acknowledge.

                                             H B Cowen
                                                    Captain.
                                             O.C. 94th M.G. Coy.

Copy No.1. 94th Infy. Bde (for information).
  "   " 2. O.C. 94nd M.G. Coy.
  "   " 3. C.O.
  "   " 4. Lieut Hill.
  "   " 5. 2nd Lieut Cant.
  "   " 6.   "   " Rex.
  "   " 7.   "   " Sykes.
  "   " 8.   "   " Derrant.
  "   " 9.   "   " Gascoine.
  "   "10. War Diary.
  "   "11. File.

Confidential

Volume ~~XIII~~ Vol 80

War Diary

91st Machine Gun Coy.   31st Division

December 1916.

WAR DIARY or INTELLIGENCE SUMMARY

(Erase heading not required.)

No. Army Form C. 2118.
No. 1 MACHINE GUN COMPANY.
No. Q/1/24
Date 2-1-17

Vol. VII

Place	Date	Hour	Summary of Events and Information	Remarks and references to Appendices
In the field	1.12.16		8 Guns in the line. (B & C sections) 8 guns in reserve (A & D sections). Issued Trench Standing Orders	Appendix No. 1 WC
do	2.12.16		Allocation of guns as before. Issued Operation Order No. 9	Appendix No. 2 WC
do	3.12.16		A section relieved B section in the right group. D section relieved C section in left group.	WC
do	4.12.16 / 5.12.16		8 Guns in the line; 8 in reserve. The sections in reserve were employed in cleaning up all guns, gear & equipment.	WC
do	6.12.16		Allocation of guns as before. Issued Operation Order No. 10. Draft of 4 Reinforcements arrived from M.G. Base Depot.	Appendix No. 3 WC
do	7.12.16		D section relieved A section in the right group. B section relieved D section in the left group.	WC
do	8.12.16 / 9.12.16		8 Guns in the line; 8 in reserve. The sections in reserve were employed in cleaning up all guns, gear & equipment.	WC
do	10.12.16		Allocation of guns as before. Issued Operation Order No. 11. Church Parade for sections in reserve.	Appendix No. 4 WC
do	11.12.16		A section relieved B section in left group. D section relieved C section in right group.	WC
do	12.12.16		8 guns in line; 8 in reserve. Draft of 2 Reinforcements arrived from M.G. Base Depot.	WC
do	13.12.16		Allocation of guns as before. Situation normal.	WC
do	14.12.16		Had an interview with O.C. Right Artillery Group with a view to co-operating M.G. fire with artillery in a gap in enemy wire at K.14.d.1.1. Arranged for a position to be put in WARRIOR trench at K.16.b.55.30 for this purpose & which is being made for a Am- proposed raid by 12th Yorks Regt. wheat trench mortars left Coy. to be ready A.D.C. to destroy A.D.C. to G.O.C. 31st Divn.	WC
do	15.12.16		Allocation of guns as before. Situation normal.	WC
do	16.12.16		Allocation of guns as before. Issued Operation Order No. 12.	Appendix No. 5 WC
do	17.12.16		Intersection relief carried out. Went to advanced Bay. HQ. in the line, to line for a few days in order to get work in hand regarding dugouts	Edward Cuff Captain

WAR DIARY
INTELLIGENCE SUMMARY

Army Form C. 2118.

(Erase heading not required.)

Instructions regarding War Diaries and Intelligence Summaries are contained in F. S. Regs., Part II. and the Staff Manual respectively. Title Pages will be prepared in manuscript.

Place	Date	Hour	Summary of Events and Information	Remarks and references to Appendices
In the field	18.12.16 19.12.16		Usual Allocation of Guns. Situation Normal.	W.E.
do	20.12.16		Situation Normal. 'C' Section in reserve constructed miniature range for training purposes, opposite Coy Billets in the DFL. 1 man Wounded in line	W.E.
do	21.12.16		Allocation of guns & Situation normal. Range-practice for sections in reserve.	W.E.
do	22.12.16		Received 914th Brigade Operation Order No 106 referring to a raid. Issued Operation Order No 13 & 14. Enemy shelled CEMETERY position	Appendices 69 & 70
do	23.12.16		Usual 6 day intersection relief. At night a raid was carried out by 914th Brigade. Our guns in FORT MARIE-LOUISE, CEMETERY & PELISSIER fired on enemy wire & trenches.	W.E.
do	24.12.16		Situation normal.	W.E.
do	25.12.16		Arrangements had been made for Christmas celebrations. Programme was as follows:- Breakfast 12:30pm – Dinner 4:30pm – Tea 6:00pm – Smoking Concert.	W.E.
do	26.12.16 27.12.16		Allocation of guns & Situation normal	W.E.
do	28.12.16		Situation normal. Issued operation order No. 15.	Appendix No 8.
do	29.12.16		Inter-Section relief successfully carried out.	W.E.
do	30.12.16 31.12.16		Situation & Allocation of guns normal.	W.E.
			N.B. From 16th to 31st the gun in position BATROSE fired in conjunction with the Royal Artillery, engaging enemy working parties etc doing excellent work.	W.E.

W R Cowan Capt

94th MACHINE GUN COMPANY.
TRENCH STANDING ORDERS.

I. ROUTINE.

1. DUTIES. A Machine Gun team in the trenches will usually consist of 1 N.C.O. & 4 men. The N.C.O. is responsible for the cleanliness, etc. of his position, the posting of sentries, & the carrying on of any work in continuity. He must see that all men are up & at their correct station at morning & evening 'stand to'. He is also responsible that the guns, ammunition etc are cleaned at least once every day.

An officer will usually be in command of from 2 to 4 guns in the trenches, & he is responsible for everything connected with such guns generally. He is responsible that these standing orders are known by all ranks under his command & that they are rigidly adhered to.

2. EMPLACEMENTS. All Machine Gun Emplacements must be kept in such a condition that they can cover the whole of the ground prescribed to them. Closed Emplacements must be maintained in perfect repair. The N.C.O. in charge must ensure by frequent testing that the loophole can be cleared quickly, & that when cleared there is no obstruction in front which would interfere with the fire effect of the gun. Unless used as a dugout nothing whatever except gun equipment will be kept in a closed position. Open emplacements must always be kept clean; the platform clear of anything other than the tripod & ammunition, & they must be concealed from possible observation by aircraft by day.

3. MACHINE GUNS. Normally in closed positions guns will be kept mounted at all times. In an open emplacement a disappearing mounting will be kept as a trench store, & the gun will be mounted at 'evening stand to' on this mounting, & kept in the lowered position, being dismounted again after morning 'stand to'. At an open emplacement, by day the gun will be kept in a chest let into the wall of the trench, near the bottom where such is available. If not available it will be kept in the dugout, near the entrance.

At all times when mounted, guns will be kept half loaded, with lock-spring released. The condenser will always be adjusted at morning 'stand to'.

4. AMMUNITION. There will always be 12 boxes of filled belts at each position, also 5 boxes of S.A.A.; the contents of one such box will be removed from bandoliers or clips & kept as an immediate supply to fill belts in case of an action; there will also be 1 box of Very Lights & 24 Bombs.

Two belt boxes will always be kept beside the gun. The remainder of the belt boxes & the reserve will be divided & kept in at least 2 ammunition stores, which should be slits cut into the trench wall & properly revetted & provided with a gas blanket to lower in case of attack. These stores should be at least 10 yards apart. In exceptional circumstances the position itself (if a closed one) may be considered to be one such store. Any undercutting of trench sides for this or any other purpose is prohibited.

5. TRENCH STORES. The following material will be kept at each position, & handed over on relief viz:

    Vermoral Sprayer - when available.
    2 Tins V.S. Solution -   "
    1 Tin of Mineral Jelly.
    Gas blankets for dugouts & ammunition stores.
    Range Card.

(Besides the above mentioned - 5000 rounds S.A.A, 1 box Very Lights & 24 Bombs) The N.C.O. in charge is responsible that any shortages are at once made known to the Section Officer who will indent on Company Hd. Qrs. to complete without delay.

6. SENTRIES. (a) In the front or support line a single sentry will be on duty at each position by day; a double sentry will be posted at night.

(b) In rear positions, a single sentry will be on duty at all times, unless an attack is considered imminent, or in other special circumstances.

(c) The length of time each sentry is on duty will generally be two hours by day & one hour by night. In particularly bad weather the periods of duty must be reduced.

(d) The N.C.O. in charge of each position will write a roster showing at what hours each man will be on duty.

(e) Most of our teams, although they may hold the rank of unpaid l/cpl are to be exercised their normal term of sentry duty.

(f) Every sentry must be regularly posted by an N.C.O., who will explain to him his duties, & make certain that the sentry knows what to do in any eventuality.

6. **SENTRIES** (contd) (g) If the emplacement is an open one the sentry will stand beside the machine gun platform, or between the platform & the gun when dismounted. If a closed one he will stand at the door of the emplacement.
(h) By day in the front or support line every sentry must be provided with a periscope, & by night they must have a Very Pistol beside them.
(i) The sentry on duty must study the enemy's trenches through his periscope. He must report anything unusual or anything of interest at once to the nearest officer.
(j) Whenever possible, a bombing post will be arranged for close beside the gun.

7. **CARE OF MACHINE GUNS, ETC.** The Section Officer will inspect all guns, revolvers, rifles & bayonets under his charge at morning & evening 'stand to' daily. He will also inspect all ammunition in belts, S.A.A. boxes, oil supplies, Vermorel Sprayers, etc. once every day. He will ensure that no two guns under his charge are being cleaned at the same time by giving each N.C.O. a specific time at which to start cleaning his gun. All guns etc. to be thoroughly cleaned by 10 a.m. each day. He will report all correct to Coy. Hd. Qrs. each day.

8. **ARMS AND EQUIPMENT** (a) Equipment will always be worn by men in the trenches.
(b) Ration & carrying parties, orderlies, etc. will wear equipment & carry arms.
(c) Except when it is necessary to fire, a round will never be kept in the chamber.
(d) The magazine will always be kept charged with 9 rounds when in the trenches.
(e) Men armed with revolvers will have their weapons loaded when on duty.
(f) By night all bayonets will be fixed.
(g) Attention of all ranks is directed to the fact that no man is to clean his rifle until both the bolt & magazine have been removed.

9. **FIRING.** No firing is allowed from the Battle position or first alternative position unless a particularly favourable target offers itself or in the case of attack, raid, etc. Any firing from front line guns should be done from the parapet some 50ˣ to the flank of the real position. After any such firing the gun engaged in it will be taken back to its battle position at once. In rear positions there will always be a special indirect fire position where necessary.

10. **WORK.** Work on all positions must be carried out in continuity. Unless work of repairing & improving existing emplacements, dugouts, parapets, & making as many alternative positions ammunition depots etc. as possible, is proceeded with at all times the state of the trenches would very soon become serious, & the health of the men would also suffer owing to lack of exercise.
Section Officers must draw up a programme of proposed work, showing times of work & number of men to be employed & they must ensure that all such work is properly carried out under the supervision of the N.C.O. at each position. On handing over positions in a relief, a list of the work being proceeded with & proposed will be given to the relieving Officer by the Officer being relieved; this will ensure all work started being carried on with.

11. **REPORTS & RETURNS.** Section Officers will send in the following reports & returns to Coy. Hd. Qrs. to reach Coy. Hd. Qrs. at the times mentioned:-
(a) Daily. 8.0 a.m:- Report of any firing done from 8.0 a.m. to 8.0 a.m.
   Situation Report   do
   Progress   do
   12.0 noon:- Certificate that inspections have been out & all found correct or otherwise.
   Trench Stores & R.E. material Required.
   1.0 p.m:- Casualties - from 12 noon to 12 noon.
(b) The day of taking over trenches:- Relief Complete.
(c) The day following taking over trenches:- List of Stores at each position.
   Programme of work proposed.
(d) The day of relief. 12 noon:- List of trench stores at each position.
   Summary of work done & being done.
   As soon as possible:- Relief complete.

12. **DEFENCE.** The manner in which the line is to be defended will be made known to Section Officers, who will take the necessary steps to see that everything affecting the guns in their charge is made known to all ranks.

13. **SANITATION, ETC.** The N.C.O. in charge at each position will see that all emplacements, dugouts, ammunition stores, also the traverse in which are the gun & dugout, are cleaned & in a sanitary condition immediately after morning 'stand to'. He is responsible that they are kept clean all day. Unless the tactical situation does not permit, all men will be washed & shaved, & have their clothing, boots & equipment brushed & clean by 10.0 a.m. daily. The Section Officer must see that this is strictly carried out, as otherwise slackness in everything will be the result.

94 Machine Gun Company
Additions to Trench Standing Orders

G.1.

(1) All guns are to be kept in the safest place possible within 15 yards at most of their battle position and not mounted in the day time unless the situation makes it imperative.
The gun must be in the bag, carrying "M.G.", or wrapped in a waterproof sheet to prevent dirt getting into mechanism.

(2) Each gun will have a sentry from the gun team watching the ground it has to cover. He must have means of alarming the team in the dug-out.

(3) Officers in charge of Sections in the line are to report daily to the O.C. Companies in the line in front of their guns, for the purpose of ascertaining all their arrangements regarding:
   (a) Patrols in "No Man's Land"
   (b) Position of Advanced Posts
   (c) Routes which will be used by carrying parties & reliefs to advanced posts, & hours when reliefs will take place.
   (d) Working parties in advance of the Red Line.

(4) Section Officers must drill their teams against time, in getting their guns into action from the dugout, on the alarm being given, and make every effort to reduce the time taken to a minimum.
This will be carried out each day & every other night, the times being taken & sent with the daily reports to Coy. H.Q.

(5) Glycerine or anti-freezing mixture will be kept in all barrel casings of guns in trenches.

(6) Every member of the gun team must know & be prepared to explain to inspecting officers:
   (a) The object with which the gun is placed there.
   (b) The direction of its fire & ranges, & names of prominent objects seen from the position.
   (c) The position & directions of fire of the guns to his right & left.
   (d) His orders in case of a bombardment, in case of attack, in case of gas attack, in case of night attack.
   (e) The arrangements for alarming gun team in dugout.
   (f) The positions of the nearest telephone,
          "   "   "   Infantry Commander
          "   "   "   belt filling depot.

(7) Special precautions are necessary for the concealment of battle positions e.g.
   (a) Never to be seen or to use a periscope from the emplacement if the same ground can be seen from another point.
   (b) Not to leave sandbags, tools, clothing etc on the parapet close to an emplacement.
   (c) To prevent cooking by day & lights or smoking by night in or near the emplacement.
   (d) To conceal the flash of the gun if the emplacement is used to repulse an attack.

F. B......
Captain
Comdg. 94th M.G.Coy.

16-12-16

Copy No 5.   SECRET

94th Machine Gun Company.
Operation Order No 8.

Map Ref 57D NE { 1/20000 }

1. No 5 Gun Team of "B" Section will relieve No 3 Gun Team of "A" Section in position FORT MARIE LOUISE on the morning of December 1st 1916.

2. No 5 Gun team will parade ready to move off at 10.30 a.m. and will move off with ration limber. Rations for the day will be carried.

3. The Gun at present in position will be taken over together with Trench Stores in the usual way.

4. On relief No 3 Gun team will proceed to billets under Sgt Blair.

Acknowledge.

                                                B. Cowan. Captain
                                                O.C. No. 94 M.G. COY.

Copy No 1 to C.O
   "   " 2 - O.C. "A" Section
   "   " 3 - O.C. "B"   "
   "   " 4 - O.C. "C"   "
   "   " 5 - War Diary.
   "   " 6 - File.

Copy No 9   94th Machine Gun Company   SECRET   G.10
                 Operation Order No 9   2-12-16.

Ref. Map {SDNE 1/20000}

1. The following inter-section relief will take place on the morning of December 3rd 1916:-
   (a) "A" Section will relieve "B" Section in right sector (positions BRISOUX, LAFAYETTE, FORT MARIE LOUISE, FORT BRIGGS)
   (b) "D" Section will relieve "C" Section in left sector (positions FAITH ST, BATEUSE, PELISSIER, CEMETERY)

2. "A" Section will parade and move off at 9 a.m. arriving at the dump HEBUTERNE at 10 a.m.
   "D" Section will parade and move off at 9.30 a.m. arriving at the dump HEBUTERNE at 10.30 a.m.
   O.C.'s "B" & "C" Sections will provide guides as usual.

3. Rations for the day will be carried by all ranks.

4. Gun boots will be drawn en route.

5. Trench stores will be handed over at each position in the usual way. Limbers will be at the dump from 8/- 11.30: to collect 12 noon.

6. Completion of relief will be reported to Coy. Hd. Qrs.

   Acknowledge.

Copy No 1 to 94th I. Bd. (for information)
     " 2 " C.O.
     " 3 " 2nd Lieut Cant ("A" Sect)
     " 4 " Lieut Howard ("B" ")
     " 5 " 2nd Lieut Sykes ("C" ")
     " 6 " Lieut Wurrest   ("D" ")
     " 7 "   Hill   (S.O)
     " 8 " War Diary
     " 9 " File.

                                    F.B.Cowen.
                                         Capt.
                        Commanding 94th M.G. Coy.

Copy No. 8   9th Machine Gun Company   SECRET.
                                                             G.10.
                        Operation Order No. 10.
                                                             6-12-16
Ref. Map 57D NE
         1/20000

1. The following intersection relief will take place on
   the morning of December 7th.
   (a) "C" Section will relieve "A" Section in right section
       position (BRISON X LAFAYETTE, FORT MARIE LOUISE &
       FORT BRIGGS)
   (b) "B" Section will relieve "D" Section in left section
       position (FAITH ST, BATEUSE, PELISSIER & CEMETERY.)

2. "C" Section will parade and move off at 9 a.m. arriving at
   the dump HEBUTERNE at 10 a.m.
   "B" Section will parade and move off at 9.30 a.m. arriving at
   the dump HEBUTERNE at 10.30 a.m.
   O.C. "A" & "D" Sections will provide guides as usual.

3. Rations for the day will be carried by all ranks.

4. Gum boots will be drawn, in route, at the store
   SAILLY, if available, if not they will be handed
   over from the trenches.

5. Trench stores will be handed over at each position
   in the usual way. Limbers will be at the dump
   for "D" Section at 11 a.m., and "A" Section at 11.30 a.m.

6. Completion of relief will be reported to Coy. H. Qrs.
   in code.

   Acknowledge.

                                    J.B.Cowen.
                                         Captain
                                Comm'd'g 9th M.G. Coy.

Copy No. 1 to 91 Inf. Bde. (for information)
     " " 2 " C.O.
     " " 3 " 2nd Lieut. Bart ("A" Sect)
     " " 4 " Lieut. Dowyard ("B" ")
     " " 5 " 2nd Lieut. Sykes ("C" ")
     " " 6 " Lieut. Edwart ("D" ")
              " Bell (S.O.)
     " " 7 " War Diary
     " " 8 " File.

COPY No 8.   94th Machine Gun Company.   SECRET.
           Operation Order No. 11   G.10
    Ref. Map 57d NE.   10-12-16.
        1/20,000.

(1). The following inter-section reliefs will take place on the morning of December 11th 1916:-
  (a) "A" Section will relieve "B" Section in left group (positions: FAITH ST, BATEUSE, PELISSIER, CEMETERY).
  (b). "D" Section will relieve "C" Section in right group, (positions BRISOUX, CAVOTTY, FORT MARIE LOUISE), with one gun in mobile reserve in the CEMETERY. This gun will ultimately occupy a position in FAITH ST. (right,- K.16.b.6.3.). In the meantime the gun team will carry on with work on this position.

(2). "D" Section will parade & move off at 9 a.m, arriving at the dump HEBUTERNE at 10 a.m.
  "A" Section will parade & move off at 9.30 a.m, arriving at the dump HEBUTERNE at 10.30 a.m.
  (b). "B" & "C" Sections will provide guides as usual.

(3). Rations for the day will be carried by all ranks.

(4). Gum Boots will be drawn "en route", at the Gum Boot Store, SAILLY, if available, if not they will be handed over in the trenches.

(5). Trench Stores will be handed over at each position in the usual way.

(6). Limbers will be at the dump, HEBUTERNE for "B" Section at 11.30 a.m., & for "C" Section at 12 noon.

(7). Completion of relief will be reported to Coy. Hd. Qrs in code.

(8). It is notified for information that the tour of duty in the line will in future be for six days.

    Acknowledge.

                                J B Caven.
                                    Captain
                              Comdg. 94th M.G. Coy.

COPY No 1. 94th Infy. Bde (for information).
  "   " 2. C.O.
  "   " 3. 2nd Lieut. Cant. ("A" Section).
  "   " 4. Lieut. Howard. ("B"   "   ).
  "   " 5. 2/Lieut. Sykes. ("C"   "   ).
  "   " 6. Lieut. Durrant. ("D"   "   ).
  "   " 7.   "   Hill. (Transport).
  "   " 8. War Diary.
  "   " 9. File.

COPY. No. 8.   94th Machine Gun Company.   SECRET.

Operation Order. No. 12.   G.10.

Ref. Map 57°NE   16.12.16.
        1/20,000.

(1). The following intersection reliefs will take place on the morning of December 17th 1916.
  (a) "C" Section will relieve 3 guns of "A" Section + 1 gun of "D" section in positions 11TH ST., BATEUSE, PELISSIER, and REVEL.
  (b) "B" Section will relieve 3 guns of "D" Section + 1 gun of "A" section in positions BRISOUX, CAVONTY, FORT MARIE LOUISE + CEMETERY.

(2) "B" section will parade + move off at 9 a.m., arriving at the dump HEBUTERNE at 10 a.m.
    "C" section will parade + move off at 9.30 a.m., arriving at the dump HEBUTERNE at 10.30 a.m.

(3) O.C. "A" + "D" sections will provide guides as usual.

(3) Rations for the day will be carried by all ranks.

(4) Gum Boots will be drawn "en route" at the Gum Boot Store, SAILLY* if available, if not they will be taken over in the trenches.

(5) Trench stores will be handed over at each position in the usual way.

(6) Limbers will be @ the dump, HEBUTERNE, for "A" section at 11.30 a.m, + for "D" section at 12 noon.

(7) Completion of relief will be reported to Coy. Hd. Qrs. in &c.

   Acknowledge.

                                        J.B.Cowen. Captain
                                        Comdg. 94th M.G. Coy.

Copy No.1. 94th Infy. Bde.(For information).
  "   " 2. C.O.
  "   " 3. 2/Lieut. Cant. ("A" Section).
  "   " 4. Lieut. Howard. ("B"   "   ).
  "   " 5. 2/ "   Sykes. ("C"   "   ).
  "   " 6. Lieut. Durrant. ("D" "   ).
  "   " 7.   "   Still. (Transport).
  "   " 8. War Diary.
  "   " 9. File.

* Brigade Gum Boot Store :- No. 69 Billet opposite present Divnl. Store.

COPY N° 8   SECRET

4th Machine Gun Company
Operation Order N° 13

REF MAP { 57D N.E.   22-12-16
         { 1/20,000

1. The following intersection reliefs will take place on the morning of December 23rd/24/16
   (a) "D" Section will relieve the guns of "C" Section in positions FAITH ST., BATEUSE, PELISSIER and REVEL.
   (b) "A" Section will relieve 4 guns of "B" Section in positions BRISEUX, CAVOUR IV, FORT MAIRIE LOUISE and CEMETERY.

2. "D" Section will parade & move off at 9 a.m., arriving at the dump HEBUTERNE at 10.15 a.m.
   "A" Section will parade & move off at 9.45 a.m., arriving at the dump HEBUTERNE at 10.45 a.m.
   O.C. "C" & "B" Sections will provide guides as usual.

3. Rations for the day will be carried by all ranks.

4. Gum Boots will be drawn en route at the Brigade Store, N° 69 Billet, SAILLY, (opposite present dump) if available, if not they will be taken over in the trenches. Sections being relieved will bring own boots out in pairs, and hand same into B. Store, N° 69, SAILLY, receipts being obtained.

5. Trench Stores will be handed over at position in the usual manner.

6. Limbers will be at the dump HEBUTERNE for "A" & "D" Sections at 1 p.m. for "C" & "B" Sections at 11 a.m.

7. Completion of relief will be reported to Coy H.Q. in Army Code. Acknowledge.

                                                                7. B. ......
                                                                Captain
                                                                Commdg 4th M.G.C.

COPY N° 1. 4th Inf. Bde. (For information)
     "   " 2. "C"
     "   " 3. 4th Bn. ("A" Section)
     "   " 4. M.G. Course (B. Section)
     "   " 5. 4/M. Bn.
     "   " 6. ...
            " ...

COPY No 8.

94th Machine Gun Company

Operation Order No 14

SECRET.

Ref Map: [illegible]

1. The following inter-section relief will take place on the morning of December 29th 1916.
   (a) "B" Section will relieve "D" Section in left group.
   (b) "C" Section will relieve "A" Section in right group.

2. "B" Section will parade & move off at 9 a.m. arriving at the dump HEBUTERNE at 10.15 a.m.
   "C" Section will parade & move off at 9.30 a.m. arriving at the dump HEBUTERNE at 10.45 a.m.
   O's.C. "A" & "D" Sections will provide guides as usual.

3. Rations for the day will be carried by all ranks.

4. Gum Boots will be drawn "en route" at the Brigade Gum Boot Store, No 17 Billet, SAILLY, (opposite present Grant Store), if available; if not they will be taken over in the trenches. Sections being relieved will have gum boots tied together in pairs, & hand same into the Brigade Gum Boot Store as they pass, receipts being obtained.

5. Trench Stores will be handed over at each position in the usual way.

6. Limbers will be at the dump HEBUTERNE, for "D" Section at 11.30 a.m. & for "C" Section at 12 noon.

7. Completion of relief will be reported to Coy. Hd. Qrs in code.

Acknowledge.

B. Cowen.
Captain,
Comdg 94th M.G. Coy.

COPY No 1. 94th Infantry Brigade (for information).
do 2. C.O.
do 3. 2/Lieut Court ("A" Section)
do 4. Lieut Howard ("B"   "   )
do 5. 2/Lieut Rep. ("C"   "   )
do 6. 2/Lieut Bothwell ("D" "   )
do 7. Lieut Gill (Transport "   )
do 8. War Diary.
do 9. File.

COPY. No. 9.   APPENDIX II.   Secret

94 Machine Gun Company Operation Order.

Ref map/ SYDEL

1. The 94th Machine Gun Company will relieve the 93rd Machine Gun Company in the section of the front from NAIRNE ST (X.23.b.4/1) to WARRIOR TRENCH (X.17.a.5/5) on the 30th October 1916.

2. Guns of the 94th M.G.C. will be divided into four groups as follows (a) Gun Position V.1 (X.23.a.95/15) will be held by No 1 Gun Team
    do   V.2 (23.a.5/5) will be held by
No 2 Gun Team, under 2nd Lt Oldfient
(b) LAFAYETTE TRENCH (X.22.b.30/25) will be held by No 3 Gun Team
    (X.22.b.35/30) do   No 4   do

Under 2nd Lt Rox
(c) FORENARI TUILE (X.16.c.55/15) will be held by No 9 Gun Team.
VERCINGETORIX (X.22.b.15/35)   do   No 10   do
CEMETERY   26.c.15/25   do   No 11   "

Under 2nd Lt Sykes
(d) PELISSIER (V.12) (X.16.c.80/40) will be held by No 12 Gun Team.
PATRIE   (V.13) (X.16.b.60/70)   do   No 7   do
    (X.16.b.5/8)   do   No 5   do
    (X.10.b.35/5)   do   No 6   do
    (X.10.b.45/30)   do   No 8   do.

Under 2nd Lt Howard
D Section will be in reserve in billets in SAILLY.

3. There will be one NCO and four men on each gun team. Each Officer will detail one man to act as runner from the reserve men of his section.

4. A Guide will be at 93rd M.G. Coy. H.Q. SAILLY at 10 am 30/10/16 to guide all gun teams to the dump in HEBUTERNE (X.15.d./5.) A guide for each gun position will be picked up here.

An additional man will be allotted to each section on going into the trenches who will find out where his Section Officer's Hd.qrs. is, the position of guns in the Section, the route to each gun. They

94th Machine Gun Company.
Alterations in Trench Standing Orders.

Para 16 is cancelled & the following substituted:-

16. GAS ALERT. As soon as "Gas Alert" is ordered all men will wear their Small Box Respirator in the "alert" position. The N.C.O. i/c at each position will inspect all Respirators & P.H. Helmets. Should any man's Box Respirator be found to be defective, a report will be sent through the Section Officer to Company Hd.Qrs., and the man will wear his P.H. Helmet pinned to his shirt in the "Ready" position. If all Small Box Respirators are found to be thoroughly effective, the P.H. Helmet will be carried in the satchel & slung from the right shoulder, so that the sling does not cross the body in such manner as to interfere with the adjustment of the Respirator, & ready to replace a Box Respirator if it becomes unserviceable.

T. Blawin.
Captain,
Comdg. 94th M.G. Coy.

be in a position to act as runners from Coy HQ to their own sections.

5. All men will be in possession of the unexpired portions of the days rations. Each gun team will send one man to the dump in HEBETURNE at 4 pm to draw the ensuing days rations.

6. Trench stores, programme of work in hand and any useful information will be taken over by the NCO at each position. A note of trench stores and work in hand will be sent to Coy HQ by each officer as early as possible.

7. Coy HQ will be in SAILLY at point J 18 b 3.

8. Completion of relief to be reported to Coy HQ as early as possible.

Acknowledge

F. Cowan H.
Comdg. 94th M.G. Coy

Copy No 1. to 94th Inf Bde (for information)
    2.   93rd M.G. Coy
    3.   C.O.
    4.   O.C. A Section
    5.   B "
    6.   C "
    7.   D "
    8.   Transport
    9.   War diary
   10.   File

CONFIDENTIAL.

Vol I

War Diary.

94th Machine Gun Company.

From:- 1st January. 1917.   To:- 31st January. 1917.

(Volume XIII)

WAR DIARY
INTELLIGENCE SUMMARY

(Erase heading not required.)

Army Form C. 2118.

MACHINE GUN COMPANY.
No. Q/1/2
Date 1-2-19
Volume XIII

Instructions regarding War Diaries and Intelligence Summaries are contained in F. S. Regs., Part II. and the Staff Manual respectively. Title Pages will be prepared in manuscript.

Place	Date	Hour	Summary of Events and Information	Remarks and references to Appendices
In the Field	1-1-19	—	8 Guns (B & D Sections) in the line. 8 Guns (A & D Sections) in reserve in SAILLY DELL. Situation: Normal. Casualties:- Nil.	N.C
do.	2-1-19	—	Allocation of Guns as before. Gun teams in reserve at range construction & firing practice. Situation:- Normal. Casualties:- Nil. Issued Operation Order No. 1.	Appendix No. 1
do.	3-1-19	—	Allocation as before. A & D Sections preparing guns etc. for relief. Situation: Normal. Casualties:- Nil.	N.C
do.	4-1-19	—	A Section relieved B Section. D Section relieved C Section in right group positions. B & C Sections took over reserve billets in SAILLY DELL. Received 94th Infy Bde Order No. 109. (Re inter-battalion relief to take place on 5th 1-16th).	N.C
do.	5-1-19	—	8 Guns in the line. 8 in reserve. Situation:- Normal. Casualties:- Nil.	N.C
do.	6-1-19	8.30 p.m.	Allocation of Guns as before. Situation in the line:- Normal. Casualties:- Nil. Enemy fired about 20 rounds 5.9" H.E. into SAILLY DELL. No Casualties.	N.C
do.	7-1-19	—	Allocation of Guns as before. B & C Sections in reserve, firing on the miniature range. Situation:- Normal. Casualties:- nil. Received 94th Infy Bde Order No. 110, concerning the relief of 31st Division by 19th Division on 11th & 12th inst, & consequent move of former into BERNAVILLE - BOULLENS - AMPLIER area for about 10 days, followed by a move into the BERNAVILLE area.	N.C
do.	8-1-19	—	Allocation of guns as before. Situation:- Normal. Casualties:- nil.	N.C
do.	9-1-19	—	As yesterday. LIEUT. J. HOWARD + 2 N.C.Os proceeded to BEAUVAL as advance party, in accordance with instructions contained in 94th Infy Bde Order No. 110. Issued Operation Order No. 2.	Appendix No. 2.
do.	10-1-19	—	Allocation of Guns as before. Situation:- Normal. Casualties:- Nil. All preparations made for relief of 11th Hy Inf 58th Machine Gun Company. Gun in BATTOSE destroyed by Enemy high fire.	N.C
do.	11-1-19	8.30 a.m.	Transport (but not required for Sections coming out of line) proceeded to new billeting area under 1/LIEUT REX, arriving about 3.0 p.m., preparing billets for the incoming sections.	N.C
		12.30 p.m.	B & C Sections paraded under LIEUT. DURRANT & Embarked at 1.0 p.m., arriving at new billets about 4.30 p.m.	
		9.0 p.m.	Remainder of transport, after relief in line, of A & D Sections by the 58th Machine Gun Company, followed to new billeting area, arriving about 12.30 a.m. on 12-1-19	

WAR DIARY
INTELLIGENCE SUMMARY
(Erase heading not required.)

Army Form C. 2118.

Place	Date	Hour	Summary of Events and Information	Remarks and references to Appendices
In the Field	11-1-19 (cont.)	11.0 p.m. 12-m.nt	A.T.D. sections paraded in full marching order, ready to "Embus" for journey to new billeting area at "Endossed" at SAILLYDELL.	N/L
do	12-1-19	2.30 a.m. 11.0 a.m.	Remainder of Coy. arrived in new billets at BEAUVAL 9 after having a hot meal, rested until Parade for cleaning of all guns & equipment.	N/L
do	13-1-19	2.0-4.0 p.m.	During the day N.V. through inspection was carried out of the equipment & small kit of every man. Talks on all guns. Sports & Games. (According to XIII Corps Scheme of Winter Training)	N/L
do	14-1-19	9.0 a.m.	Parade for issue to complete, if all clothing & of the pack. Received 94th Infy Bde Order No.111, stating that the 31st Division is in G.H.Q. reserve & that the 94th Infy Bde will be prepared to begin to entrain at 24 hours' notice at CANDAS station.	N/L
do	15-1-19	9.0 a.m. 10.0 a.m. to 12.45 p.m. 2.0-4.0 p.m.	Training carried out, in, & in vicinity of billets at BEAUVAL as follows:- Squad Drill by sections & objects of instruction; Saluting Drill; Rifle Exercises; Inspections; lecture;- Machine gun training & objects of instruction. Baths for whole Company.	N/L
do	16-1-19	9.0 a.m. 10.0 a.m. 11.0 a.m. 2-4 p.m.	Physical Drill. Inspection of Coy. in skeleton order, without Transport - by C.O. " " in billets with guns & gun equipment by C.O. Sports and Games.	N/L
do	17-1-19	9-9.30 a.m. 9.40 a.m. to 12.15 p.m.	Physical Drill. Training as follows:- General Description of Gun; Squad Drill; Gun Drill; Saluting Drill; Inspection Sports & Games in afternoon.	N/L
do	18-1-19	9.0 a.m. 10-12.30 p.m.	Progressive Training as follows:- Physical Drill; Mechanism; Squad Drill; Instruction on Barr-Stroud Range-finder; Care, Stripping & Cleaning of Gun; followed in the afternoon by Sports & Games.	N/L
do	19-1-19	9.0 a.m. to 12.30 p.m.	Expected visit of Army Commander. Sections being differently Employed at same time:- Physical Drill; following Training was carried out;- of gun; mechanism; Elementary Gun Drill; Visual Training, & in afternoon Sports & Games. General Description Received Operation 94th Infy. Brigade Order No. 112 regarding the move of the 31st Division into the BERNAVILLE Training area, m.22-1-19, this Company being detailed to billets at DOMES MOINT.	N/L

W. Stamper C.A.

WAR DIARY
INTELLIGENCE SUMMARY

(Erase heading not required.)

Army Form C. 2118.

Instructions regarding War Diaries and Intelligence Summaries are contained in F.S. Regs., Part II. and the Staff Manual respectively. Title Pages will be prepared in manuscript.

Place	Date	Hour	Summary of Events and Information	Remarks and references to Appendices
In the Field	20-1-17	9.0 a.m -12.30 p.m	Progressive Training as follows:- Physical Drill; Mechanism; Stripping & cleaning of gun. Gun Drill; Rifle Exercises; Squad Drill; Guards; Saluting Drill; Inspections.	M.L.
do.	21-1-17	10.0 a.m 10.30 a.m	Billet inspection by C.O. Kit Inspection by Section Officers. Received 94th Infy. Bde Order No. 112, regarding move on 22/1/17 into BERNAVILLE area.	M.L.
do.	22-1-17	7.30 a.m 9.0 a.m	Advance party under LIEUT. T. HOWARD proceeded in motor lorry with Coy.Stores to new billets at DOMESMONT. Coy. moved off on march to new billeting area, where it arrived at 11.30 p.m. Rest of day spent in kit & attention to billets.	M.L.
do.	23-1-17	9.0 a.m -12.30 p.m	Training carried out as follows:- Physical Drill; Immediate action before & Squad Drill; Instruction on guard duties. Lecture: Trench Warfare, embracing attack & defence; Saluting Drill.	M.L.
do.	24-1-17	9.0 a.m 10.30 a.m 2.0 p.m	Training as follows:- Physical Drill; Squad Drill; Rifle Exercises; Saluting; Immediate action. Guards; Lecture:- "Fire Orders & Fire Control." Shots & Games.	M.L.
do.	25-1-17	9.0 a.m -11.45 a.m 11.45 a.m 2.0 p.m	Route march & full marching Order (without transport owing to severe frost) Route followed :- Start from billets at DOMESMONT - W. to RIBEAUCOURT - hence to BERNAVILLE & back to billets. Mechanism; Immediate action stoppages. Shoots & Games.	M.L.
do.	26-1-17	9.0 a.m -12.30 p.m 2.0 p.m	Training as follows:- Physical Drill; Squad Drill & Section Route March; Lecture: Fire Orders - Range-Cards; Company Drill & Rifle Exercises; Inspections. Shoots & Games. LIEUT. J.H. WILSON joined for duty from M.G.C. Base Depot.	M.L.
do.	27-1-17	9.0 a.m -12.30 p.m 5.0 p.m 3.0 p.m	Training as follows:- Physical Drill; Immediate action & Stoppages; Company Drill; Lecture:- Range Discipline; Points before, during & after fire; Stripping & Cleaning. Shots & Games. Several officers of the company attended a lecture by the Corps Commander at AUXIMCOURT. Received 94th Infy. Bde Order No. 114.	M.L.
do.	28-1-17	10.0 a.m 10.30 a.m	Billet inspection by C.O. Kit Inspection by Section Officers. Received 94th Infy. Bde Order No. 115.	Extracts Appendix No.3.
do.	29-1-17	8.0 a.m 10.0 a.m 1.0 p.m 3.0 p.m	Parade for packing Stores & S.A.A. & cleaning up of billets. LIEUT. V. St. G. HILL, accompanied by two cyclists proceeded to new billets at MONTRELET. Company moved off to proceed to new billeting area at MONTRELET. Company arrived in new billets at MONTRELET, & after a hot meal, spent remainder of day in tidying.	M.L.

WAR DIARY
INTELLIGENCE SUMMARY
(Erase heading not required.)

Army Form C. 2118.

Instructions regarding War Diaries and Intelligence Summaries are contained in F. S. Regs., Part II. and the Staff Manual respectively. Title Pages will be prepared in manuscript.

Place	Date	Hour	Summary of Events and Information	Remarks and references to Appendices
In the Field	30-1-17	9.0 a.m. 9.0 a.m.-12.30 p.m. 6.0 p.m.	C.O., 2/Lieut. CANT (O.C "A" Section) reconnoitred the M.G. range. Coy. training as follows:- Physical Drill; "Range Cards"; Practice in making these for attack & defence; use of No-stand Rangefinder; "Lecture: Gun Emplacements for Defence: Theory of Direct fire & Practice in gun-laying by Drill methods. LIEUT. V. ST. C. HILL (A.V.O.), & Transport N.C.Os attended a lecture on "Horse Management," by A.D.V.S. at BONNEVILLE.	[initials]
do.	31-1-17	9.0 a.m.-12.30 p.m. 2-4 p.m.	"A" Section was firing on the Range. Remainder of Coy. employed as follows:- Squad Drill; Immediate Action & Stoppages; Advanced Gun Drill; Machine guns in the attack; Consolidation of newly won positions. Sports & Games.	[initials]

W. Cant C.A.
Cmdg. 94th M.G. Coy.

• COPY No 8   <u>Appendix No 1.</u>
        <u>94th Machine Gun Company</u>
           <u>Operation Order No. 1</u>

   Ref. Map. { 57D NE.
              { 1/20,000   2.1.17.

1. The following intersection reliefs will take place on the morning of ~~December~~ January 4th 1917:—
   A Section will relieve B section in left group.
   D   "   "   " C   "   " right group.
2. A Section will move off at 8.30 a.m.
   D   "   "   "   " " 9.0 a.m.
   O.C. B & C Sections will provide guides as usual.
3. All other arrangements will be as usual.
4. Limbers for B & C sections will be at the dump HEBUTERNE at 11.0 a.m. & 11.30 a.m. respectively.
5. Completion of relief will be reported.

   Acknowledge.

                                    T Beaven
                                        Captain,
                                  Comdg. 94th M.G. Coy.

COPY No 1. 44th Infantry Brigade (for information).
  "   " 2. C.O.
  "   " 3. 2/Lt. Cant. ("A" Section)
  "   " 4. Lt. Howard ("B"   "   )
  "   " 5. 2/Lt. Rey. ("C"   "   )
  "   " 6. 2/Lt. Bothwell ("D" ")
  "   " 7. Lt. Hill (Transp't ")
  "   " 8. War Diary.
  "   " 9. File.

Copy No:- 8.   Appendix No. 2.   SECRET.
9th Machine Gun Company.
Operation Order No. 2.

Ref. Map { 57D N.E / 1/10,000 }

1/ RELIEF.

The 9th Machine Gun Company will be relieved by the 58th Machine Gun Company on 11th January 1917.

2/ GUIDES.

No. 6. "A" & "I" Sections will have a guide for each position at road junction K.16.a.9.3. at 12 noon, 11.1.17. These guides will report to an officer from the Battalion in the line who will be in charge of all guides.

On arrival of relieving Company's limbers, they will take them to the dump and thence to various positions. Each guide will be in possession of a chit stating for which position he is guide.

The N.C.O. i/c. at each position will hand over all trench stores to the relieving N.C.O. in the usual way, obtaining a receipt for everything so handed over.

All tripods, belt boxes, and disappearing mountings will be brought out.

3/ HANDING OVER

Section Officers will ensure that all emplacements and dug-outs are handed over in a clean and sanitary state. They are responsible that the N.C.O. i/c. at each position has full instructions regarding the handing over of his position. All particulars such as direction of fire, any firing done, the enemy's attitude, range-cards, order-cards and other useful information must be handed over.

5/ ADVANCED HD. QTRS.

2/Lt Bant will hand over all Trench Stores in the line to Senior Officer of 58th M.G. Coy at Advance Coy. Hd. Qrs., the list being prepared on A.F.W. 3405 in triplicate and signed by an officer of the 58th M.G. One copy of this form will be handed to the Officer of 58th M.G. Coy and the other two will be handed to Orderly Room, on completion of relief.

6. SIGNALLERS.

The signallers will hand over the line to signallers of 58th M.G. Coy. and after doing so will pack their instrument and return to Coy. H.Q.trs.

7. TRANSPORT

After being relieved "A" & "D" Sections will be marched back to Coy. H.Q.trs.

Limbers will be at the dump as follows:-
For "A" Section. 2 Limbers at 3.30 p.m.
" "D" " " " " 3.45 p.m.

8. GUM BOOTS

All Gum Boots will be handed in to Brigade Boot Store, SAILLY, receipts being obtained.

9. COMPLETION OF RELIEF

As soon as relief is complete and everything satisfactorily handed over, 2/Lt Cant will return to Coy. H.Q.trs., and report completion of the relief to C.O.

<u>Acknowledge</u>

F.B.Craven.
Captain
Comdg. 9uth M.G.Coy

Copy No 1. :- 9uth Infy Bde (For information)
" " 2 :- O.C. 58th M.G.Coy.
" " 3 :- C.O.
" " 4 :- 2/Lt. Cant ("A" Section)
" " 5 :- Lieut. Howard ("B" Sect.)
" " 6 :- 2/Lt. Rex ("C" Section)
" " 7 :- 2/Lt. Bothwell ("D" Sect.)
" " 8 :- War Diary
" " 9 :- File

FBC

SECRET   Appendix No. 3   Copy No. 5.

94th Infantry Brigade Order No. 155.

Ref. Map,)
L ENS 11,)
1/100,000)   28.1.17.

1. The following moves of Units of the Brigade will take place tomorrow, 29-1-17:-

     94 Machine Gun Coy.   DOMESMONT to MONTRELET.

2. The following will be the routes to be followed:
     (a). 94 Machine Gun Coy.— BERNAVILLE— thence by road running N. and S. through the first E of BERNAVILLE, to cross-rds half-mile W. by N.W of the M of MONTRELET— MONTRELET; leaving Coy. H.Qrs. at 10 a.m.
     (b). — — — —
     (c). — — — —
     (d). — — — —

3. 200-yds distance will be maintained between Coys & Transport on the march.

4. First Line Transport ~~will be maint~~ & baggage wagons will accompany units.

5. Transport. (a). Additional G.S. wagons or lorries will be supplied to units for blankets etc.
     (b). — — — —

6. Billeting parties from each Unit will report to the Staff Captain at the Town Major's office at BONNEVILLE at 8.a.m. tomorrow.

7. — — — —

8. Completion of move will be reported to Bde. H.Q. by special D.R.

           Signed. I. G. Sorby. Captain,
               for Brigade Major,
                   94th Infantry Brigade.

Amendments.

Recipients of   G. 34/B.
94 Bde. Order 115.   28.1.17.

     The following amendments are made to Brigade Order No. 115, dated 28.1.17:-

     Para 2 (a).   For 10 a.m. read 1.0 p.m.
     " 2 (b). — — — —
     " 2 (c). — — — —
     " 2 (d). — — — —

     Add sub-para (e).— "No troops to enter MONTRELET or FIEFFES before 2.0 p.m."

     Para 6. (Billeting parties). For "8 a.m." read "10 a.m."

B.M.Q.   Signed. W. Carter. Captain,
28-1-17.   Brigade Major,
                               94th Infantry Brigade.

APPENDIX II

COMPANY ORDERS.

BY : CAPTAIN F.S.COWEN.

No. 82.   COMMANDING 94th. MACHINE GUN COMPANY.

1. **DETAIL.**   Orderly Officer for 19.3.17.————Lieut. J.H.WILSON.
   Next for duty——————————— 2nd.Lt. A.M. CANT.

2. **PARADES.**   9.a.m,————— C.O's Orderly Room.
   9.45 a.m.————— Parade ready to move off.

3. **DRESS.**
   Marching order less packs, waterbottles full, haversacks on back, canteen on back of haversack, Steel helmets on on the left side, waterproof sheet on belt, box respirators to be carried by all ranks.

4. **ORDER OF MARCH.**
   "A" Section.   "B" Section.
   "C" Section.   "D" Section.
   Transport.———— Mess-cart leading followed by Section limbers in above order, H.Q. Limber S.A.A. Limbers and Water Cart.

5. **TRANSPORT.**
   All transport will leave the column at BEAUQUESNE and HULEUX and continue the journey to BEAUVAL via TERRAMESNIL.

6. **BLANKETS.**
   All blankets will be rolled by Sections and handed to Q.M. Stores by 7.30. a.m. A limber will be detailed to take these to DUMP at BUS where a receipt will be obtained. On this limber's return it will be repacked immediately.

7. **MOVE.**
   The Brigade is moving to a new area by march route, which will probably take 5 days hard marching.
   The C.O. hopes that all ranks will do their utmost as regards smart and soldierly appearance, attention to march discipline etc.
   The Company will be inspected at certain points by Officers from the General Staff.
   No man will the ranks without the written permission of an officer. All drivers will dismount at recognised halts, when limber poles will also be lowered.
   The Orderly Officer is responsible that the camp is left in a clean and sanitary state. He will also ensure that, immediately on arrival at the new billets, the cooks start preparing a hot meal.

8. **DISPLINE.**
   LOADED REVOLVERS. As an accident has recently occurred owing to an officer leaving his revolver loaded when in billets, attention is drawn to Brigade Routine Order No. 299 dated 6-2-16 which is republished below.
   All officers, when returning to billets from the trenches, will unload their revolvers before removing their equipment.
   D.R.O. 299.- DISCIPLINE
   D.R.O. No. 1098 dated 25.5.16., is republished for information
   "Accidents have lately happened owing to the
   "carelessness of Officers, who on return to their
   "billets, leave revolvers loaded. Orders will be
   "issued by Brigades and Divisional units to the effect
   "that disciplinary action will be taken against any
   " officer, who, by leaving his revolver loaded,
   " causes an accident".

(Sd). F. S. COWEN, Captain.

Comdg. 94 M. G. Coy.

CONFIDENTIAL

War Diary.

94th Machine Gun Company

From. 1st February 1917 – To 28th February 1917

Volume XIV

Vol 10

Army Form C. 2118.

WAR DIARY
of
INTELLIGENCE SUMMARY.
(Erase heading not required.)

No. 94 MACHINE GUN COMPANY.
No. Q./22
Date 12.3.17

Instructions regarding War Diaries and Intelligence Summaries are contained in F.S. Regs., Part II. and the Staff Manual respectively. Title pages will be prepared in manuscript.

Place	Date	Hour	Summary of Events and Information	Remarks and references to Appendices
In the field	1.2.17	—	In billets at MONTRELET. Very severe frosty weather.	YH
do	2.2.17	9/1230 9/1430 8/1430	"C" Section were on the range. The remainder of Company as follows: Squad Drill; Saluting Drill; lecture on deflection of shots holes; lecture; preceded against sides. Drill with new gun appliances. The afternoon devoted to sports & games.	YH
do	2.2.17	9.05 12.30 p.m 2.24	"B" Section on the range all morning. Rest of Company did Saluting Drill; advanced Gun Drill, including mounting and dismounting in concealed positions, conversational signs and laying of guns for indirect fire. Sports & Games.	YH
do	3.2.17	—	Frost still continues. "D" Section on the Range all morning. Remainder of Company did Company Drill; Picking of limbers; advancing over rough ground and coming into action on hastily improvised positions. Sports & Games.	YH
do	4.2.17	2.30 p.m.	In the morning Church Services were held for different denominations. Went to ward and 1 O.R. proceeded to U.K. on short leave.	YH
do	5.2.17	9am to 12.30 12.30 to 4	Two guns of "D" Section under Lieut. J. de Kilian practiced an attack on trench system with 1st Bn. York Regt. Remainder trained as follows: Physical Drill; lecture; Employment of M.G. Section in attack from MONTRELET; Immediate Action and stoppages; Village fighting; taking up positions for action without being seen. In the afternoon an hour Bomb throwing and an hour Bayonet fighting was done.	YH
do	6.2.17	—	"D" Section were on the range all morning. Two guns of "C" Section under 2/Lt. E. S. Rex co-operated with 13th Bn. Yorkshires in practice attack on German trenches. Remainder as follows: Square Drill; Packing of spare parts; Belt filling by machine; lecture on trench H. Gun; French Orders; Employment of M.G. in demonstration of principles of cross-fire for defence. Bombing & Bayonet fighting. 2/Lt REX attended a lecture at BEAUVAL by Col. FOULKESON. Sen. Stokes Mortars.	YH
do	7.2.17	9am/11am	Elementary Gun Drill including Mounting etc. Immediate Action, Stoppages and an hour cleaning of guns, gun equipment and clothing and Equipment. Two guns of "A" Section under the CAPT. carried out a practice attack on trench system. Lieut. N.W. DURRANT & 3 N.C.Os left to go to Advanced Course at M.G.C School GAMBIERS. Sgt. WARD left to take up duties as instructor at Base.	YH

[signature] Major Capt

WAR DIARY

INTELLIGENCE SUMMARY

(Erase heading not required.)

Army Form C. 2118.

Place	Date	Hour	Summary of Events and Information	Remarks and references to Appendices
Authie Buildings	8.2.19	9am/2.30	"C" Section went on the Range carrying out Advanced M.S. Practices. Rest of Company did Elementary Gun Drill, Saluting Drill and open fighting between Montrelet & N.W. outskirts of Ramades. Training area. Practices carrying into action from limbers. Gun Section chosen a competition was held to decide which Section would represent 9th M.G. Coy in Corps Commanders M.G. Competition. "D" Section were selected.	H/-
do	9.2.19		Training was carried out as usual. Two N.C.O.s left to join an Officers Cadet unit in U.K. 2/Lt REX & R.O.R.s left to go to Egypt and on short leave respectively (2 O.R.s joined on duty from A.H.T. Depot)	H/-
do	10.2.19		A Section on the range all morning. Remainder of Company had Arms Drill, Aiming & Range finding, Making of Range Charts and practice in distance, use of Aerial Sights: Indirect fire Barrage: Judging & without indirect fire angles & Scantings: Indirect fire Barrages.	H/-
do	11.2.19	12 noon	Church Services were held for different denominations. The 5.0 to 9 pm. In (antry Rod) impaired the billets of this Company.	H/-
do	12.2.19		"B" Section on Range all morning. Rest of Coy did a route march. Bomb Throwing, Bayonet fighting, Shorts, Games & the A & G. Hand Left for XIIIrd Corps H.Q. to be temp. A.D.C. to Corps Commander.	H/-
do	13.2.19	9am/2.30	Training included Physical Drill, Company Drill, Exercise with Packmules. The afternoon was devoted to Games.	H/-
do	14.2.19	2.30/3 pm	In the morning the Coy took part in a Brigade tactical exercise, assaulting a marked system of trenches. Bayonet fighting, Bombing, Shorts, Games	H/-
do	15.2.19		A Section went on Detachment to provide an Anti-Aircraft guard. 2 Guns under 2/Lt CANT proceeding to PUCHVILLERS & 2 Guns under 2/Lt BOTHWELL to AUTHUIL. B Section were tested for Corps Commander's Competition. Rest of Coy employed building Horse Stand.	H/- J. Mansard Capt

Army Form C. 2118.

WAR DIARY
INTELLIGENCE SUMMARY.
(Erase heading not required.)

Instructions regarding War Diaries and Intelligence Summaries are contained in F.S. Regs., Part II. and the Staff Manual respectively. Title pages will be prepared in manuscript.

Place	Date	Hour	Summary of Events and Information	Remarks and references to Appendices
In the field	17.2.17		'B' Section out training with 11th Batt. East Lancs Regt. 'D' Section with 1st Batt. Northants. Rest of Company had Baths and were employed on building stove standings	
do	18.2.17	11 a.m.	Church Services were held for the different denomination. This set in. 2.D. Officers V.M.C.A attended a lecture by Captain GRAY, Intelligence Officer, G.H.Q. on CENSORSHIP' at the School BERTAVILLE at 11 a.m. 2/Lt. G.E. RICHARDSON joined for duty	
do	19.2.17		Received orders to move to forward area. Day spent in preparations for moving. 'D' Section were declared winners of Corps Commanders competition	
do	20.2.17		Lieut. Hill proceeded on in advance to BEAUQUESNE to arrange billets. Company started to march at 10 a.m. arriving at destination at 2 p.m. Rest of day resting.	
do	21.2.17		Lieut. Hill proceeded to COUIN and arranged billets for Company who marched in at 2 p.m.	
	22.2.17 23.2.17 24.2.17		In Billets at COUIN. The Company was employed in overhauling gun gear and getting everything in readiness for the line. On the 23rd 2/Lt. R. ENESHING joined for duty	
	25.2.17		Rec'd R.A.E Order No. 60 Offensive & revised Warning Order 11° 1 (offensive.) Lieut. N. St. C. HILL left to proceed to M.G.C. School CAMIERS	Offensive Offensive Appendix
	26.2.17 27.2.17 28.2.17		All three days were spent in the vicinity of village of COUIN. Training in open fighting and gas lectures & demonstrations being given	Appendix

J. Hayward
for Capt.

CONFIDENTIAL.

(Original)

War Diary

9th Machine Gun Company

From 1-3-17 To 31-3-17

Volume XV

95
IX

WAR DIARY
or
INTELLIGENCE SUMMARY.

(Erase heading not required.)

Army Form. C. 2118.

No. 94 MACHINE GUN COMPANY.

MAP REF sheet 2
LENS 11 edt 2

Place	Date	Hour	Summary of Events and Information	Remarks and references to Appendices
In the field	MARCH 1917		2/Lt A.J.C. HANDS reported from being temporary A.D.C. to XIII Corps Commander. Company employed in similar section tactical schemes employing pack mules for transport. Received instructions verbally from B.G.C. Major that 9th Machine Gun Company would relieve the 93rd M.G. Coy in the line tomorrow 2-3-17 and to report to 93rd Brigade 3rd Div. BAYENCOURT 2E 9 am in order to make all arrangements and final details for the relief. Received Brigade Order No 120 relating to this relief, which stated that the 9th M.G. Coy will come under the orders of the A.D. of 93rd Infantry Brigade until S.O. 6 9th Infantry Brigade assumes command of the section. Draft of 3.O.R. arrived from M.G.C. Base Depot.	M.C.
- do -	2nd	9 am	Reported to B.G.C. 93rd Infantry Brigade at BAYENCOURT to fix up details of relief. Met Major WINDLER Commanding 4 Coy and entered into details with him. Informed that 4 Battalion (18th D.I) of 93rd Infantry Brigade were to make an attack on the 1st GARDE STELLUNG i.e K 5 a 5 & to K 5 a 8.7. Informed to turned out a fatigue day so that the 18 pounders could effectually cut the barbed wire entanglement. Issued Operation Order N° 3 to the effect that the whole Coy of 16 guns would be employed as follows:— 2 guns of B Section under 2/Lt RICHARDSON (late German Hut) at points K5 a 50.25, K5 a 26, K5 a 24. 2 guns of C Section under Lieut WILSON (late German 2nd 3rd line) at points K 11a 8.2, K 11a 50.25. 2 guns D Section under 2/Lt NESLING (late German 3rd line) at posts K 11 a 4.7 K 11a 65.45. A Section under 2/Lt CANT in positions at following locats:— K 10 d 35.50; K 10 d 99.22, K 16 b 40.30 K 10 c 99.99. 2 guns of B Section under 2/Lt BOTHWELL in old R line at K 9 c 48.85, K 9 d 65.55.	M.C.
		10.15 am	Remainder of Coy viz 2 guns C & 2 guns D section in reserve at Advanced Coy H.Q. X was as HERUTERNE K 9 a 90.02. X was ordered to have the Company ready to move off with orders for Lieutenant HUNT (2nd Dragoons, who had previously been instructed to have the Company ready to move off) with orders for him to proceed as far as Advanced Coy H.Q. & await further instructs.	
		10.30am	Proceeded with O.C. 93 M.G. Coy to Bn H.Q. of 18 D.L.I. in German old front line at about K 11 a 3.6.	
		11.15am	Saw operation order for the attack which did not allow time for the barbed wire to be cut. The attack was relieved, therefore, and arranged for these guns to stand by but await orders.	
		11.45am	Attack postponed owing to snowy weather. Returned to Advanced H.Q. with O.C. 93rd.	

WAR DIARY or INTELLIGENCE SUMMARY

Army Form C. 2118.

Place	Date	Hour	Summary of Events and Information	Remarks and references to Appendices
In the field	2 (cont)	1.15pm	Machine Gun Coy who got into touch with En. Brigade and as head of the relief of the forward guns was to be proceeded with. Sections rapidly relieved. Sections began to arrive at advanced Coy Qrs. All guns except the new situation & forward guns picked up guides and proceeded to their positions. Situation normal.	MC
do	3	12.15am	Information received that the 18th Kent York Regt. had captured Rossignol Wood information issued to O.C. 93rd M.G. Coy. and at the same time orders to take over defensive positions in N.W. corner of Wood. Information ultimately relieved by 9th M.G. Coy. also orders taken information rec'd that the relief had to be carried on with the 9th.	
		1.15am	Information rec'd that the relief had to be carried on with. Owing to fog, guns having to go forward to Rossignol Wood this entailed detailing two guns for reserve section under 2/Lt T.B. Smith with to take on the duties previously assigned to 2/Lt Nesling while the latter went further forward to Rossignol Wood.	
		2.15am	Arrangements for relief complete and guides advanced. 2nd Sec. Seaton moved off. Lieut Seaton & Sec. 18th West Yorks Regt. and interviewed with O.C. that Regt. into informed me of the general situation and asked for the two guns to be placed so as to be able to sweep lote apr. m. K. 6. c.od. to the N.W. flank. Orders to this effect written	MC
		5.45pm	and sent to 2/Lt Nesling proceeded to Rossignol Wood via Sunken Road & Bulow Weg to S.W. corner of the wood. Enemy in attitude very quiet with the exception of a little M.G. rifle fire. Got into touch with 2/Lt Nesling and new guns into positions. Returned by same route to German Front Line, thence along Front Line to HQ QRS 18th D.L.I. There no further orders re attack had been received. They had information Lewis Gun the one of their patrols had made its way up Pioneer Alley to the Grande Stellung where strong opposition was met with.	
		9.30am	Returned to Coy QRS on new Heauterne-Bucquoy road. Issued orders for 2/Lt Cant to withdraw his two light guns from position K.16.c.no.30;K.10a.99.22 to reserve at Coy Qrs QRS. Two O.R. wounded while carrying ammunition forward.	
			The relief of 93 M.G. Coy was smoothly carried out and does confers at 4.35am. Owing to the heavy state of the ground it was arranged between the two Company Commanders to hand over and take over all 8 Belt Boxes and Tripods for the forward guns. This was done.	MC

WAR DIARY
or
INTELLIGENCE SUMMARY
(Erase heading not required.)

Army Form C. 2118.

Place	Date	Hour	Summary of Events and Information	Remarks and references to Appendices
In the field	4	2.30am	Information received from 2/Lt BOTHWELL that one tripod was out of action. Arrangements made to have this replaced.	
		7.30am	Orders issued to LIEUT HOWARD at Bge Hd Qrs re sending up of rations.	
		8.0am	Reports received from Section Officers. 2/Lt NESLING reported for duty. Showing of his guns at K.12 & 65.30 and K.11 & 2a approximately, and 2/Lt BOTHWELL stated that 1st & 2nd Garde Stellungs had been captured and acting under orders from O.C. 16 West Yorks, had pushed his Hot gun up to positions K.6.C.A1 and K.6.C.5.0.5. Towards afterwards one, which were duly despatched to Bde H.Q. Quarters. Further report from 2/Lt NESLING stated that he had observed 4 Germans working at point K.6.C.10.10 which was suspected to be a strong point and according by reported to the Infantry. This post was subsequently rushed. Casualties NIL.	
		3.30p	8/old Operation Order No 4 to the effect that 2 guns of "C" Section at present in reserve at Advanced Coy Hd Qrs would relieve 2 guns of "B" Section in left group. 2 guns of "B" Section at present in Old British R lines to evacuate their positions and return to be in reserve at Advanced Coy Hd Qrs. This arrangement being left, Company disposition as follows:- "A" Section 2 guns in reserve; 2 guns in Old British R line "B" Section in reserve; "D" Section in British new Front line "C" Section was ordered to have a gun placed in vicinity of K.12.C.96 to fire on aeroplanes with.	
		5.30p	Made out a report for 94th Infantry Brigade on reconnaissance carried out in morning suggested that all guns in Old British R line be withdrawn to reserve and that Coy Hd Qrs be moved forward to about point K.11 to 7 where one section could be in reserve, the second reserve section remaining at HEBUTERNE. Reported also the following alteration in disposition viz. 1 gun from ROSSIGNAL WOOD. (K.12.d.15.30) moved to UHLEN IEL GRABEN at about point K.7.d.75.20	
-do-	5	8.30am	Received message from Bde Hd Qrs that the 94th Inf Bde is to relieve the Brigade at present on the left of 92nd Infantry Brigade today. Warden to meet guide at SUCERIE to reconnoitre M.G. emplacements told. Proceeded at once to the rendezvous and got into touch with O.C. 9/Kings Co. who was in the line with 20 K.92 Fy Bde, the Brigade to be relieved. Made all arrangements for relief, later message from Bde reads "Withdraw your guns at 10 am today and move	

McGowan Col.

WAR DIARY
or
INTELLIGENCE SUMMARY

Army Form C. 2118.

(Erase heading not required.)

Place	Date March	Hour	Summary of Events and Information	Remarks and references to Appendices
Inchadield	5 (contd)		to COUIN and You will not go into line today and ends. Necessary arrangements made at the withdrawal. All guns were withdrawn and arrived at billets at COUIN at 8.45pm 5.3.17.	MC
-do-	6		Day devoted to cleaning up. Section Officers submitted indents for all clothes, equipment & spare parts to complete their sections. Reported at Bde. Hd Qtrs (O.2.c.H.6) and had interview with Brigade Major.	MC
		8.45pm	Received orders to reconnoitre, with a view to relieving 91 M.G. Coy at the MOUSETRAP (K.35.a. central) with all available officers, the Brigade front, the following officers to attend. To start at 8.30am: LIEUT J.H. WILSON. 2/LT. A.M. CANT 2/LT J.E. RICHARDSON + 2/LT J.R. BOTHWELL	
-do-	7		Reported to O.C. 91st M.G. Coy in accordance with order. Section Officers reconnoitred the front. Made all arrangements for relief. The 91st M.G. Coy had 16 guns in the line but more of these are too far back to be of any use. Decided to relieve only one gun at M.G. Coy had pushed 1 gun further forward toward the line of posts and to keep 8 guns in reserve at the MOUSETRAP. Provided this was agreed to by Brigade. Had an interview with Brigade Major and this was agreed to. Returned to Company Headquarters and would O.O. No. 5.	MC
do	8		Company moved into the line in accordance with Operation Order No. 5. Relief was completed at 10.35pm. A draft of 7 O.R. joined from M.G.C. Base.	MC
do	9		In trenches carried out a thorough reconnaissance of the Brigade front. Guns placed in positions as under: 1. L.Bd. 70.35 2. L.15d. 05.25 3. L.15c. 25.70 4. L.15c. 30.65 'A' Section 5. L.21.a.9.5 6. L.21.c.6.4 7. L.21.B.2.4 8. L.27.B.2.6 'C' Section under 2/LT CANT with HD.QTRS at L.14a.30.95 under LIEUT WILSON with HD QTRS at L. 20.c.9.1 The remainder of the Company was disposed as follows, 'B' Section under 2/LT RICHARDSON in reserve in dugouts at the MOUSETRAP (K.35.A.55) 'D' Section under 2/LT BOTHWELL in reserve in dugouts at SERRE (K.36 central) Advanced Coy. Headquarters at K.35.a. central. Q.M. stores at moved from COUIN to COURCELLES (with the exception of the machinery the morning). Decided to move advanced Coy. Headquarters to PUISIEUX about L.4.30.d.2.6 tomorrow 2/LT BOTHWELL reconnoitred PUSIEUX for dugouts with a view to moving half his section into close reserve. A made dugout was found and occupied by one gun team. Both dugouts were found but required some cleaning. These dugouts are situated through were carried on with. Shelling. Enemy artillery fairly active especially around PUSIEUX in dugouts of A Section. Night quiet	MC

WAR DIARY
or
INTELLIGENCE SUMMARY.

Army Form C. 2118.

(Erase heading not required.)

Place	Date March	Hour	Summary of Events and Information	Remarks and references to Appendices
In the field	10th	6.15am	Received orders to report at advanced Brigade Headquarters at 10am. (L.28.a.1.4) Proceeded to Bde. Hqrs. and reported that they had occupied the dugouts directed upon an advanced day. Bde. Hqrs. accordingly the move advanced by the dug-outs arranged for war signalled. Had interview with G.O.C. 94th Infantry Brigade, instructing to take four of the 2 × M.G. guns into positions for the defence of the following (approximately) positions and should moved forward. Reconnoitered L.27.b.2.5; L.21.c.8.3; L.20.a.2.9; L21.c.7.8. Issued orders to 2/Lt. Bothwell to take up these positions with "D" section as soon as the move up completed and to report when the move up completed. Arranged for "B" Section to take over the dug out in SERRE evacuated in consequence of "D" Section moving thereout. Had interview with Lieut. Wilson and 2/Lt Cant M. Gun Officer. M Gun Officers in the line and found everything correct. CASUALTIES. Nil.	
		2.30pm	Part of 94th T.M.B. came to dug out BCS and took over a portion of our dugout accommodation	
		3.0pm	Received order 12th Infantry Brigade, showing dispositions of troops in Brigade on importance of consolidation of every part established or captured.	
		10.30pm	Received copy of enemy Pocket Book from Corps M.G. 13 Corps. Situation during the past 24 hours normal a certain amount of shelling on the SERRE-PUSIEUX Road but PUSIEUX was not so heavily shelled as yesterday. Shell fire seemed to be from LONGEST WOOD. A number of being rifle notable.	
	11	10 am	Received report from 2/Lt. Bothwell to the effect that "D" Section had occupied positions as follows: L.20.d.1.9; L.21.c.1.8; L.27.b.6.7; L.27.b.40.99, this HDQTRS being in PUSIEUX.	
		11 a.m	G.C. 94th M.G. Coy arrived at advanced dug dug out and stated it was probable that this company would relieve the 4th tele guns of 12th instant. I reviewed the positions etc. with him and gave him list of all co-ordinates.	
		11.30am	Reported to Bde. on the new positions occupied by "D" section.	
		12 n	Read Divisional orders.	
		2.0 pm	Received order from Brigade to have all the M.G. positions on the left, sent in preparation report to Brigade issued the necessary instruction to 2/Lt. Cant, to take over during next 24 hours the teams cleaning and inspecting all positions in the line and having casualties. Mounded and constructing shelters.	
		2.30 pm	Received information from Brigade that the teams situated in Right Bn. sub sector (i.e. "C" section) would be relieved tonight. I issued orders to this effect to Lt/Lt Wilson instructing him to proceed to dug out in SERRE on completion of relief.	
		5.30 pm	An officer from 94th M.G. Coy reported and stated that his company would	

P. Brownlow

WAR DIARY
or
INTELLIGENCE SUMMARY.

(Erase heading not required.)

Army Form C. 2118.

Instructions regarding War Diaries and Intelligence Summaries are contained in F.S. Regs., Part II. and the Staff Manual respectively. Title pages will be prepared in manuscript.

Place	Date	Hour	Summary of Events and Information	Remarks and references to Appendices
In the field	March 11 (cont)		relieve Lewis gun in the early morning of the 12th int the relief to be completed by 9 am. Arrangements for guides etc made. Our Artillery was very active all day & specially round about BUCQUOY. The enemy put up feeble retaliation & PUSIEUX was lightly dealt with by parties, were shelling at intervals the forward situation normal. We desultory MG fire when shelling all round by enemy, snipers active all day & from day break to dusk. Enemy Anti-aircraft Artillery very active against our planes.	T.C.
do	12th	1.30am	Received wire from Brigade stating that the relief of the MG sections would take place tonight. Arranged relief for 'C' Section. Orders to be issued forward by 9 oclock with a note that Lieut NIXON informing him of the movement of the relief.	T.C.
		9.30am	Received reports from sections Officers. Progress on positions. 'A' Section 4 positions throughly wired and further consolidated by being dug in further. 'B' Section improvements to all emplacements. 'C' Section were hindered owing to heavy rain. Living to trail water continually & at and alternative emplacement was constructed at L.22.a.1.9.	
		2.30pm	Received telephone message from Brigade Major to carry on with the relief of guns arranged with 91st MG Coy yesterday according to shared attention of to this Document to the effect that the relief must be completed by 9 am. Guides for all positions to be at NE of SERRE (K.30.c.5.5) at 5 am. Parties of 'D' Section after being taken over by 91st MG (G.O.) to be evacuated tonight. 'C' Section Officer to report at advanced Coy HQ Bn. on completion of relief to receive further order as to where to proceed to. Arrangements made for transport to bring guns, stores Pack mules. On 'A' & 'D' sections limbers for 'B' Section.	
	2.45pm		O.C. 208th M.G. Coy came to advanced HQ, 'B' Section. Conferred with him and he finally decided that the guns went into the gun pits dug at positions on his withdrawal, the rights, south end of PUSIEUX (L.20.c.4.8) at 4.30 am. Made arrangements for guides to be at formed Operation Order No.7 which instructed, Lieut NIXON to withdraw his gun on net being relieved at 5.30 am 13/3/17 to PUSIEUX where they would be joined there by the 3rd being relieved and where pack animals would be waiting at 6.30 am. Pack animals their equipment tack. Ordered Lieut NIXON to report at 208th M.G. Coy HQ Q.R.S. on his way out and to proceed to billets at COURCELLES, showed 208th MG Coy not arrive by 6.15 am 'C' Section must evacuate in order to make relief complete by 9 am.	N.C. Cameron G.M.

A5834. Wt. W4973/M687. 750,000. 8/16. D.D. & L. Ltd. Forms/C.2118/13.

WAR DIARY
or
INTELLIGENCE SUMMARY.
(Erase heading not required.)

Army Form C. 2118.

Place	Date	Hour	Summary of Events and Information	Remarks and references to Appendices
In the Field	12.	3.25p 5.80p 9pm 9.40pm	Had telephone conversation with Bde Major who stated that all arrangements made for relief. Received Brigade Order No 125 which stated that this company would march to COURCELLES, and proceed to BUS at 2.30 the same day 13/3/17. Received message from Brigade that the battalion (6th) A.& L Division now in line would be relieved to day by the enemy wire from 4.11 A 32 to 4. 8. B.7 at frequent intervals from midnight to day light in order to present retain being handed over with Batn Head Quarters of the Battalion in the trenches, who stated that the firing was not now replied to. being to entrenches being cut	T.C.
do.	13.	4. 45am 6.30am 7.15am 8.15am 8.45am 10.30am 2.30p.m. 5.30p.m.	9.15 M.G. Coy arrived to take over. B. Section proceeded to COURCELLES. D. Section (2 guns) relief being complete, and their portions that by had left, which section forward to billets under. That BOTHWELL. A. Section having been relieved arrived at Coy HD QTRS and proceeded to billets. C. Section proceeded to billets. The relief was complete at 7.45am and reported to BDE accordingly. Coy HD QTRS arrived at MOUSE POINT and everything having been satisfactorily handed over. 9p.m. M.G. Coy proceeded to COURCELLES. The 208 M.G. Coy and not turn up, therefore the gun position on the my lt was evacuated at 6.15am in accordance with Operation Order No 1 (yesterday all sections had arrived at billets at COURCELLES where lunches were packed. Started to march to BUS in order at half hour intervals in following order. D.C. A followed by B.M.G. sections S.A.A. etc. B. Section leading and remanded by Coy all arrived at Bus and comfortably settled	T.C.
-do-	14.	6 pm 9.30pm	In huts JUNIPER CAMP, BUS. The day was devoted to cleaning and overhauling all guns equipment, equipment, clothing, boots and other necessaries were used. Also spare parts for guns. Sergt Duncan left to join the X ARMY SCHOOL of Instruction in A. Edens as instructor. A Lecture arrived at the huts where the following Pte STEVENSON Pte BIRD Pte STOCKLEY Pte WILFORD the Journey, namely:- "OR PTE BIRD sum an officers Batman and was engaged in cleaning the officers rifle which was apparently loaded, and went off wounding BIRD himself and three other men comfort at this was forwarded to HD QTRS 19th Infantry Brigade Received order from Brigade that the sick now on was to be transferred from the X ARMY to be 1st ARMY concentrating in the BOUQUEMAISON area by the 20th inst	T.C.

WAR DIARY
or
INTELLIGENCE SUMMARY

(Erase heading not required.)

Army Form C. 2118.

Place	Date MARCH	Hour	Summary of Events and Information	Remarks and references to Appendices
In the field	14.		Forwarded to BRIGADE a report on certain N.C.O.s and men who were considered inefficient in their present employment and recommended that they be transferred either to the Infantry or to the 3rd Battn.	MC
-do-	15th		Morning devoted to testing all guns on the range. Firing of lettos and generally finishing the work of cleaning started yesterday. A Court of Enquiry assembled at H.Q.T.R.S of the 93rd FIELD AMB. to enquire into the accident that occurred yesterday wounding L/Cpl WILFORD another three men. LIEUT WILSON detailed as member. Sgt KING, Sgt DUNBAR, Cpl DUTTON & Pte DUFFY detailed to attend as witnesses.	MC
		2 Pm	Instructions received for No 27640 Sgt FENTON to proceed to No 13 M.G.Coy to take up duties of C.Q.M.S. Necessary orders given and he left during the afternoon. Afternoon devoted to square drill & general cleaning of equipment. Received verbal instructions from the Brigade that the Battalion was under 4 hours notice to move into the line, in the area recently left. Issued warning Order No. 3.	Appendix I
do	16th	3 Pm		
		9 Pm	In view of the instructions issued regarding a move at short notice issued yesterday easy training in the vicinity of the camp was carried out, including lectures etc. At 4 a.m. we received that L/Cpl WILFORD had died of the wounds received accidentally on the 14th inst. Funeral took place at the Cemetery Couin D 25 a. 8.1 at 2.30 pm. The C.O. & Lieut DURRANT also a number of N.C.O.s and men were given leave to attend. Reported orders that the BRIGADE would move to the BEAUVAL area in the 19th inst.	MC
do	17th		Day spent as yesterday viz:- Easy training in vicinity of Lines. Received B.O. No 126 regarding move to BRUAY ALQuy area, also probable itinerary of the move. Received instructions regarding move, which placed that a motor lorry would probably be available for transport of blankets to the new area, following the Company and also all part of blankets & stores. Blankets to be dumped at BUS. In the camp of the 12th Battn YORK & LANCS. Returned all equipment etc. Received some notes from BRIGADE re loading of vehicles and agmt note 1/10,000 & 1/20,000 & 1/40,000 of the 5th ARMY area. to F.D.E H.Q. as left as possible, which were ordered to be returned left.	MC

WAR DIARY

INTELLIGENCE SUMMARY

Army Form C. 2118.

(Erase heading not required.)

Instructions regarding War Diaries and Intelligence Summaries are contained in F.S. Regs., Part II. and the Staff Manual respectively. Title pages will be prepared in manuscript.

Place	Date March	Hour	Summary of Events and Information	Remarks and references to Appendices
Wadicul	18th		Blanket per man and entire stores were dumped as instructed in the administration instructions for the move returned yesterday. Capt. Harley F. & 1/Cpl. McGinn went to the Camiers for the first series of M.G. Courses with A.G.'s letter No. 1/6804 of 8.3.16. Pte Green. A. Clarke. C.W. Pickles. R. Reeves. W. Smith. G.A.	M.C. REF MAP LENS. II
		4 pm	Received A.G's March Table A which showed that the 94th M.G. Coy. had to leave the station point for the march to Road Junction 1½ N. of E in Authie at 11.15 am and proceed to take billets at Beauval occupied by January during the morning and meet the staff captain at 12 noon re billeting. Issued Well order (to move re company Orders 1st & 2nd order issued from here depot	(? Authie II)
do	19th		Marched to Beauval in accordance with order route Authie–Marieux–Beauquesne, thence to Beauval by road arriving there at 3.6 pm and occupied the same billets as those occupied by January. Received instructions that we would be billeted in Petit Bouret with Carncr. & 1st Howard proceeded to Prevent to meet the staff captain to arrange billets.	M.C.
		7 pm	Received orders that an early start would be made in the morning	
		9.45 pm	Received March Table B which detailed this unit to pass the starting point Beauval Station at 8.6am.	
do	20th	2.15 am	Received instructions from Brigade that all units would pass the starting point ½ an hour later than detailed on March Table 'B'. Also instructions regarding filling	M.C.
		6.10 am	marched out of billeting area and proceeded on the march via Douvenes. Bouquemaisen–Mon Leniard–Bouret. Owing to traffic the march was very slow	
		3.5 pm	Arrived at our billets, especially along Douvenes & Bouquemaison. During the heat two days the weather has had a slight effect on the men, and the company owing to the fact that the cooks had to unload the stew meat before they could light a fire had to wait a considerable time later	
		7.0 pm	applied to Brigade asking if a cooker could be applied	
		11.45 am	Lieut Howard went to Groiy the billeting area for tomorrow, to arrange billets with the staff captain. Received orders from Brigade that the company was to start & arrive at 8 am in Bogret: at 200 × N of E in Bogret. A rendezvous and the necessary orders	

WAR DIARY

INTELLIGENCE SUMMARY

Army Form C. 2118.

Place	Date MARCH	Hour	Summary of Events and Information	Remarks and references to Appendices
In the Field	21	10.30am	Received orders from Brigade. March Table "C" which shewed that the 9th M.G.Coy would march the lead of the Brigade & the starting point 200W of U in BOMETZ Sq. marched out of billets and 1.15pm. Lieut Howard proceeded to SACHIN tomorrow billeting area to arrange billets. at 7.00am	MC
""	22		Marched out and proceeded via ST POL - VAL HUON - FAUX-to billets at SACHIN-LE-BUCQ arriving there at 1/2.30pm.	MC
			Brigade Routine received from Brigade stated that we would march on the 23-3-17.	MC
			Brigade Routine Order dated 24.3.17 shewed that the following distances had been covered by this Company during the march viz: 19th March 10½ miles, 20th March 12½ miles	MC
""	23		Resting in Billets at SACHIN. Clearing of all gun and gun equipment, etc. Received Brigade March Table F, shewing that this Company had to march past the starting point (Cross Roads 500° N of Y in CAUCHY) at 8.6 am	MC
""	24	6.36am	Marched out at 6.36am and proceeded via PERNES-FERFAY-A'MES-LIERES, StHILAIRE to billets at BOUREG arriving there at 10.45am	MC
		2.30pm	Received Brigade March Table F shewing time of passing 8.30am order in column to be advanced one hour, eleven p.m. becoming 12 midnight point to be road junction 500° N of S in LILLERS. Lieut. T HOWARD proceeded to MERVILLE to meet the Staff Captain to arrange for billets. Received notice that summer time would start today at 11 p.m. that all limbered (would make the start one hour earlier this therefore made the	MC
""	25	7	Marched out at 7.45 (summer time) and proceeded via LILLERS-BUSNES. ROBECQ to billets at REGNIER arriving there at 12.15pm BRO. shewed the following distances to have been covered over March 19th 8½ miles, 24th 10 miles, 25 - 11¾ miles after making a total	MC
""	26		Parades ordered for cleaning of gun and equipment, also overhaul of limbered wagons and generally getting all gear to be in readiness to proceed to the trenches. The Company was paid out during the afternoon	MC
""	27th to 31st		Training in vicinity of billets carried on with one Section lying in a 50 yards range daily. Orders received that the Brigade to be in G.H.Q. reserve and to be ready to move at short notice	MC

R Cower all.

SECRET   APPENDIX I   Copy No 7

94th Machine-Gun Company. Warning Orders No 3

15th March 1917.

1. Information has been received that the 21st. Division is to be transferred to the FIRST ARMY concentrating in the BOUQUEMAISON area on the 20th. instant.

2. As it is most probable that no additional transport will be available Section Officers will go very carefully into the question of what is being carried. Any surplus stores must be handed into the Quartermaster's Stores without delay to enable such to be disposed of. Officers must endeavour to cut down their kits to the absolute minimum. Any winter clothing etc. not now required should be despatched through Messrs. Cox & Co. as early as possible.

3. Section Officers are responsible that their limbers are carefully and properly packed so that the following are carried on each limber, viz:- Two Guns, Tripods, Spare parts etc. Belt Boxes, Officers Valise, Packs and Blankets of two gun teams. It may also be necessary for a certain quantity of other stores to be put on Section Limbers.

4. The Transport Officer will go into the question of Transport equipment and driver's kits to ensure that nothing more than is absolutely necessary is carried to the new area.

5. Further orders have been received that the 94th. Machine Gun Company must be prepared to move into the trenches recently left on four hours notice.
In the event of orders to move being received, a temporary dump will be established at the present Quartermaster's Store, and all Officer's kits, packs and blankets etc. will be dumped there and left under the charge of a small rear party. The Company will move to the forward area in Fighting Order. Section Officers are responsible that their Sections are ready to move immediately on receipt of orders.

W. Blower.
Captain,
Commanding 94th. M.G.Coy.

Copy No. 1 - C. O.
" " 2 - O.C. "A" Section.
" " 3 - O.C. "B" Section.
" " 4 - O.C. "C" Section.
" " 5 - O.C. "D" Section.
" " 6 TRANSPORT
" " 7 &8 VEARDIARS
" " 9 FILE

CONFIDENTIAL.

Vol 12

WAR-DIARY
(Original)
OF
94th MACHINE GUN COMPANY

From: 1st April 1917   To: 30th April 1917

(Volume XVI)

WAR DIARY
INTELLIGENCE SUMMARY

Army Form C. 2118.

No. 94 MACHINE GUN COMPANY.

Place	Date April	Hour	Summary of Events and Information	Remarks and references to Appendices
In the field	1		In billets at REGNIER-LA-CLERC (Ref. Map. France Sheet 36A K 35 a.1.1) Training was carried out in the vicinity of the billets.	JJPler
do	2		As yesterday. A conference of Commanding Officers was held at Brigade Headquarters (MERVILLE) at 5.30 pm at which forth coming operations were discussed.	JJPler
do	3 4 5		Training carried on with, including Section Schemes and firing on range.	JJPler
do	6		Training carried on with. Received Brigade Order No. 128, which shewed that the Bgde would march to the MARLES-LEZ-MINES - BETHUNE area on the 8th inst. Draft of 10 O.R. reported.	JJPler
do	7		Carried out a Company advanced guard scheme. Order No. 128 cancelling that received yesterday but the move comes under that of A.S.C.R. 146 & 348 of 4.4.17 (being a further code) after notification was received that Lieut E. PRICE Royal Inniskilling Fus. 119th M.G. Coy. had been appointed 2nd in command of the Company. No. 7581 Pte Jones left in time.	JJPler
do	noon 4 pm		Received orders from Bde that 2 guns of this company would take over afternoon 1 Anti-aircraft duties in area of TRESIENNES from CORPS CAVALRY at 12 noon. Issued Operation Order No. 8.	JJPler
do	8		These guns detailed in Operation Order No. 8 left billets at 8 am to take up Anti-aircraft duties. Marched out of billets area at 9.45 having the starting point Road Junction Q 11 B. 6.1. at 11.30 am. Marched by route PACAUT - HINGES - VENDIN-LEZ-BETHUNE - OBLINGHEM-ANNEZIN arriving there at 2.20 pm.	JJPler
do	9		In Billets at ANNEZIN. Training was carried on with during the day.	JJPler
do	10		In billets at ANNEZIN. Training carried on with. Lieut V Sr C HILL rejoined from Depot. Received a warning order from Bde stating that the Coy would be moving tomorrow morning to ETAPLES.	JJPler

J.O. Whistler L/m
Lt OC MGCoy

WAR DIARY
or
INTELLIGENCE SUMMARY.
(Erase heading not required.)

Army Form C. 2118.

Place	Date April	Hour	Summary of Events and Information	Remarks and references to Appendices
In the field	11		Received Brigade Order No 130 stating that we would move to the BRUAY area today the unit being billeted in NOEUX-LES-MINE. Starting point - road junction 650* N.E.) of that of ANNEZIN, which this Bn had to pass at 1.12 pm. Paraded and marched out of Billets at 12.45 pm and proceeded by route ANNEZIN - BETHUNE to billets in NOEUX-LES-MINES, arriving there at 2.10 pm. A.A. Order No. 130 also stated that on arrival at the new billets the Brigade would come under the orders of G.O.C. 1st CORPS and would be prepared to move at 2 hours notice.	J.S.P.4
		8.30 p	Received instructions from Brigade that Officers and N.C.O's must make themselves thoroughly acquainted with the M.G. emplacements in and immediately in front of the village line and for this purpose guides would be provided tomorrow from the 11th & 14th Batteries. M.G. reporting at Bde H.Q. at 9 am. Each guide to take a party of 1 Officer 2 N.C.O's to reconnoitre the frontage of one Infantry Brigade. All parties to report at Bde. H.Q. concerned before commencing the reconnaissance.	
do	12.	9 am	In billets at NOEUX-LES-MINES (Trench Ref. Map sheet 36.b - K.18 & 29) Guides from the 11th, 14th M.M.G. Batteries reported in accordance with instructions received from Brigade last night. Officer with 2 N.C.O's ex detailed to reconnoitre the camps of the Brigades as follows:- 13th Infantry Brigade (HQ at AIX NOULETTE) Lieut Cant, 17th Infantry Brigade (HQ at BULLY GRENAY) Capt HEATH, Sub Section Lieut NILSON. 12th Infantry Brigade (BULLY GRENAY) 8/C SUB SECTION 2/LT BOTHWELL. 91st Infantry Brigade (LES BREBIS) Lieut DURRANT. 184 Infantry Brigade (MBZINGARBE) Lieut HOWARD. 71st Infantry Brigade (PHILOSOPHE) Lieut HOWARD. The reconnaissances duly carried out. Instructions concerning R.T. RICHARDSON of the H.Q. detachment on Anti-Aircraft work would be released at 3 pm today to rejoin his unit at NOEUX-LES-MINES tonight.	J.S.P.4
		8.30 p	Received instructions from Bde. that a second reconnaissance would be carried out today by officers & parties to those detailed.	
do	13		Detailed Officers with 2 N.C.O's each to reconnoitre Brigades as follows:- 13th Inf Bde, A.17.17 (3rd Inf) Bde. 14.1.P. BOTHWELL - 12th Inf Bde Lieut HOWARD - 14th Inf Bde Lieut WILSON - 9th Inf Bde Lt WILSON. The reconnaissance was duly carried out.	J.S.P.4

WAR DIARY
INTELLIGENCE SUMMARY
(Erase heading not required.)

Army Form C. 2118.

Place	Date APRIL	Hour	Summary of Events and Information	Remarks and references to Appendices
In the field	13 (cont)	11 a.m.	Mr RICHARDSON reported that his detachment had been relieved and had arrived at billets	J.P.W
		12 noon	Received Warning Order from Brigade stating that we would be moving tomorrow morning	
		5.30 p.m 11.45 p.m	Lieut J.E. PEIRCE joined for duty as second in command (vice 119 R.M.G.Coy). Received Brigade Order No. 131 which stated that the 31st Division would move to the area shown on P area tomorrow starting to take to B.R.15. at 3.6 (Ref Sheet 36 b) the unit parading at 9 a.m. that move ordering parade for 8.45 a.m. Issued the necessary orders	J.P.W
- do -	14	8.45	Marched out of billets at NOEUX-LES-MINES and proceeded via BARLIN-CITÉ LIAUTEY - MAISNIL LES RUITZ - Road junction H 35 a W 3 - PH 4 2.6 - RAINCHICOURT - LA COMPTE - to billets at HOUVELIN (Lieut V.F.C. HILL was sent in advance to arrange billets and met the Coy on the outskirts of the village) arrived at 1.45 p.m. Location Sheet 12 HOUVELIN O 29 c 40	J.P.W
- do -	15		The morning was devoted to cleaning up of guns and gun equipment. Orders were received to clean up of the area we had to move with drawn a range was allotted to (the Company at points G 35 a.b.c. which was reconnoitered by Lieut WILSON) Lieut CAMT proceeded to the 31st Army School to attend the gas course. assembling at P.O.W.G.S today	J.P.W
- do -	16	1.45 p.m	Training was carried out during the morning. "C" Section was on the range and the other sections carried out simple tactical exercises. Received order to be prepared to move at short notice	
		2 p.m	Received further orders that the Coys would move probably to MINGOVAL during the afternoon	J.P.W
		4.0 p.m	Received definite orders to move today to MINGOVAL. Ordered parade for 5.30 p.m	
		5.30 p.m	Paraded and moved off arriving at the new billets at 7.55 p.m. (Lieut's HILL & HOWARD to proceed in advance to arrange for billets with the town Major of) Location 36.G v 23 6.66	
- do -	17	12.15 a.m	Received orders from XIII Corps to move to ANZIN - ST. AUBIN taking over billets from the 36th Division. Major there also received instructions regarding refilling	
		10.30 a.m	Paraded today and moved off arriving at the new billets at 3.20 p.m.	J.P.W J.E.W

WAR DIARY
or
INTELLIGENCE SUMMARY.
(Erase heading not required.)

Army Form C. 2118.

Instructions regarding War Diaries and Intelligence Summaries are contained in F.S. Regs., Part II. and the Staff Manual respectively. Title pages will be prepared in manuscript.

Place	Date April	Hour	Summary of Events and Information	Remarks and references to Appendices
Sulzbach	17 contd	3.45p	Had interviews with both Machine Gun Officers XIII Corps who went into the board scheme of the forthcoming operations which this company will be taking part in and stated that orders would be issued as soon as trench mortally fought, regarding the dispositions of guns and ammunition etc.	J.S.P.W.
-do-	18.		No further orders were received yesterday regarding dispositions for the (attack) contemplated, therefore the company was ordered to standby ready to move out at short notice in big hurry order while Lieut J. Howard 7/L. Bott H.W.F.H with 2 N.C.Os were detailed to carry out a reconnaissance of the ground to be able to judge the gun teams into positions (and also to discover the best route to the trenches for either wheeled or pack transport.	J.B.P.W.
-do	19.		Standing by at billets prepared to move out on receipt of orders. No orders however were received. Lieut. N.St C. Hill proceeded to Bere (a.lit qu.In Rd. OD 193)	J.S.P.W.
-do-	20.		Morning in vicinity of billets. Orders were received by O.C. Coys (from Lieut (M.G.O XIII Corps and communicated to O.C. C 92nd and 94th and S Companies relating to the further coming operations. Issued operation order No 9	appendix II J.S.P.W.
-do-	21st	6.30p	Carried out a reconnaissance to approximately locate positions for the 16 guns of this company. Owing to the proximity of infantry posts and outposts there had to be some care given to ensure that the correct angle of safety could not be obtained, and also to the fact that the both M.G.Os with regard to this matter, who decided to alter the ... using eight guns in positions as detailed for is group with the same (target) eight group to be employed, to ... vicinity of road in D 28 62.d	(appx II)
		8.30p	Had further interviews with both M.G.O who owing to the fact that the distance of some 600 yds in action on the line of road in D 28 8.d.- a ... thus left only and decided to cancel guns of this company therefore to ... received further orders from the company to employ — and also for gun company to be employed tomorrow. Leaving ... (Received from 7 ...) ... direction etc., from each gun.	J.S.P.W.

WAR DIARY
or
INTELLIGENCE SUMMARY.
(Erase heading not required.)

Army Form C. 2118.

Place	Date April 1917	Hour	Summary of Events and Information	Remarks and references to Appendices
Inchy-Buld	22	9.30am	Received further orders together with operation Order No 10 from Brig M.G.C.	appendix
		3pm	"B" Section under Lieut. J.H. Wilson & 2/Lieut R. Bothwell marched out with transport. On arrival at the dump, too many prepared, and after dark the gun teams proceeded to take up positions lifting in wire complete by midnight.	III J.B.M.
-do-	23	5.45am	Zero hour. Our Barrage started whereupon the Germans heavily retaliated on the position of this Company being heavily bombarded. A number of other ranks were wounded very early on during the final. No 1238H S/S. BROWNE S.K. 30944 t/Sgt. RICHARDS P.T. were killed by a direct hit from a shell. Shortly after Lieut J.H. Wilson received a shrapnel wound in the arm but remained at duty till his section had finished the task allotted to it. 9/47 J.R. BOTHWELL was also slightly wounded on the leg, but remained at duty. Total casualties were. Officers wounded = 2, O.R. killed = 2, O.R. wounded = 10. Many of the other ranks wounded were only slightly injured and remained at their duty, until their section moved back. Showing great devotion to duty and a splendid example to the other men were No 28148 4/Cpl MARKHAM J, 25009 Pte BRUMPTON C.B.F., 54684 Pte NEWLAND W.F, Pte HARRISON J., 83861 Pte LINDSEY J., 30812 Pte	J.B.M.
		7.30am	As a result of orders from H.Q. 190 Bde officer to evacuate their positions and return to the dump. Sections were all out and clear of the dump by 10am. and returned to billets at ANZIN-St-AUBIN.	J.B.M.
-do-	24		The day was spent in cleaning up of guns and ammunition etc by the sections that were in action yesterday, and in cleaning by the other sections. A carrying party was detailed to go up to Pontoon Sub C and D sections yesterday, to collect a number of belt boxes that had to be left there.	J.B.M.
-do-	25		Received order from F.M.G.O. to Infantry programme of work to send to Bde H.Q. from 26.28th inst. inclusive. Work done but the training that billets was carried out. A Party was detailed to mend limbered wagons which work and good progress was made.	J.B.M.

WAR DIARY

INTELLIGENCE SUMMARY

(Erase heading not required.)

Army Form C. 2118.

Instructions regarding War Diaries and Intelligence Summaries are contained in F. S. Regs., Part II. and the Staff Manual respectively. Title pages will be prepared in manuscript.

Place	Date APRIL	Hour	Summary of Events and Information	Remarks and references to Appendices
Snellegem	26	10.30am	Training as per detailed programme was carried out. A German aeroplane shot down one of our observation Balloons about 500' from the Billets. The machine descended to a height of 900 feet had three attempts before succeeding in bringing it down to engage this aeroplane by m.g. our a.a. gun which was mounted for a.a. w/c [?] of work. Prior to its lighting [?] [?] the balloon and the balloon had landed. The aeroplane disappeared into the clouds flying very fast.	J.S.P. Lt
-do-	26 cont		Sgt interviews with Corps M.G.O. who gave some details and a copy of scheme containing same further instructions, a blank copy — Appx. Attached which [?] all the [?] of this [?] as he explained in [?] [?] [?] [?] for [?]	APPENDIX IV
		9.30pm	3rd [?] [?] [?] were very [?] out further orders were necessary. After having a [?] party from the into [?] [?] having [?] to its [?] from the Infantry to assist him in getting all they required to its [?] handle that the gun would have to make good during the operations in order [?] [?] [?] [?] [?] [?] [?] [?] crossing [?] [?] the [?] [?] [?] will be some 3000'- 3500' [?] Coln M.G.O. [?] that for 4 men the gun is to be attacked [?] this [?] of movements will only allow of 5 men in the [?] [?] the [?] [?] [?] which is absolutely insufficient for the [?] [?] [?] [?] [?]	J.S.P. Lt
-do-	27	1.30pm	Limbers were packed ready for moving. Received instructions [?] [?] that moving [?] can be made in [?] with the [?] [?]	J.S.P. Lt
-do-	27 cont		Ground Operation Order No.6. (attached) [?] moved out in accordance therewith and arrived at the dump at about 8pm.	APPENDIX V
-do-	28	4.25am 6.15am	Zero hour. 10 [?] guns opened heavy fire. Received reports [?] [?] [?] officers stating that [?] had [?] up [?] [?] a body for action almost 2.30 am	J.S.P. Lt [?]

A 5834 Wt. W4973/M687 750,000 8/16 D. D. & L. Ltd. Forms/C 2118/13.

Army Form C. 2118.

WAR DIARY
or
INTELLIGENCE SUMMARY.
(Erase heading not required.)

Instructions regarding War Diaries and Intelligence Summaries are contained in F.S. Regs., Part II. and the Staff Manual respectively. Title pages will be prepared in manuscript.

Place	Date	Hour	Summary of Events and Information	Remarks and references to Appendices
Sailly Sail	28 APRIL cont	9.30am	Runner reported at advanced Coy H.Q. with casualty reports, etc. Casualties up to date 1 O.R. wounded. Group Commanders reported that it had been impossible to move guns forward, owing to very heavy shelling, therefore they had laid all guns on the lines indicated for barrage, and counter attack from their original positions. Replied to this order ordering Section Officers to stay in their present position until the situation became clearer.	J.G.P.
		10.30	One of the men detailed as orderly Bearer reported at adv. Coy H.Q. and reported that all guns, ammunition and rations had been got up to the positions.	
	cont	11 noon	Reported "Estimated casualties" to H.Q. 6th & 3rd Inf. Bde and 99th Inf. Bde. as 1 Wounded O.R. 2 "	
		3.0pm	The Runner who was detached to Section Officers with orders to counter attack reported that order had been delivered.	
		5.30pm	Note giving position was sent heavy around all gun positions to H.Q. 6th & 3rd Inf. Bde stating that the guns of this company would be withdrawing at 8pm, unless orders to the contrary were received from Corps, in accordance with XIII Corps Letter No CM 9/3/19 of 27.4.19. Reported all correct at same time.	J.G.P.
		6.50pm	Issued orders to Lieut J.F. PRICE to send up the transport as soon after 10.0pm as possible.	
		7.45pm	Received the following message from 99th M.G. Coy. "You are on no account to leave your present positions. Orders from Brigade are following. This is most urgent. Please sign this and return." Signed from O.C. Troops Copy sent into Section Officers forthwith, and copy sent to H.Q. 19th Bde. in conformation and XIII Corps willing for keeping in touch with 99th Bde. had handed over to 99th Infantry Brigade.	
		9.30pm	Received orders from 9th Bde. had handed over to 99th Infantry Brigade and to report at their Head Quarters (situated on B 21 a 7.6) for full instructions also that all guns must stand fast until chief withdrawal signal given. Orders to Lieut PRICE to bring up rations and water as early as possible, and	
		10.30	Reported to O.C. 99th Infantry Brigade binding together other details and received a copy of operation Order No 231 which attached (2nd Division forms 3rd Bde will attack 99th & 3rd Bde (p.t.o.) and capture	J. Gilroy Lieut

A5834 Wt. W4973/M687 750,000 8/16 D. D. & L. Ltd. Forms/C.2118/13.

WAR DIARY
INTELLIGENCE SUMMARY

Army Form C. 2118.

Place	Date	Hour	Summary of Events and Information	Remarks and references to Appendices
In the field	April 28 cont.	10.30 pm	German front and support lines between right of Divisional Boundary B.18 d & B.18 b & d & 63rd Division on the left. G.O.C. 99 of Infantry Brigade sent verbal orders regarding the parts to be played by the guns of the Coys (C & D) which were to fire on same targets as yesterday from Zero + 6 m. till artillery barrage ceases. Then to start by starting (from B.13 central) to get to the south thus notifying the southern side of the village of OPPY. Formed Orders to Section Commanders embodying the above points.	J.E.Rie Zus
		11.30 pm 11.35 pm	Received report by runner that all guns had been withdrawn. The order previously issued at 1.15 pm leaving apparently one section of S gun commanders before they had reached said out — Runner to instruct them to go forward to support or advance Coys D & C as met had reached 99th M.G. Coy that guns had withdrawn before the later order reached them and that it was not expected that they could begin in position by 2 am hours.	
do -	29	12.25 am 1.30 am	Reported to H.Q. 99th Inf. Bde. that guns had withdrawn. Received information (from 99th Inf. Bde.) C Coy which detailed targets to be engaged by this Coy.	J.S.L.Z
		1.35 am	C Coy had withdrawn after the orders and again pointed out that all guns of the Coy had not reached their positions by Zero according to previous orders issued and would probably not reach their positions by Zero	
		10 am 8.15 am	Secured the following message from O.C. 99th Inf. Bde. "Have received no information of reports from front of 99th Inf Bde. C.19 Scouts report no change of Barrage reached trench line B.13 d from OPPY to GAVRELLE leading from OPPY to GAVRELLE inclusive as much as possible can March carefully all round south of OPPY to about C.19 central down to get any information in regards to enemy or movement at once. Absolutely no (firm attack or occupation by the enemy acknowledge) (SD) R.O KELLEY (Brig Genl) Comdg DRAYSTON (99th Inf Bde) 1.20 am at the same time a runner reported from the enemy at about B.23 muskets &c. The bullets that the Coy	J.Blair Zus

WAR DIARY or INTELLIGENCE SUMMARY

Army Form C. 2118.

Place	Date	Hour	Summary of Events and Information	Remarks and references to Appendices
In the field	29 April cont		had arrived there at 2.0 a.m. this morning and that up to the time of his starting, none of the orders issued yesterday had been received (from Lrach a/gce.) which orders to Lt PRICE J to get the Lts sent at (Pritchett to do the work contained in the above orders) had not arrived. Reported the state of affairs to 99th Inf Bde stating that guns are expected to be in positions very shortly.	
		6.30 a.m		
		8.45 a.m	Lieut T. HOWARD reported als personally to Old Bn. He arranged the situation with him and arranged for the guns of the Bn. to move forward when they arrive at the dump to position (about B.23 c.5.) to the place to cover HILL 80 and the ground round about it, also to be able to take on the Barrage target.	
		10.30 p.m	Received message from 99th Inf Bde. H.Q. that S.O.S. had been given from our front line and that all guns will need to be ready to shoot.	
		1.15 p.m	Runner reported from Bulleely with memo from Lt F. PRICE stating that the 4 guns were on the move and due at the dump and gained orders to be able to take Hill 80 and Sunk.En forward to position in B.23 c.5.	
		4.85 p.m	Received return from 9th. BOTHWELL, stating that 4 guns HQs had taken up positions in B.23 c at 5.25 p.m.	
		6.25 p.m	Reported to 99th Inf Bde. that guns were in position and asked (or orders) re withdrawal.	
		8.10 p.m	Received orders from 99th Inf Bde. to remain in our position (or to-night).	
		10.30 p.m	Received 99th Inf Bde Order No. 135 which stated that the 13th EAST YORKS Regt will take over the whole of the 2nd Division front to-night; also stating that the 9th M.G. Coy is available under the orders of 99th Inf. Bde. Received memo from o.c. 99th M.G. Coy asking (not to be this boy) Replied giving necessary particulars. (like to position of my own guns, men were reported short of rations, and the remainder of the M.G. Coy like the gun under the men were being conveyed by tram and A.M.M. etc.	

WAR DIARY
INTELLIGENCE SUMMARY

Army Form C. 2118.

Place	Date APRIL	Hour	Summary of Events and Information	Remarks and references to Appendices
In the field	30	12.30am 8.30am	S.O.S. signal was given from front line. Received report from 2/1/ Bgd M Gun stating that his guns had (with a belt of each on the S.O.S. call) fired that his positions had been very heavily shelled with gas shells for 2½ hours last night.	JBM
		10.15am	Received from 99th Inf Bde transport to 93rd Bde H Q at 5 H I a 3 4 for onward passing Centre.	
		11.20am	Reported at and found that the advanced Bde HQ (93 Inf Bde) were actually at H3 a 59 no forward there that interviews with SO of 93rd Inf Bde and received instructions to meet OC 190 M Gun Coy & 93rd Inf Bde together. Major & ADC OC 190 M G Coy in the line with him & assumed the details fallen.	APPENDIX VI
		1.30pm	Returned to adv log A Q and resumed Operation Order No.12/Appendix.	

John Lewis
OC 95th M G Coy

WAR DIARY
or
INTELLIGENCE SUMMARY.
(Erase heading not required.)

Army Form C. 2118.

No. 94 MACHINE GUN COMPANY.
No. 21/22
Date 2.5.17

Place	Date	Hour	Summary of Events and Information	Remarks and references to Appendices
In the Field	30/4/17 continued	2.15 pm	Reported to 99th Infantry Brigade the orders given by G.O.C. 93rd Infantry Brigade, and stated that all guns of this Company would withdraw at midnight tonight. Asked for confirmation which is to follow.	J.T.R.
		10.15 pm	Issued orders to 2/Lt BOTHWELL to withdraw the four guns under his command to the region of MAISON BLEU COTE, reporting to himself on completion of the move.	

J.T.McLean /lt
OC 94th MGC

APPENDIX I

SECRET.   Copy No. 7

94th MACHINE GUN COMPANY.   OPERATION ORDER No.8.

Ref Map, France Sheet 36a.

1. 2 guns of the 94th Machine Gun Company will relieve 2 guns of the CORPS CAVALRY at TREIZENNES (N.6 a 9.7.) taking over the Anti-Aircraft defence of that area, at 12 noon on the 8th inst.

2. 2 guns of "B" Section under 2/Lt. G.E. RICHARDSON will take up these duties.

3. The sub-section will parade at "B" Section's billet with transport, ready to move off, at 8-0 a.m. and will proceed via. Cross-road opposite billet to canal bank, thence along road by canal - ST VENANT - Cross-road P.5 d 9.0.- Drawbridge O 12.c - HOLINGHEM - TREIZENNES - N 6 a 9.7.

4. The unexpended portion of the days rations will be carried by all ranks, and in addition one more days forage and rations will be carried on the limbers.

5. 4,000 rounds reserve S.A.A. will be taken. Blankets will be carried on the limbers.

6. 2/Lt. G.E. Richardson will take over all particulars of the duties from the Officer being relieved and he will wire ROFE direct immediately the duties have been taken over.

7. Further arrangements regarding rations will be notified as soon as known.

Acknowledge.

                                                                    Captain,
                                                          Comdg. 94th M.G.Coy.

Copy No. 1 : 94th Inf Bde
         2 : O.C.
         3 : O.C. "B" Sect.
         4 : 2/Lt G.E. Richardson.
         5 : P.O.
     6 & 7 : War Diary.
         8 : File.

APPENDIX II

SECRET

94th MACHINE GUN COMPANY OPERATION ORDER NO.

1. The 94th Machine Gun Company will be taking part in some forthcoming operations, the date of which will be notified later, providing a covering indirect fire barrage on the enemy's trenches, and bringing fire to bear on points behind his lines.

2. The following shows the grouping of guns of 94th Machine Gun Company, and the targets allotted:

"F" Group: 4 guns to search enemy's trench from B.30.c.3.7. to B.30.b.3.4.

"G" Group: 4 guns to search enemy's trench from B.30.a.3.3. to B.30.a.4.5. – firing from B.24.c.0.4.

"H" Group: 8 guns to enfilade enemy's front line in B.24.a. to B.30.a. – firing from H.3.a.5.0.

These groups will be provided by sections as follows:
"F" Group: "D" Section.
"G" Group: "C" Section.
"H" Group: (a) "B" Section, in positions approximately line of road B.5.d. to B.5.c.3.9. sweeping target from B.24.a.15.100 to B.24.a.8.4.

(b) "A" Section, in positions approximately line of road in B.5.d. sweeping target from B.24.c.0.0 to B.30a.7.4.

3. All guns will commence firing immediately the Artillery barrage opens and will fire one belt on to the above targets, after which they will traverse eastwards to SAVEELLE, maintaining 500 yards in front of the Artillery Barrage, particulars of which will be issued as soon as known. All guns will cease fire at 2400 yards range. The rate of fire will be about one belt per gun every five minutes.

4. Gun teams will consist of one N.C.O. and three men each, i.e. two on the gun, and two some distance in rear filling belts. In addition to this one more man per gun will be concentrated somewhere in the vicinity of advanced Company Headquarters.
There will be 18 boxes of belts and 2 boxes of spare S.A.A carried by each gun team.

5. Telephones will be installed from Headquarters Section to headquarters of Divisional Machine Gun Group. Telephones also to the advanced Coy. H.Q. Each section O.C. will have communication with him, to take orders and reports to advanced Coy. H.Q.
O.C. "D" Section will be responsible for connecting his section with a telephone to act as observer between "F" and "G" Groups. O.C. "B" Section will do the same for "H" Group.

6. Dumps of ammunition will be made for the use of Company as follows:
(1) At MAISON DE LA CORNE 40,000 rounds
(2) At FOND DE TOUR 40,000

Each belt messenger car will be issued up to these dumps in addition, before operations, one "D" and "C" sections, and four for "B" Group (H section).

SECRET   Copy No. 8.

APPENDIX III

24th. MACHINE GUN COMPANY OPERATION ORDER NO.10
                                                    22-4-17

1.   The 63rd. Division is going to attack the line from
SATILEUL – GAVRELLE railway on B.?.d. to a line from H.?.?.?.
to H.8.b.9.6.

2.   This order is issued as an amendment to Operation
Order No 9.

3.   Reference para 3 of that order, the only guns of
this company that will be engaged will be C and D Sections
all the guns of which sections will be in position in the tri-
angle formed between the following co-ordinates:-
        B.17.c.8.8.   B.17.d.6.5.3.   B.17.c.9.0.

4.   All guns will open fire immediately after the Artillery
barrage at Zero and will fire one belt.
        They will subsequently lift to 300 yards beyond the
artillery barrage, maintaining that distance in front of it.
Particulars of this barrage have been issued to Section Officers.
        The rate of fire will be one belt per gun per five
minutes.
        After the first lift guns will lift at the rate of
100 yards per four minutes.
        The barrage will be maintained on the last line until
Zero plus 72 minutes when all guns will cease fire.

5.   New worn barrels will be used. The legs of and tripods
will be firmly embedded in the ground before opening fire.
        Each gun commander will have clearly written on the
forms provided the results of the calculations for elevation
and direction for each lift of that gun.

6.   Gun teams will consist of 1 N.C.O. and three men.
In addition a carrying party of another four men per gun will be
provided to carry up ammunition etc. This party on the
completion of their task will return to Billets.
        12 boxes of belts and 2 boxes reserve S.A.A. will be
carried to each position.

7.   Os C "C" and "D" Sections will each have two runners
with their sections. They will forward the following reports
to advanced Company Headquarters:-
        (1) As soon as all guns are dug in and ready to open fire –
            " . " Section Ready for action."
        (ii) At Zero plus 30 minutes (a) Casualty Report
                                      (b) Anything of Interest.

        Orders as to the withdrawal of guns will be sent back
to Section Officers as early as possible by these runners.
        The location of advanced Company Headquarters will be
in the Railway Cutting at HEAPES FOND DE LA MAISON BLANCHE.
(H.1.a.5.6.)

8.   Para 7 of Operation Order No 9 will remain unaltered
with the exception that parade will be at ?.?.?. a.m. on "Y" day

9.   Section Officers will arrange to have their watches
synchronised at advanced Coy HQ at ?.?.? a.m. on "Y" day
        Zero hour will be ?.?.?. a.m.

                                              Commanding 24th M.G. Coy.

APPENDIX IV

SECRET.   Copy.

G.S.,

2nd Division.

1. Scheme for the employment of Machine Guns of the 2nd Div. and 2 companys 31st Division in attack OPPY- ARLEUX.

It is understood that M.G. of 99 M.G.Coy. will be attached to 5 and 6 Brigades for operations.

In conjunction with the Bde. schemes including 99 Bde M.G the following targets will be dealt with by 92nd & 94th M.G.Co

Orders will be issued for carrying out of these operation by C.M.G.O. to 92 and 94 Coys.

They will be attached to 2nd Division from m.n. Y-Z night who will arrange for communicating with them in case of alterations to programme through H.Q., Right Bde and Btn. H.Q. at B.17.d. 5.5.

92 and 94 M.G.Coys. will be withdrawn at dusk on Z night unless special application is made by 2nd Division to XIII Corps for their retention in line.

Targets.(Ref 51 b N.W.)

Unit	Location firing from	firing at
8 guns 92	B.17.d.	1st Target- B.12.b.5.0. to B.12.b.4.5.
8 guns 92	C.23.b.0.8.	2nd Target- C.1. b.& d. B.12.d. 8.5. to C.1.a.5.0.
8 guns 94	C.23.b.	B.18.b.2.6. to C.7.4.7.
8 guns 94	C.23.a & c.	C.13.c.0.3. to C.13.b. 9.6.
also possibly ? guns from 63rd Div.	B.30.c.	B.18.d. 9.0.to C.13.c.3.7.

Until Art. lift from German Support Line.

Barrages will be arranged by timed schedule to maintain 300 yards beyond Art. creeping barrage.

Watches will be synchronised at 6th Bde. H.Q.

Canadian Corps will be asked to co- operate in their own areas and N. of Hill 60 in C.1.

It is requested that 2nd Division will forward copies of

(1) 2nd Division Op. Orders.
(2)   "   Artillery

Barrage table as soon as possible.

APPENIX V

SECRET   Copy No 4
           94th MACHINE GUN COMPANY OPERATION ORDER No.
                                                           27.4.17

1.   The 94th Machine Gun Company will co-operate
with the attack of the 2nd Division by engaging the special
targets below:-
     "C" Group -   "B" and "D" Sections under Lieut T Howard
     8 guns firing from   at: Target:
     ------------------   ---   -------
        B.28.b   Firing at B.18.c.2.6 to
                                       C.7.c.4.7.

     "D" Group -   "C" and "D" Sections under 2/Lt Richardson
     8 guns firing from   at: Target:
     ------------------   ---   -------
        B.28.d   Firing at C.13.c.0.3. to
                                       C.13.b.9.0. and new trench
                                       C.13.c.5.5. to C.13.c.1.9.

2.   At Zero plus 30 minutes both groups will move forward
to positions about our jumping off trenches from which they can
form a protective barrage on the following points in event of
S.O.S. signal being given.
     Group: Target:
     ------   -------
        C   500 yards beyond Brown line in C.14.a.
        D   500 yards beyond Brown line in C.14.b.d.

3.   94th Machine Gun Company will be attached to 2nd
Division from 12 midnight Y-Z night
           They will withdraw at dusk on Z night unless orders
to the contrary are received from XIII Corps.

4.   Details of lifts of the barrage have been given to
Section Officers.

5.   Gun Teams will consist of 1 N.C.O. and 3 men
10 boxes of belts will be taken to each position
As much reserve S.A.A. as possible will also be taken to the
positions.

6.   On O. Groups will each have two runners from each
Section.   They will forward the following reports to advanced
Coy H.Q.   position of which will be notified later:-
      (1) As soon as all guns are dug in and ready to fire —
           "Group ready for action"
      (ii) At Zero plus 180 minutes (a) Casualty Report
                                    (b) New Positions taken up.

7.   Two stretcher bearers with one stretcher will be
detailed for each group.

8.   Times of parades on Y day have been detailed.
Particulars regarding synchronisation of watches will be issued
later

9.   Facilities for establishments have been arranged
through 6th Brigade Headquarters at B.17.d.5 2nd Bn. H.Q.
           One runner will be at Battalion H.Q. from 12 m.n
Y-Z night

10.   Zero hour will be notified

           Acknowledge
                                         B Crisp
                                         Captain,
                                         Comdg. 94th M.G. Coy

Copy No 1 to O.C.
      " 2 " Lieut T Howard
      " 3 " 2/Lt.G.E.Richardson
      " 4 " War Diary
      " 5 " File

Secret.   APPENDIX VI   Copy No. 5

94th MACHINE GUN COMPANY.   OPERATION ORDER No. 12.
30-4-17.

Ref Map. 51 B.N.W.

1. The 94th Machine Gun Company will relieve 190th M.G.Coy. tomorrow May 1st 1917, the relief commencing at 1-30.p.m. On completion of relief 94th Machine Gun Company will come under the orders of O.C. 93rd Infantry Brigade.

2. Dispositions will be as follows :-
   (a) "A" Section under Lieut. B.E.Durrant will be in positions on Hill 80 between B.23.C.5.7. and B.23.b.0.5.
   (b) "B" Section under Lieut. T.Howard will be in positions on the immediate left of "A" Section stretching as far as B.23.b.8.4. 2 guns of "C" Section will also come under Lieut. Howard taking up positions at about B.23.a.9.0.
   (c) Remainder of Company (viz. 4 guns and 4 teams) under 2/Lt. Richardson will be in reserve in RAILWAY CUTTING.
   (x) Arrangements for accomodation are being made by Staff Captain, 93rd Infantry Brigade (probably about B.1.d.5.
   (d) Advanced Coy. H.Q. will be at B.21.d.4.1.

3. All men not actually on duty with the forward guns will be withdrawn by day to a dugout at B.29.a.5.9. where they will get as much rest as possible. Only a sentry per gun will be on each gun by day : by night the whole team will be in position with the guns.

4. All guns mentioned in para 2(a) (b) will be held in reserve to provide an Indirect Fire Barrage on the S.O.S. Signal being given, covering the square contained between the following reference C.13.central to SUNKEN RD. (C.1 .a.3.0) down SUNKEN RD. to point 64 (C.13.c.1.) and thence to Southern End of practice Trenches C.13.d.5.1.

   This will be sub-divided between Sections as follows :-
   "A" Section - New trench running through C.13.c.1.4. to practice trenches at C.13.d.1.7. (inclusive) and all ground to Southern boundary of square.
   "B" Section - All ground North of above mentioned trench.
   "C" Section - SUNKEN ROAD C.13.a.3.0. to point 64.

   Section Officers will have the result of their calculations clearly written on a card, and will ensure that each Gun Team Commander throughly understands his duty.

   Fire will be opened immediately the S.O.S. is given.

5. Guides from 190th M.G.Coy. will be provided as follows :-
   (a) For all forward positions and reserve dugout at B.29.a.5 at MAISON de la COTE at 1-30.p.m. 1-5-17.
   (b) For Coy.H.Q. at present Coy.H.Q. (B.27.a.2.0.)at 1-30.p.

6. Completion of relief will be reported to Adv.Coy.H.Q. as early as possible by runner.

7. Six belts per gun will be taken forward to each position. On completion of relief all those belt boxes now at B.27.c. will be taken to the new positions making each gun up to 10 belt boxes.

   Section Officers will arrange to collect as much reserve S.A.A. as possible from the vicinity of their positions.

8. Rations and Water will be sent up daily as early as possible to a point on the road about B.26.b.1.6. where they will be collected by a carrying party detailed from the reserve teams, who will carry all rations for Forward Guns and Coy. H.Q. to Adv. Coy. Each gun team will have one man at advanced Coy. H.Q. at 6-0.p.m. each night to carry rations and water to his position.

Acknowledge.

(Sd) F.D.COHEN,   Captain,
Comdg. 94th M.G.Coy.

Copy No.1 - 93rd Inf Bde.(for information)
     "   2 - O.C.190 M.G.C.   "   "
     "   3)
     "   4) Section Officers.
     "   6 - War Diary.
     "   7 - File.

Confidential

Volume XVII

Vol 13

War Diary.

94th Machine Gun Company   31st Division

May 1917.

WAR DIARY

INTELLIGENCE SUMMARY

(Erase heading not required.)

Army Form C. 2118.

Place	Date	Hour	Summary of Events and Information	Remarks and references to Appendices
In the Field	1-5-17	5.45 a.m.	(Ref: Map 51.B.N.W. 1/20000) 2/Lieut Bothwell reported that his guns had been withdrawn to H.Q. trench near MAISON de la COTE, without any casualty.	
	12 noon		Lieuts Hannan and Durrant reported at Advanced Company Headquarters. Discussed the proceedure with them and made all necessary arrangements for the move etc.	
	1.30 p.m.		Guides reported in accordance with Company Operation Order No 12. The relief of 190th Coy Company was commenced.	
	2.15 p.m.		Company Headquarters moved forward to B.27.c.6.37 and took over from 190th Company.	
	6.15 p.m.		Relief of 190th Machine Gun Company reported to be complete. Proceeded to Headquarters 93rd Infantry Brigade (Location HAYSTACK – H.3.a.5.9) and had interview with B.O.C. 93rd Brigade. Pointed out to him that the guns and their present positions are of no real use except for offensive Harass Barrage work. Also how small a number of Machine Guns are more than ample. Positions for the defence of the line were accordingly asked if at least a certain number of the guns of this Company could be withdrawn into reserve. The matter was referred to Corps Headquarters who stated that this Unit would have to be under the orders of the 93rd Infantry Brigade from 12 midnight	

JCC. Cpt.

Army Form C. 2118.

WAR DIARY
or
INTELLIGENCE SUMMARY.
(Erase heading not required.)

Instructions regarding War Diaries and Intelligence Summaries are contained in F. S. Regs., Part II. and the Staff Manual respectively. Title pages will be prepared in manuscript.

Place	Date	Hour	Summary of Events and Information	Remarks and references to Appendices
In the Field	15.9.17	6.15 p.m.	Target. Further instruction were received the orders of the 92nd Infantry Brigade Commander was invited to report at their Headquarters (B.21.a.6.8.) either tonight or tomorrow for further information regarding route. B.O.C. 92nd Infantry Brigade gave his permission for one guide to be sent on reconnaissance from the line tonight as to ensure a good service too.	
		7.50 p.m.	Reported at Headquarters 92nd Infantry Brigade and had an interview with B.O.C. and Brigade Major. It was decided to telephone to B.S. 3rd Division asking what orders were given to the Coy, as they were known that they should be relieved at no later than the night of May 29/30th and subsequently and further operations against OPPY:— (a) 8 guns located at B.17.C.4.0 with targets (1) OPPY - NEUVIREUIL ROAD (2) OPPY Support trench. (b) 8 guns located at B.23.a. with targets C.13.C. Asked where the men of the Company would have to go to for tonight and tomorrow morning, pointing out that if the men be moved back to billets at ANZIN ST AUBIN, great hardship would have to ensue — as men going in very shattered state now — and the march up agunnered position too too much for men at the men.	

A.5834 Wt. W4973/M687 750,000 8/16 D.D. & L. Ltd. Forms/C.2118/13.

Army Form C. 2118.

WAR DIARY
INTELLIGENCE SUMMARY.
(Erase heading not required.)

Instructions regarding War Diaries and Intelligence Summaries are contained in F. S. Regs., Part II. and the Staff Manual respectively. Title pages will be prepared in manuscript.

Place	Date	Hour	Summary of Events and Information	Remarks and references to Appendices
In the Field	1-5-17	7.50 p.m.	Was given permission to reconnoitre all the men in advance at B 28 a.5.9. entering road to get into the new positions.	
		8.15 p.m.	Returned to advanced Company Headquarters and wrote orders to Lieut. HOWARD and DURRANT to reconnoitre all guns and personnel to this dug out, and to ensure that all men got as much rest as possible tonight and tomorrow. Orders sent Lieut. HOWARD in charge of the intake party.	J.S.L. Cpl.
		9.0. p.m.	Our Artillery put up a heavy barrage lasting approximately.	
		10.30 p.m.	Lieut. DURRANT reported move to new quarters complete.	
	2-5-17		During the morning the following casualties occurred:— PRIVATE - SELF. KILLED. CAPTN. COWEN. WOUNDED. LIEUT. HOWARD takes up command of the Company until the arrival of LIEUT. PRICE.	J.S.L. Cpl.

Army Form C. 2118.

WAR DIARY
of
INTELLIGENCE SUMMARY.
(Erase heading not required.)

Instructions regarding War Diaries and Intelligence Summaries are contained in F. S. Regs., Part II. and the Staff Manual respectively. Title pages will be prepared in manuscript.

Place	Date	Hour	Summary of Events and Information	Remarks and references to Appendices
In the Field.	2-5-17	5.30 p.m.	LIEUT. PRICE paid a visit orders for the Company/Coy in the attack (Operation Order No. 13). O.C. proceeds to final interview with G.O.C. 92nd INFANTRY BDE.	Appendix I.
		9.30 p.m.	A.B and C. SECTIONS moved forward under LIEUT. DURRANT and 2/LIEUT. BOTHWELL and occupied the position indicated upon by O.C. COMPANY.	
	3-5-17	12.45 a.m.	(Ref to 2nd/3rd) General report from LIEUT. DURRANT that guns were in position and ready for action.	
		3.25 a.m.	Similar report from 2/LIEUT. BOTHWELL.	
		3.45 a.m.	ZERO.	
		5.40 a.m.	Received report from LIEUT. DURRANT Barrage was being successfully carried out. Two guns temporarily out of action (portage stoppage)	
		5.45 a.m.	Similar report of satisfactory work from 2/LIEUT. BOTHWELL. No casualties on completion. Attack unsuccessful, all guns at once taken as promptly arranged to protect the front. Seven guns at 9.2nd M. G. Coy. composite in defence scheme – MAJOR CONLEY	9.30 YP

A 5834 Wt. W 4973/M687 750,000 8/16 D.D. & L. Ltd. Forms/C.2118/13.

WAR DIARY of INTELLIGENCE SUMMARY

Army Form C. 2118.

(Erase heading not required.)

Place	Date	Hour	Summary of Events and Information	Remarks and references to Appendices
In the Field	3-5-17	6.30 a.m.	92nd M.G. Coy assuming command of the guns.	
		7.0 p.m.	B.O.C 92nd BRIGADE advised OFFICERS COMDG. 92nd and 94th M.G. Coys. to submit a plan of defence for the protection of the line.	J.B.P. Cyr
			Proposals submitted with lines of fire to B.O.C. as arranged.	
		11.0 p.m.	Four guns are left in the line to co-operate with 92nd M.G. Coy. 8 guns in all being considered sufficient for the task. Remaining guns occupy dug-outs in or near reserve line. Replacement completed at 3 a.m.	
			NOTE:- Communications are present by runners in pairs. Left numerous in map nearer Bonnes Froez aux mur to factory.	
			Draft of 28 men arrived and were absorbed into the sections to make up numerical strength required.	
	4-5-17		Received orders that 94th BDE. would take over defence of the line in the right of 92nd BDE. Three Army the 93rd BDE. 94th Coy. less 1 Section (with unit 93rd BDE.) to release 93rd M. Coy. Line arrangement with O.C. 93rd M.G. Coy not disturbed dispositions were made so as to impart to this stretch of line an Infantry more careful and undertakings. There are interior.	

WAR DIARY
INTELLIGENCE SUMMARY
(Erase heading not required.)

Army Form C. 2118.

Place	Date	Hour	Summary of Events and Information	Remarks and references to Appendices
In the Field	4/3/17		with B.O.C. 93rd and 94th BDES. and BDE MAJORS who agreed. That the MACHINE GUNS reconnect noted night of 5th/6th MAR.	
		5.0 p.m.	2/Lieut PHILBIN joins the Company in the line.	
	5/3/17		PTE. CLIFFE recovered (remained at cuty with "A" SECTION under LIEUT. DURRANT who was still attached to 92nd BDE.) Men of Company prepare Guns and Equipment for the line. Reconnaissance of new posts to be taken over is made by O.C. Coy. and plans of defence arranged for.	
		4.0 p.m.	O.C. Coy. had interview with G.O.C. 94th BDE. Reports disposition of Guns are placed before him and approved. Operation Order No. 14 is issued for the relief. Relief commenced at 9 p.m. completed without any casualties by 12 midnight. "A" SECTION relieved by 92nd BDE. Relief completed without incident by 3 a.m. "A" and "C" SECTIONS remain in reserve.	Appendix II

Army Form C. 2118.

WAR DIARY
or
INTELLIGENCE SUMMARY.
(Erase heading not required.)

Place	Date	Hour	Summary of Events and Information	Remarks and references to Appendices
In the Field	6/5/17		Position in the line are improved and improvements are formed with BDE. Back area. Rear H.Q. small present and having remained at ANZIN-ST-AUBIN is ordered forward into BDE. back area. NIGHT 6/7/17. Work in the line proceeds. During the night one gun and tripod of D' SECTION receives a direct hit by a shell and totally disappears. No casualties to the gunners.	
	7/5/17	3.25 a.m.	Received Operation Order from H.Q. 93rd BDE. directing the relief of D' one half B SECTION by 93rd M.G. COR. Lower Operation Order at 10.15 p.m. their into effect.	Appendix VII
		7.0 p.m.	"A" and "C" SECTIONS now back in BDE. back area. Transport and Cor. kit left them at ANZIN ST AUBIN are now taken during the day to BDE. BRICK AREA under Lieut. DURRANT.	
		8.0 p.m.	Receive information that Lieut. HOWARD is admitted to hospital. During the morning a portion of the trench vacancy to receive officers mornings trenches line and 50 yards away drew heavy gunfire.	
			EVENING 7/8/5 MAY. 93rd M.G. COR. with two sections occupy night PICQUUNL SECTOR. this relieves the seconds of the gun IN & Cor. ammunition in operation	J.S. Cpt.

WAR DIARY
INTELLIGENCE SUMMARY

(Erase heading not required.)

Army Form C. 2118.

Instructions regarding War Diaries and Intelligence Summaries are contained in F. S. Regs., Part II. and the Staff Manual respectively. Title pages will be prepared in manuscript.

Place	Date	Hour	Summary of Events and Information	Remarks and references to Appendices
In the Field	8/5/17		Orders No.15. Trips and Belt Boxes being handed over representing this relief which was complete by 3.25 a.m. Section relieves together with Cor. H.Q. one then went to engage Gun pits at B.22.C.72. During the day sections relieved guns and equipment. O.C. meets O.C. 92nd M.B.Coy and makes arrangements for relief of 2nd M.B.Coy by the 94th M.B.Coy in left Divisional sector for the night 8/9th.	Appendix II
		9.30 p.m.	Army Operation Order No.16 arrived to put this into effect. Rcvd. Cor. H.Qrs. with "A" and "C" SECTIONS remain in BDE. Sub area.	J.F.Cpt
		11.30 a.m.	Relief of 92rd M.A.Cpt Minor to start – Relief delayed 2 hrs through heavy hostile barrage of H.E. and GAS SHELLS.	
		1.0 a.m.	Relief completed, and comfortable without incident by 2.a.m.	
	9/5/17	12.30 a.m.	Having trips and maps for impending new garrisoned received and considered. "C" Section arrive from BDE back area at Coy H.Q. as reserve action. During the day Section in reserve performs interior duties and provides carrying for Anti Aircraft work. Officers both in the line now at Coy H.Q. consists	J.F.Cpt

Army Form C. 2118.

WAR DIARY
or
INTELLIGENCE SUMMARY.
(Erase heading not required.)

Instructions regarding War Diaries and Intelligence Summaries are contained in F. S. Regs., Part II. and the Staff Manual respectively. Title pages will be prepared in manuscript.

Place	Date	Hour	Summary of Events and Information	Remarks and references to Appendices
In the Field	9/5/17		Plans of Action.	
		2.45 a.m.	Operation Orders No. 17 issued, directing "C" Section to relieve "B" Section in the line.	Appendix V.
		11.30 p.m.	"B" Section relieved by "C" Section. Rain delayed owing to heavy shelling. Completed at 2 a.m. without any casualties. "B" Section remain in reserve at Bn. H.Q.	J.H.C.[?]
	10/5/17		B Section cleaned guns and equipment and new gun for Anti-Aircraft work. C.O. visits the two machine gun positions and examines the whole of the country with the INFANTRY COMMANDERS. C.O. suggest plans of employment and INFANTRY C.O. LEFT SECTOR for men machine guns on night 10/11/17.	
		8.30 p.m.	Gunner LEFT SECTOR reported to S.O.S. signal from INFANTRY of LEFT SECTOR and also German LEFT SECTOR reported it S.O.S. signal from [?]. Rumor engagement with our guns 400.	
		5.30 to 11 p.m.	Heavy shelling by both sides of front most supports lines.	
		11.15 p.m.	Strong hostile raid on our "A" Section relieved "D" Section in LEFT SECTOR. Relief complete 1 a.m. (11/5/17) no casualties	J.H.C.[?]

Army Form C. 2118.

WAR DIARY
or
INTELLIGENCE SUMMARY.
(Erase heading not required.)

Instructions regarding War Diaries and Intelligence Summaries are contained in F. S. Regs., Part II. and the Staff Manual respectively. Title pages will be prepared in manuscript.

Place	Date	Hour	Summary of Events and Information	Remarks and references to Appendices
In the Field	10/5/17	12.0 p.m.	B.SECTION remove back to REAR COY H.Q.	
	11/5/17		REAR COY H.Qs remove from BDE, back over to BDE TRANSPORT LINES	
			D SECTION remain in reserve at COY H.Qs, cleaning guns and equipment and men rest through June.	
		11.0 a.m.	C.O. visits BRIGADE H.Qs to discuss certain details with the STAFF.	
		12.0 noon 12.10 p.m.		
		5.15	COY. H.Qs bombarded with 5.9s - several direct hits on dug out - no casualties	
		4.15 p.m.	2/LIEUT G.H. BALL reports to C.O. for duty in the line. He effectively the COY at TRANSPORT LINES on the Job.	
		6.30 p.m.	2/LIEUTS. RICHARDSON and BALL proceed to the line in relief of 2/LIEUTS	
			BOTHWELL and PHILBIN.	
		9.0 p.m.	2/LIEUTS. BOTHWELL and PHILBIN again for H.Qs on relief from the line.	

A5834 Wt. W4973/M687 750,000 8/16 D. D. & L. Ltd. Forms/C.2118/13.

WAR DIARY
INTELLIGENCE SUMMARY
(Erase heading not required.)

Army Form C. 2118.

Instructions regarding War Diaries and Intelligence Summaries are contained in F. S. Regs., Part II. and the Staff Manual respectively. Title pages will be prepared in manuscript.

Place	Date	Hour	Summary of Events and Information	Remarks and references to Appendices
Souttre Fosse	13/1/17		"D" Section. no reserve. clean guns and equipment and perform Anti-Aircraft duties.	J.S.P. Captⁿ
		2.0 p.m	LIEUT BALL reports to Col. H. Qs. on his appointment as SECOND-IN-COMMAND. Remains during the day and evening to discuss details with the C.O.	
			NOTE. 2/LIEUT PHILBIN returned to TRANSPORT LINES.	
		7.30 p.m	"B" Section arrive from TRANSPORT LINES with rations relieving "D" Section in reserve at Col. H. Qs. "D" Section return to TRANSPORT LINES at 9 p.m.	
		10.0 p.m	"B" Section and all available men at H. Qs. employed carrying ammunition into the line, completing their task about 5 a.m. 13th May. No Casualties.	
			Anti-Aircraft mountings prepared during the day of the 12th were carried into the line and fitted up in the night 12th/13th.	
			NIGHT 12th/13th Guns on the line heavily shelled - emplacements and trenches damaged. No Casualties.	

WAR DIARY
INTELLIGENCE SUMMARY
(Erase heading not required.)

Army Form C. 2118.

Instructions regarding War Diaries and Intelligence Summaries are contained in F.S. Regs., Part II. and the Staff Manual respectively. Title pages will be prepared in manuscript.

Place	Date	Hour	Summary of Events and Information	Remarks and references to Appendices
In the Field	13/5/17		"B" SECTION cleaning guns and equipment and new Anti-Aircraft gun-sunk in the line shelter out antennas arranging trenches and emplacements.	
		7.30 p.m.	N° 86038 PTE HALLETT, G, who had just arrived for duty from TRANSPORT LINES wounded in hand by shell fire (aerorials)	
		7.45 p.m.	COY. H.Q. shelled for 15 minutes. No further casualties.	
		9.0 p.m.	"B" SECTION proceed to the line to relieve "C" SECTION.	
		2 a.m.	"C" SECTION proceed to the line to carry ammunition for a outpost being formed returning to H.Q. at 4.30 a.m.	
		NIGHT of 13th/14th	COY H.Q. heavily shelled for half an hour. No casualties.	
	14/5/17		"A" and "B" SECTIONS in the line. Hostile Aircraft engaged by "A" SECTION who drove them off front line. "C" SECTION remain in reserve at COY H.Q's, clean guns and equipment and perform Anti-Aircraft duties.	

WAR DIARY
or
INTELLIGENCE SUMMARY.
(Erase heading not required.)

Army Form C. 2118.

Place	Date	Hour	Summary of Events and Information	Remarks and references to Appendices
In the Field.	14/3/17		C.O. prepares plans for reengagement of guns in the line and for night firing operations.	
		8.0 p.m.	"D" SECTION arrive from TRANSPORT LINES.	
		9.0 p.m.	"D" SECTION proceed to relieve "A" SECTION in the line also 2/Lieut BOTHWELL proceeds to reconnoitre new positions being taken over in the line. On completion of reconnaissance he relieves 2/Lieut BALL.	
		11.0 p.m.	"A" SECTION returns from the line to Coy H.Q.	
		noon	"A" SECTION carry ammunition down to 100 Lane 2 guns. During afternoon and night Coy. H.Q. letter. No casualties.	J.N.Yt
	15/3/17	7.30 a.m.	2/Lieut BALL reports at Coy H.Q. from the line. During the day "A" SECTION perform Anti-Aircraft duty, clean guns and equipment - are change MARK I for MARK II down to in the yard.	
		11.30 a.m.	C.O. meets C.M.B.O. and Coy COMMANDERS of 92nd and 137th M.G. Coys. at conference to consider details of plan of our impending attack; afterwards making reconnaissance of the line.	J.N.Yt

Army Form C. 2118.

WAR DIARY
or
INTELLIGENCE SUMMARY.

(Erase heading not required.)

Instructions regarding War Diaries and Intelligence Summaries are contained in F. S. Regs., Part II. and the Staff Manual respectively. Title pages will be prepared in manuscript.

Place	Date	Hour	Summary of Events and Information	Remarks and references to Appendices
In the Field	18/3/17	12.45 p.m.	C.O. discussed plans with BRIGADIER and BRIGADE MAJOR 94th BRIGADE.	
		4.30 p.m.	2/LIEUT PHILBIN reports at Coy H.Qs. from the TRANSPORT LINES & proceeds in the line and afterwards proceeds to relieve 2/LIEUT RICHARDSON.	
		10.0 p.m.	2/LIEUT RICHARDSON arrives from the line at Coy H.Qs.	
			NIGHT 18th/19th Guns in line subjected to frequent shelling.	
		12.05 to 1.15 a.m.	One gun employed in night firing on LINK MAZE – L Bel & Fieu	
	19/3/17	8.30 a.m.	C.O. reports to BRIGADE H.Qs. and receives further instructions regarding the impending operations.	
		12.0 noon	"C." SECTION ordered up from TRANSPORT LINES, owing to return of "A" Section to the line this cancelled.	
		2.0 p.m.	2/Lieu gun positions visited. Orders despatched to 2/LIEUTS BOTHWELL & PHILBIN warning them of the impending operations and giving the necessary preliminary orders.	
		7.0 p.m.	2/LIEUT BALL reports at Coy H.Qs. from TRANSPORT LINES.	

Army Form C. 2118.

WAR DIARY
or
INTELLIGENCE SUMMARY.
(Erase heading not required.)

Instructions regarding War Diaries and Intelligence Summaries are contained in F. S. Regs., Part II. and the Staff Manual respectively. Title pages will be prepared in manuscript.

Place	Date	Hour	Summary of Events and Information	Remarks and references to Appendices
In the Field	16/5/17	7.30 p.m.	C.O. interviews BRIGADIER and receives verbal instructions cancelling the evacuation of the positions by the reserve sections tonight. This confirmed by written message at 8.30. C.O. has interview with BRIGADIER and lays complete plans before him.	
		8.0 p.m.	Amended instructions despatched to 2/Lieut BOTHWELL and PHILBIN cancelling the cancellation and indicating further orders received from the BRIGADE H.Qrs. C. SECTION arrives from TRANSPORT LINES.	
		NIGHT 16/5/17	2/Lieut BOTHWELL reconnoitred and occupied MISSY POINT at B.19.c.30.49. Sergt PUGH and rest of "B" SECTION on lorry relieved on the NORTHERN SECTA. Much ammunition & Sm Arms S.A.A. was cut down during the night from C.O.T. H.Qrs to 2/Lieut BOTHWELL's pos. 2/Lieut BOTHWELL's pos. H.Qrs heavily shelled during the night – no casualties.	J.S.L.Y.[?]
	17/5/17	9.30 a.m.	"A" and "C" SECTIONS overhaul guns and equipment in anticipation of coming operations. During the day "D" SECTION perform Anti aircraft duties. C.O. has consultation with BRIGADIER to discuss final adjustment of plans.	
		2.0 p.m.	Special Operation Order received. Operation Order of 92nd and 93rd BRIGADES derived[?] which renders exchange in the disposition and assignment action of the guns of the 94th M.G. Coy. C.O. discussed the matter with H.Qrs. 94th BRIGADE and arranged plans are revised upon which results in Operation Order No. 18 being issued.	J.S.L.Y.[?]

A5834 Wt.W4973/M687. 750,000 8/16 D.D.&L. Ltd. Forms/C.2118/13.

Army Form C. 2118.

WAR DIARY
INTELLIGENCE SUMMARY.
(Erase heading not required.)

Instructions regarding War Diaries and Intelligence Summaries are contained in F.S. Regs., Part II. and the Staff Manual respectively. Title pages will be prepared in manuscript.

Place	Date	Hour	Summary of Events and Information	Remarks and references to Appendices
In the Field	17/5/17.		During the afternoon the following casualties occurred :— 86244 PTE TOWLER. A. Wounded in hand by shell fire. seriously. P5-895 " SEELEY. C. Shell Shock. Remained on duty. 27565 " HIND. W.C. Wounded and Shell Shock. 85973 " TILLBROOKE. E. Wounded right thigh.	
		9.30 p.m.	Guns are moved forward into positions recorded by survey party with S.A.A. from the INFANTRY.	for C/S
		11.0 p.m.	Report received that all ready for action.	
		12.30 a.m.	NIGHT 17th/18th. ZERO opens and guns fire ones to start with, later, as guns, one Results of recent disturbance by shell fire, springs and plates and joints. Demonstration by M.R. carried out according to programme. Guns remaining in occupation of the position during remainder of the night were concealed during the whole of the next day flts. batteries	
	1. a.m. to 3 a.m.	Coy. H.Qs. heavily shelled. No casualties.	
	18/5/17.	5.a.m.	Report received from four Commanders of the various sectors concerning personnel this effort. No casualties occurred and guns were employed successfully according to programme.	for C/S
		9.30 a.m.	C.O. reports to BRIGADE H. Qs. result of operations.	

Army Form C. 2118.

WAR DIARY
INTELLIGENCE SUMMARY.
(Erase heading not required.)

Instructions regarding War Diaries and Intelligence Summaries are contained in F. S. Regs., Part II. and the Staff Manual respectively. Title pages will be prepared in manuscript.

Place	Date	Hour	Summary of Events and Information	Remarks and references to Appendices
In the Field.	18/6/17	8.0 p.m.	2/Lieut MARSLAND arrives at REAR H.Qs and reports to 2nd i/c for duty. Wire received from BRIGADE H. Qs. authorising withdrawal of "A" and "B" SECTIONS after dusk.	
		9.30 p.m.	"A" SECTION moves back to H.Qs. "C" SECTION under 2/LIEUT BALL proceed to GAVRELLE SECTOR to relieve "B" SECTION.	
		11.40 p.m.	Warning received from BRIGADE asking for special alertness on the part of all troops. Precautionary measures taken to ensure quick turn out of Reserve Sections. H. Qs. shelter during night. No casualties.	2/L C/L
		12.0 (m.n.)	"B" SECTION arrive on completion of relief. During the night of 18th/19th guns in both sectors subjected to a fair amount of shelling.	
	19/6/17	9.0 a.m.	"A" and "B" SECTIONS clean guns and equipment and perform Anti-Aircraft sentries. C.O. meets C.O. of relieving Coy. Morning spent in discussing and arranging details of relief.	
		2.0 p.m.	2/LIEUT BOTHWELL reports to Coy. H. Qs. after being relieved by 2/LIEUT BALL.	2/L P Coy

Army Form C. 2118.

WAR DIARY
of
INTELLIGENCE SUMMARY.
(Erase heading not required.)

Instructions regarding War Diaries and Intelligence Summaries are contained in F. S. Regs., Part II. and the Staff Manual respectively. Title pages will be prepared in manuscript.

Place	Date	Hour	Summary of Events and Information	Remarks and references to Appendices
In the Field	19/9/17	2.30 p.m.	C.O reports at BRIGADE H.Qrs.	
		8.0 p.m.	Report received from 2/Lieut BALL of the following casualties:— 30647 Cpl. BARRETT. H. 57347 L/Cpl. COOK. A. } All wounded 65410 Pte. HENDERSON. L. 25020 " DENT. L. } Missing The casualties occurred on the night 18th/19th at the WINDMILL DEFENCES. The men missing were separated from the STRONG POINT by SECTION OFFICER with intention of the casualties station 3 and 4 a.m. and failed to reach his destination. During the day gun in the line and the gun in reserve on Anti-Aircraft mountings were in use off hostile aircraft.	1st Cpt [?]
		9.0 p.m.	2/Lieut RICHARDSON proceeds to relieve 2/Lieut PHILBIN. One gun team of "A" Section is responsible to GAVRELLE SECTOR to replace casualties in "D" SECTION— "A" SECTION less one gun team (plus one gun team of "B" SECTION) proceed to Northern Sector to relieve "D" Section. "B" SECTION less one gun team (plus one gun team of "A" SECTION attached) carry S.A.A. to GAVRELLE SECTOR. Cpl H. Reavine usual intention from hostile shelling day & night 19th/20th. No casualties.	
		11.0 p.m.	2/Lieut PHILBIN returns to Coy. H. Qrs.	

Army Form C. 2118.

WAR DIARY
of
INTELLIGENCE SUMMARY.
(Erase heading not required.)

Instructions regarding War Diaries and Intelligence Summaries are contained in F. S. Regs., Part II. and the Staff Manual respectively. Title pages will be prepared in manuscript.

Place	Date	Hour	Summary of Events and Information	Remarks and references to Appendices
In the Field	29/8/17	7.0 a.m.	Reinforcement from 2/Lieut BALL that CPL BARRETT and 4/CPL COOK died of wounds within an hour of this being hit. PTE HENDERSON suffering from shell shock only. PTE DENT two apparently two taken prisoner by being pushed into the German lines in error	
		9.30 a.m.	O.C. C.rspns & BRIGADE H.Q. are receiving details of Cor. work with BDE. MAJOR and staff Captain.	
		12.0 (noon)	A German flight of 5 machines noticed at a height of about 5000 or 6000 feet closely one of our machines. Anti-Aircraft gun at H.Q. opened fire, caused the German formation to break up and their persuit to be abandoned.	Appendices VII
		12.30 p.m.	2/Lieut HANDS rejoins the Coy. for duty from course at M.G. School. Operation Orders No 19 are issued to all concerned for the relief on night of 29/22— During the day Anti-Aircraft guns on the line very active. During the morning PTE ALLIETT on duty with Anti-Aircraft gun in GAVRELLE SECTOR burned in arms at a nice being prompt - Sup out in time by the STRETCHER BEARERS of STAFF.	
		9.30 p.m.	A complete gun team from H.Q. augmented to relieve a gun team in GAVRELLE SECTOR. 2/LIEUT PHILBIN and "B" SECTION (less one gun team) proceed to Northern Section and relieve "A" SECTION under 2/LIEUT RICHARDSON	95 "C" Y
		10.0 p.m.	Two Officers and 8 Sections of the 190th M.G. Coy arrive to be attached to 9th M.G. Coy on the line for one day previous to 190th M.G. Coy taking over.	

WAR DIARY
INTELLIGENCE SUMMARY.
(Erase heading not required.)

Army Form C. 2118.

Place	Date	Hour	Summary of Events and Information	Remarks and references to Appendices
In the Field	20/5/17	11.0 p.m.	2/Lieut RICHARDSON and "A" SECTION less one gun team report to Coy H.Qrs.	
		11.30 p.m.	Officers and Guides of 190th M.B. Coy proceed to the line to join their respective positions.	
		3. a.m.	2/Lieut RICHARDSON and "A" SECTION complete proceed to TRANSPORT LINES in anticipation of the Coy's relief on the line. "D" SECTION remaining in reserve at Coy H.Qrs.	
		NIGHT 20th/21st	Generally quiet.	
	21/5/17	morning	"D" SECTION clean guns and equipment and perform Anti-Aircraft duties. Hostile Aircraft engaged on two occasions.	
		9.0 p.m.	Officers of 190th M.B. Coy report for relief.	
		9.30 p.m.	Relief commences. Completed at 4.20 a.m. without casualties. Sections returning independently to TRANSPORT LINES after reporting to H.Qrs.	
	22/5/17	9.0 a.m.	Coy Hqrs "A" SECTION and TRANSPORT move off from TRANSPORT LINES to MAROEUIL to Billets arriving at 11.15 a.m.	
		1 p.m.	TRANSPORT and "A" SECTION arrive.	
		2 p.m.	LIEUT HANDS regains BRIGADE H.Q. for duty as Orderly Officer. LIEUT HOWARD and PTE JOHNSTON proceed to 1st ARMY SCHOOL OF INSTRN. PTE BARLOW proceeds to 1st ARMY REST CAMP.	

Army Form C. 2118.

WAR DIARY
INTELLIGENCE SUMMARY.
(Erase heading not required.)

Instructions regarding War Diaries and Intelligence Summaries are contained in F. S. Regs., Part II. and the Staff Manual respectively. Title pages will be prepared in manuscript.

Place	Date	Hour	Summary of Events and Information	Remarks and references to Appendices
In the Field	23/5/17	2.0 pm to 4.30 pm	Coy. overhaul guns and generally clean up for Armourers inspection in the afternoon. Men have baths and clean clothes.	JSP Cpt
	24/5/17		COMPANY carry out training in vicinity of billets the following being the programme for the day :— 9.0 a.m. to 10.0 a.m. — Physical Training and Drill. 10.0 a.m. to 12.30 p.m. — Complete overhaul of gun equipment and personal kit; Cleaning and repairing belts, ammunition etc. 2.0 pm to 4.0 pm — Rapid laying — Rapid adjustment of elevating and traversing wheels. Special training for new Draft 9.0 a.m. to 12.30 pm } 2.0 pm to 4.0 pm } Inventing and dismounting, Loading and unloading, Laying, Ammunition Rates. Care and cleaning.	JSP Cpt

Army Form C. 2118.

WAR DIARY
or
INTELLIGENCE SUMMARY.
(Erase heading not required.)

Instructions regarding War Diaries and Intelligence Summaries are contained in F. S. Regs., Part II. and the Staff Manual respectively. Title pages will be prepared in manuscript.

Place	Date	Hour	Summary of Events and Information	Remarks and references to Appendices
In the Field	25/5/17.		Training continued with the following programme:-	
		9.15 a.m. to 10.0 a.m.	Physical Drill.	
		10.0 a.m. to 11.15 a.m.	Drill.	
		11.15 a.m. to 12.30 p.m.	Immediate Action.	
		2.0 p.m. to 3.0 p.m.	Quick bayonet	
		3.0 p.m. to 4.0 p.m.	Use of Elevating and Traversing Drills.	
			Programme of work modified for new men.	
			Leave being proposed no man dispatched on leave.	
			27562. Sgt THOMPSON. A. proceeds to Divisional Lewis School.	Yes Off
	26/5/17.		Training continued with the following programme:-	
		9.15 a.m.	C.O's inspection.	
		9.30 a.m. to 10.0 a.m.	Infantry Drill.	
		10.0 a.m. to 11.0 a.m.	Immediate Action.	
		11.30 a.m. to 12.30 p.m.	Aim Drill.	
		2.0 p.m. to 3.0 p.m.	Use of Elevating and Traversing Drills.	
		3.0 p.m. to 4.0 p.m.	2nd term of Elevating wheel and aligned traversing.	
			For new men demons alone but simplified to suit beginners.	
			RANGE TAKERS	
		10.0 a.m. to 11.15 a.m.	} Testing and adjusting H.I. on ZERO.	
		11.30 a.m. to 12.30 p.m.		
		2.0 p.m. to 3.0 p.m.	Ranging on distant marks.	
		3.0 p.m. to 4.0 p.m.	Study of ground.	Yes Off

WAR DIARY
INTELLIGENCE SUMMARY

Army Form C. 2118.

Place	Date	Hour	Summary of Events and Information	Remarks and references to Appendices
In the Field	27/5/17		Training continued with the following programme:—	
		7.0. a.m.	R.C. parade for Mass at 7.15 a.m. at MARŒUIL Church.	
		7.30 a.m.	Holy Communion (Voluntary).	
		9.0. a.m.	Cleaning all guns and equipment.	
		10.40 a.m.	Church Parade for service at 11.0 a.m. in Empire Hall.	
		12.30 p.m.	Inspection of billets by C.O.	JSP Cpt
			Leave kept in progress. Draws despatched on leave.	
	28/5/17		Training continued with the following programme:—	
			TRAINED MEN	
		9.15 a.m. to 12.30 p.m.	Cleaning and entry of fighting knives	
		2.0 p.m. to 3.0 p.m.	Use of Traversing and Elevating dials.	
		3.0 p.m. to 4.10 p.m.	Traversing and searching practice.	
			NEW DRAFT.	
		9.15 a.m. to 10.15 a.m.	Mounting, loading and laying gun.	
		10.15 a.m. to 11.15 a.m.	Immediate Action.	
		11.15 a.m. to 12.30 a.m.	Stripping, repair and adjustment.	
		2.0 p.m. to 3.0 p.m.	Use of Traversing and Elevating dials	
		3.0 p.m. to 4.0 p.m.	Traversing and searching practice.	JSP Cpt

Army Form C. 2118.

WAR DIARY
or
INTELLIGENCE SUMMARY.
(Erase heading not required.)

Place	Date	Hour	Summary of Events and Information	Remarks and references to Appendices
In the Field	28/5/17		RANGETAKERS.	WSP Cyp
		9.15 a.m to 11.15 a.m.	Testing and adjusting M.I. and ZERO.	
		11.15 a.m to 12.30 p.m	Ranging on direct marks.	
		2.0 p.m to 3.0 p.m	Construction of Range Cards.	
		3.0 p.m to 4.0 p.m	Ranging through mirage.	
			LIEUT DURRANT proceeds for attachment to Divisional Coy A.S.C. in connection with transport duties.	
			Leave long in progress 1 Officer and 4. O.R. despatched on leave.	
			27562 Sgt THOMPSON returns from Divisional Gas School.	
	29/5/17		Training continued with the following programme:—	J6 Cyp
			ALL PARTIES.	
		9.15 a.m to 10.0 a.m	Physical Drill	
		10.0 a.m to 11.15 a.m	Infantry Drill	
		11.15 a.m to 12.0 (noon)	Immediate Action (see Range Takers)	
		12.0 (noon) to 12.30 p.m	Gun Drill (" — do —)	
			TRAINED MEN.	
		2.15 p.m to 3.15 p.m	Sketch of ground	
		3.15 p.m to 4.30 p.m	Mounting guns in prone position.	
			NEW DRAFT	
		2.30 p.m to 4.30 p.m	Range (Holding and Grouping)	

Army Form C. 2118.

WAR DIARY
or
INTELLIGENCE SUMMARY.
(Erase heading not required.)

Place	Date	Hour	Summary of Events and Information	Remarks and references to Appendices
In the Field	29/3/17		RANGE TAKERS	
		11.15 a.m to 12.0 noon	Testing H.I. and checking ZERO at measured distances.	
		12.0 (noon) to 12.30 p.m	Advanced ranging.	
		2.15 p.m to 3.15 p.m	Study of ground (unit company)	
		3.15 p.m	Advanced ranging with range cards.	
			27562. 7/Sgt THOMPSON returns from Divisional Gas School. This man reported on leave.	
	30/3/17		Training continued with the following programme:-	
			ALL PARTIES	
		9.15 a.m to 10.0 a.m.	Physical Training.	
			RANGE TAKERS	
		10.0 a.m to 11.0 a.m	Testing and adjusting H.I. and ZERO.	
		11.15 a.m to 12.0 noon	Advanced ranging.	
		12.0 noon to 12.30 p.m	Construction of Range cards.	
		2.0 p.m to 3.0 p.m	Ranging from cover.	
		3.0 p.m to 4.0 p.m	Testing ZERO and 2 points in opposite directions.	
			TRAINED MEN	
		10.0 a.m to 11.0 a.m	Immediate Action	
		11.15 a.m to 12.0 noon	Mounting Gun in prone position	
		12.0 noon to 12.30 p.m	Reaction drill	
		2.0 p.m to 3.0 p.m	Range finder drill	
		3.0 p.m to 4.0 p.m	Visual training and judging distance.	

WAR DIARY
or
INTELLIGENCE SUMMARY.

(Erase heading not required.)

Army Form C. 2118.

Place	Date	Hour	Summary of Events and Information	Remarks and references to Appendices
In the Field	30/5/17		DRAFT.	
		10.0 a.m. to 11.0 a.m.	Innoculation Parade.	
		11.15 a.m. to 12.0 noon	Infantry drill - steady drill.	
		12.0 noon to 12.30 p.m.	Repairs and adjustments.	
		2.0 p.m. to 4.0 p.m.	Range - Holding and grouping.	
	31/5/17		Training continued with the following programme.	
			ALL PARTIES.	
		9.15 a.m. to 10.0 a.m.	Physical training	
			TRAINED MEN.	
		10.0 a.m. to 11.0 a.m.	Immediate Action (Blindfolded)	
		11.15 a.m. to 12.0 noon	Infantry gun in prone position.	
		12.0 noon to 12.30 p.m.	Aiming drill.	
		2.0 p.m. to 3.0 p.m.	Theory of group.	
		3.0 p.m. to 4.0 p.m.	Rough ground drill.	
			DRAFT.	
		10.0 a.m. to 11.0 a.m.	Innoculation Parade.	
		11.15 a.m. to 12.0 noon	Dismantling and Layout.	
		12.0 noon to 12.30 p.m.	Repairs and adjustments.	
		2.0 p.m. to 4.0 p.m.	Range - Holding and grouping.	

Army Form C. 2118.

WAR DIARY
or
INTELLIGENCE SUMMARY.
(Erase heading not required).

Place	Date	Hour	Summary of Events and Information	Remarks and references to Appendices
In the Field.	31/5/17		RANGE TAKERS.	
		10.0 a.m. to 11.0 a.m.	Taking ranges from maps.	
		11.15 a.m. to 12.0 noon.	Checking H.I. and ZERO.	
		12.0 noon to 12.30 p.m.	Taking memory of maps ranges.	
		2.0 p.m. to 4.0 p.m.	Actual ranges with use of journal	
	1.6.17.			

E.W.O'Sullivan
for O.C. 9th Machine Gun Coy

SECRET.

Appendix I

COPY NO.:-

94th MACHINE GUN COMPANY- OPERATION ORDER No.13.

Map Ref. 51 B.N.W.

1. The 94th Machine Gun Company will take part in an attack on the line C.7.a.7.1. to C.13.b.8.1.
2. <u>Gun Positions</u> - Gun positions will be taken up as follows :-
   "A" Section and ½ of "C" Section under Lieut. DURRANT in B.23 a.
   "B" Section and ½ of "C" Section under 2/Lt. BOTHWELL in 17 c 9.6.
3. <u>TARGETS</u>.- Targets to be engaged as follows :-
   "A" Section and ½ of "C" Section. 3 guns to fire on LINK TRENCH C.13.c.8.5. to C.14.a.2.2. 3 guns to fire on OPPY- NEUVIREUIL ROAD C.13.b.0.8. to C.8.c.1.1.
   "B" Section and ½ of "C" Section. 6 guns firing between B.12 d 5.6 and C.13.c.5.4.
   At ZERO all guns will place a barrage on their respective targets. The first barrage will be 300 yards beyond the artillery barrage, the table of which has been seen by all Officers.
   Each subsequent lift be 100 yards every four minutes until the limit of OPPY SUPPORT TRENCH is reached
   Fire will be raised 500 yards and maintained until the time table is complete.
   All guns will remain in position until further orders are received and will be prepared to put a barrage on 500 yards beyond OPPY SUPPORT TRENCH on S.O.S. being sent up.
4. <u>Ammunition Dump</u>. Ammunition supply will be arranged under Sgt. LUCCOCK at B.23 d and 17 c in rear of each Gun-Team.
5. <u>RATE OF FIRE</u>. During the barrage guns will fire at the rate of one belt every four minutes. The rate of fire on the S.O.S. being given will be increased on the discretion of Section Officers.
6. <u>COY. H.Q</u>. Coy. H.Q. will be established at B.21 d 4.1. to which all reports will be sent.
7. <u>REPORTS</u>. Reports will be sent to Coy. H.Q. when guns are in position. After ZERO reports will be sent in as frequently as possible. Reports whether NIL or otherwise will be despatched to H.Q. at least every hour.

Acknowledge.

Lieut. Captain,
O.C. 94th M. G. Coy.

2-5-17.
8-45.p.m.

Secret.   Appendix I.
                       Copy No:- ....

94th Machine Gun Company. Operation Order
No. 14.~

1. The 94th Machine Gun Company less one section will relieve the 93rd Machine Gun Company in the CAVRELLE SECTOR on the night 5th/6th May.

2. Guides will be detailed by O.C. 93rd Machine Gun Coy to meet the gun teams at a point selected by O.C's 93rd and 94th Coys and notified to gun team commanders later.

3. <u>Detail.</u> "D" Section under 2/LIEUT. BOTHWELL will relieve the guns now in position at C.25.c.5,2. and B.30.c.55,40.
"B" Section under 2/LIEUT PHILBIN will relieve the guns now in position at B.24.d.3,5 and B.30.a.7,7. 2/Lieut PHILBIN will go with LIEUT HOWARD to assist in taking over the line.
"C" Section under SERGT. LUCCOCK will remain in reserve at B.28.a.6,9.
"A" Section under LIEUT DURRANT will remain attached to and under orders of G.O.C. 92nd BRIGADE.

4. Relief will commence at 8.45 p.m. Section commanders will report to Coy H.Q's when relief complete. Coy H.Q's will move to H.4.a.5,2. at 8.45 p.m.
Section commanders will as soon as possible after taking over, send to Coy H.Q's the exact positions of their guns and arcs of fire. Any stores taken over will be notified to Coy H.Q's

5. "C" Section will assist "B" and "D" Sections in carrying the kit into the line.

6. <u>Reports.</u> Section commanders will send into Coy H.Q's by 7. A.M. a report on the situation and will continue to send in reports each morning while in the line. Special information will be despatched at once.

7. Exchange of tripods and belt boxes will be affected if it is possible to arrange it.

                                    J E Bull Capt
                                    O.C 94th M.G. Coy

4 May 1917.

Secret   Appendix III   Copy No:..........

94th Machine Gun Company. - Operation Orders No. 15.

1. Owing to readjustment of Brigade Front the following reliefs will take place:- "D" Section 94th Machine Gun Coy under 2/Lieut BOTHWELL and the 2 Southern guns of "B" Section about B.30.a.60.80. will be relieved tonight by the 93rd Machine Gun Coy.

2. Guides will be detailed as follows:-
   To report to advanced Coy. H.Qs at 9.50 P.M. tonight,
        One guide from Nos 1 and 2 guns.
        One guide from 3.
        One guide from 4.
        One guide between 5 and 6.
   Guns are numbered from right to left of the line. Guides will be careful to let the relieving team know the number of the gun position they represent.

3. Belts, Boxes and tripods will be handed over to the relieving teams.
   Lists in duplicate of Trench Stores will be made out and receipts obtained by Gun commanders from the relieving team.
   Petrol tins belonging to the Coy will be brought out of the line with the teams concerned.
   Teams when relieved will make their way each under their Gun commanders and report to advanced Coy H.Qs. They will then proceed to the gun pits previously occupied by "A" and "C" Sections where they will spend the night.
   Rations will be awaiting them at the gun pits.
   2/LIEUT PHILBIN will remain in command of the two gun teams not relieved. Orderlies from these teams will be despatched to the gun pits above described for their rations as usual.

4. Gun commanders will hand over range cards showing, Ranges, Arcs of fire, Q.E. and night lines of their respective guns.

5. Pists will be handed over in a clean condition and a note to that effect entered above the signature of the Gun Commander taking over.

                                                Lieut
                               Commanding 94th Machine Gun Coy.

3. p.m.
7-5-17.

Appendix No. IV.

Secret.   Copy No. _____

94th Machine Gun Company - Operation Orders No. 16.

1. Following the redistribution of the front taken over by the BRIGADE, the following relief will take place on night 8th/9th May.

2. "D" SECTION and ½ "B" SECTION under 2/LIEUT BOTHWELL will relieve the two Sections of the 92nd BRIGADE now holding the line. The guns will be allotted positions in the line according to instructions issued separately to 2/LIEUT BOTHWELL.

3. Teams will move forward at a time to be detailed later with interval of five minutes between the last man of one team and the leading man of the succeeding one. Guns will be carried in the least ostentatious manner and not more than two men will move together.

4. Belt Boxes will be taken over from the relieving teams receipts being given for the same.

5. 2/LIEUT BOTHWELL will report by Orderly when relief is complete.

6. Work for improvement of the line will be put in hand at once and work reports forwarded to reach Coy H.Q. at 6 A.M.

7. Rations will be sent up to the gun positions on their arrival.

8. Dispositions of guns, arcs of fire and night lines will be recorded and despatched to Coy H.Q. in accordance with orders issued direct by O.C. Coy to 2/LIEUT BOTHWELL.

J. E. Price Coples
Lieut.
O.C. 94th Machine Gun Coy.

4.0 p.m.
8/5/17.

Secret.   Appendix No V.   Copy No..........

94th Machine Gun Company. Operation Orders No 17.

1. Inter Company relief will take place tonight 9th/10th May as follows:-

   ½ "C" Section will relieve ½ "B" Section in right Sector. 2/Lieut PHILBIN will remain in command of this post until further orders.

   ½ "C" Section will relieve ½ "B" Section in left Sector. 2/Lieut BOTHWELL will command this post and the ½ Section forming its garrison. The N.C.O. in command of the ½ Section of "B" in left Sector will report personally to 2/Lieut BOTHWELL when he has taken over his post.

2. Guides from each gun team will be sent tonight to Coy H.Q. by 9.p.m.

3. Tripods & Belt Boxes will be handed over by the teams being relieved and the usual Certificates between commanders completed.

4. "A" Section will provide the carrying party for rations and water from Rear H.Qrs to Advanced H.Qrs. Gun teams will each despatch one man per team to report to Coy H.Qs for the rations of their respective teams. 2/Lieut BOTHWELL will despatch one man from his H.Qs for his rations.

   The teams relieving the posts will bring their rations with them. It is pointed out that unless the greatest care is taken to return the petrol tins, the water supply cannot be kept up. Gun commanders are held responsible that this is done. Rations will arrive at Coy H.Qs about 9.P.M.

5. On completion of relief the teams relieved will return to Coy H.Qs, the gun commanders reporting personally to the C.O.

                                        J.A. Price Cooper
                                        Lieut
                                        O.C. 94th Machine Gun Coy.

2-45 p.m.
9-5-17.

Appendix VI.

Secret.   Copy No. _____

94th Machine Gun Company. Operation Order No. 18.

Intention — An attack will be made on GAVRELLE TRENCH which runs about C.19.c.9.5.00 to about C.25.b.15.30.

The left will be joined up with the WINDMILL DEFENCES about C.19.c.8.3. as soon as possible.

Disposition of Guns.

Machine Guns of 92nd and 93rd BRIGADES and guns from XVIIth CORPS have been allotted duties on the front of the attack.

The 94th M.G. Coy. will assist by demonstrating against OPPY WOOD & VILLAGE. The guns to carry out this demonstration will be "A" and "C" Sections under 2/LIEUTS. RICHARDSON and BALL. They will take up positions about B.23.d.20.30 and will employ their fire in accordance with orders issued separately to these Officers (APPENDIX I.).

2/LIEUT PHILBIN will occupy his normal positions but will take no part in the action.

Nº 92 and 93. Coys will place 8 guns East of 2/LIEUT PHILBIN'S position on a line from B.17.a.6.6 to B.23.b.6.7 for defence of the left BRIGADE front.

2/LIEUT PHILBIN will arrange to send from his Northern guns 20 Belt Boxes with a guide who will be sent to him for use of "A" and "C" Sections.

2/LIEUT BOTHWELL will occupy the WINDMILL DEFENCES tonight after dusk and also the STRONG POINT already held by him. These two guns are for defence only and will not open fire unless their line is attacked.

The gun at B.24.d.13.71 will open fire against OPPY WOOD in the demonstration on a Magnetic Bearing of 50°18' and an elevation equal to 1600ˣ. Should our line be attacked this gun will join in the defence of its sector firing still on the same bearing but reduce range to 1200ˣ.

2/LIEUT BOTHWELL will send in a report that the WINDMILL DEFENCES are occupied as soon after dusk as he can. This orderly must return to 2/LIEUT BOTHWELL before 11.30 P.M. If 2/LIEUT BOTHWELL cannot get the message to Coy. H.Qs. he must report its occupation to O.C. BATTN. H.Qs. in his sector.

J.E. Vrie Copld
Lieut
O.C. 94th Machine Gun Coy.

4-47. p.m.
17.5.17.

Appendix I. to Operation Order No 18.

All guns will open fire at ZERO on the targets given below and fire at the rate of one belt per gun per 3 minutes for 30 minutes. Fire will then gradually die away and cease at ZERO + 40 unless S.O.S. goes up when it will be continued.

CO-ORDINATE of gun position	TARGET	M.B.	RANGE.	Q.E. USED.
On a line from B 23 a 08,38 to B 23 a 42,20	OPPY WOOD & VILLAGE.	50° Parallel lines of fire.	2,000 2,100 2,200 2,300 for each Section.	4° 48' 5° 22' 6° 6° 4'

J E Pine Coyle
Lieut
O.C. 94th Machine Gun Coy.

7.35 P.M.
17-5-17.

Appendix VII.

Secret.   Copy No. ....

94th Machine Gun Company. Operation Order No. 19.

1. **Relief.**

   The 94th Machine Gun Coy will be relieved by the 190th Machine Gun Coy on the night 21st/22nd May.

2. **Times of Relief**

   The guides from the 190th Machine Gun Coy (attached to the 94th Machine Gun Coy from the night 20/21st May) accompanied by guides from the 94th Machine Gun Coy will report to the Coy H.Qs at 9.30 p.m. night 21st/22nd May as follows:-

   Guides from Nos 3, 4, 5 and 7 teams.

   The guides of No. 3 team will in addition to guiding their own relief also act as guides to Nos 1 and 2 teams.

   These latter teams will be taken to Section Officer's H.Qs. in GAVRELLE SECTOR. At these H.Qs guides from 1 and 2 teams will be waiting to pilot their teams to their respective posts.

   No. 5 Guides will also bring back No. 6 team and No. 7 will bring No. 8 with their own team.

   Handing over.

   Gun team commanders will hand over posts & trench stores to the incoming teams taking & giving receipts on the slips sent out to them. These slips when completed will be handed to their Section Officer.

   The following Company stores will be handed over to the 190th Coy:-

   Tripods, Belt Boxes, Anti-Aircraft Mountings, Anti-aircraft Sights. One petrol tin will be left for gun.

   Posts will be left clean and sanitary.

   Completion of Relief

   On completion of relief Section Officers will move their Sections back to Coy H.Qs. taking the usual precautions for safety in the method of advance.

On arrival at Coy H.Qs Section Officers will hand in the completed lists of Stores handed over to O.C. Coy. They will then without loss of time move their Sections to the dump on the MAISON DE LA COTE ROAD.

Sections arriving here before the arrival of the limbers will leave their guns and equipment under an N.C.O. and two men who will load up on the arrival of the limbers. Sections will then move independently under Section Officers to the Coy Transport Lines.

The following time table is calculated on the probable times of arrival with normal conditions prevailing.

"D" Section arrives at dump . . 11. p.m.
"   "   "   " Transport Lines 1. A.M.
"B" "   "   " dump . . 12. M.N.
"   "   "   " Transport Lines . 2. A.M.
"C" "   "   " dump . . 2. A.M.
"   "   "   " Transport Lines . 4. A.M.

Limbers

Two limbers will be at ration dump at MAISON de la COTE at 2 A.M. to remove the following stores :- 12 guns 4 tripods 64 Belt Boxes 40 petrol tins (approx:) and few extras H.Qs Stores and kit.

Transport Officer will use his discretion in despatching a third limber should he consider it necessary.

On arrival at Transport Lines each section will be provided with a hot meal.

Movement to Billets at MARŒUIL.

The Company will fall in to march to Billets at MARŒUIL at 10. A.M. Breakfast at 8.0 A.M. Lines to be left clean and 2nd/i.c. to make the necessary arrangements for handing over the Transport Lines to the 190th Machine Gun Coy; the disposal of the incoming Section of the 94th Machine Gun Coy from the line prior to their moving off to Billets will be arranged mutually between the Officers 2nd/i.c. of the respective Companies.

Taking over kits.

The Transport Officer of the 94th Machine Gun Coy will arrange to take over from the Transport Officer of the 190th Machine Gun Coy the equivalent number of Belt Boxes, tripods and other stores in exchange for those handed over by the 94th Coy to the 190th Coy in the line. Actual quantities will be notified to Transport Officer on arrival of O.C. 94th Coy from the line.

J E Pres Capt.
O.C. 94th Machine Gun Coy.

4.30. P.M.
20-5-17.
Copies to all concerned.

Confidential

Volume XVIII
Vol 14

War Diary.

94th Machine Gun Coy.   31st Division

June 1917

Army Form C. 2118.

WAR DIARY
or
INTELLIGENCE SUMMARY
(Erase heading not required.)

Instructions regarding War Diaries and Intelligence Summaries are contained in F. S. Regs., Part II. and the Staff Manual respectively. Title pages will be prepared in manuscript.

Place	Date	Hour	Summary of Events and Information	Remarks and references to Appendices
In the Field	June 1st		Reference Map F.21.C.10.50. Training continued with the following programme:—	
			ALL PARTIES	
			8.45 a.m. to 9.15 a.m. Physical Training	
			9.30 a.m. to 10.30 a.m. Baths	
			10.30 a.m. to 11.15 a.m.	
			"A" SECTION.— Range.— Grouping, application and quick application at various targets.	
			"B" & "D" SECTIONS.— Rough Barrel Drill.	
			DRAFT. Drill.— Traversing	
			11.15 a.m. to 12.0 noon.	
			"A" SECTION. Range. — DRAFT Immediate Action.	
			"B" & "C" SECTIONS. Repairs adjustments to and preparing guns for firing.	
			"D" SECTION. Immediate Action. (Blindfolded)	
			12.0 noon to 1.30 p.m.	
			"A" SECTION. Cleaning guns and equipment	
			"B" SECTION. Range (Same programme as "A")	
			"C" SECTION. Drives. "D" SECTION. Revolver Drill. DRAFT. Quick laying	
			1.30 p.m. to 3.0 p.m.	
			"C" SECTION. on range carrying out similar practices as previous section.	

A5834 Wt. W4973/M687 750,000 8/16 D. D. & L. Ltd. Forms/C.2118/13.

Army Form C. 2118.

WAR DIARY
of
INTELLIGENCE SUMMARY.
(Erase heading not required.)

Instructions regarding War Diaries and Intelligence Summaries are contained in F. S. Regs., Part II. and the Staff Manual respectively. Title pages will be prepared in manuscript.

Place	Date	Hour	Summary of Events and Information	Remarks and references to Appendices
In the Field	June 1.	2.0 pm to 3.0 pm	"A" SECTION. Tactical Section exercise (A).	
			"D" SECTION. Repairs adjustments and preparing guns for firing.	
			DRAFT. Combined Drill.	
		3.0 pm to 4.0 pm	"A" SECTION and DRAFT. Use of traversing and elevating dials.	
			"B" and "C" SECTIONS. Cleaning guns — Use of traversing and elevating dials.	
		3.0 pm to 4.30 pm	"D" SECTION on range carrying out guns programme as for other Sections.	
			RANGE-TAKERS fired with their section — Work when not firing — Unaimed ranging & range cards.	
	2.		Training continued with the following programme:—	
			ALL PARTIES	
		9.15 A.M. to 10.0 A.M.	Physical Training	
			TRAINED MEN.	
		10.0 a.m. to 11.0 a.m.	Immediate Action (Blanckfontein)	
		11.15 am to 12noon	Section Exercises (A).	
		12.0 am to 12.30 pm	— do —	
		2.0 pm to 3.0 pm	Study of ground	
		3.0 pm to 4.0 pm	Judging distance and Revolver Drill.	

A 5834. Wt. W4973/M687 750,000 8/16 D. D. & L. Ltd. Forms/C.2118/13.

Army Form C. 2118.

WAR DIARY
or
INTELLIGENCE SUMMARY.
(Erase heading not required.)

Instructions regarding War Diaries and Intelligence Summaries are contained in F.S. Regs, Part II. and the Staff Manual respectively. Title pages will be prepared in manuscript.

Place	Date	Hour	Summary of Events and Information	Remarks and references to Appendices
In the Field.	June 2.		DRAFT.	
		10.0 a.m. to 11.0 a.m.	Immediate Action.	
		11.15 a.m. to 12.0 noon	Drill - Rapid Application.	
		12.0 noon to 12.30 p.m.	Practice in Belt Filling.	
		2.0 p.m. to 4.0 p.m.	Range - Application practices	Jt'gp
			RANGE-TAKERS.	
		10.0 a.m. to 11.0 a.m.	Advanced ranging	
		11.15 a.m. to 12.0 noon	Use of prone	
		12.0 noon to 12.30 p.m.	Cleaning instrument	
		2.0 p.m. to 3.30 p.m.	Advanced ranging	
		3.30 p.m. to 4.0 p.m.	Revolver drill.	
	3.		Training continued with the following programme:-	
			Guns, Huts and Billets cleaned during the morning	
		8.45 a.m.	R.C. parade under Sgt COLLINS.	
		9.15 a.m.	Nonconformists parade under S/Lieut RICHARDSON.	
		11.15 a.m.	C.F.B. parade.	
			Eight reinforcements arrived from M.R. Base Depot.	Jt'Sgt
			Leave keeping progress - 3 men reported in leave.	

Army Form C. 2118.

WAR DIARY
INTELLIGENCE SUMMARY.
(Erase heading not required.)

Instructions regarding War Diaries and Intelligence Summaries are contained in F. S. Regs., Part II. and the Staff Manual respectively. Title pages will be prepared in manuscript.

Place	Date	Hour	Summary of Events and Information	Remarks and references to Appendices
In the Field	June 4.		Training continued with the following programme :—	
			ALL PARTIES	
		9.15 am to 10.0 am	Physical Training.	
			TRAINED MEN	
		10.0 am to 11.0 am	Immediate Action (Blindfolded)	
		11.15 am to 12.0 noon	⎫	
		12.0 noon to 12.30 pm	⎬ Tactical fire section Exercises (A)	
		2.0 pm to 3.0 pm	Bisic Rapid loading.	
		3.0 pm to 4.0 pm	Use of Elevation and Traversing Drills	
			DRAFT.	
		10.0 am to 11.0 am	Immediate Action.	
		11.15 am to 12.0 noon	Control Drill.	
		12.0 noon to 12.30 pm	Care, cleaning & repairs.	
		2.0 pm to 3.0 pm	Drill Traversing	
		3.0 pm to 4.0 pm	Use of Elevation and Traversing scales.	
			RANGE TAKERS	
		10.0 am to 12.0 noon	Testing and adjusting H.I. and ZERO.	
		12.0 noon to 12.30 pm	Care and cleaning of instruments.	
		2.0 pm to 4.0 pm	Quarries, ranges, overrange cards.	

WAR DIARY
INTELLIGENCE SUMMARY
(Erase heading not required.)

Army Form C. 2118.

Instructions regarding War Diaries and Intelligence Summaries are contained in F. S. Regs., Part II. and the Staff Manual respectively. Title pages will be prepared in manuscript.

Place	Date	Hour	Summary of Events and Information	Remarks and references to Appendices
In the Field	June 5.		Training continued with the following programme:-	
		9.15 A.M. to 10.0 A.M.	Physical training for all.	
		10.0 A.M. to 11.0 A.M.	Immediate Action and lock repairs for transverses - Immediate Action for drafts - Testing H.I. and ZERO for Range finders.	
		11.15 A.M. to 12.30 p.m.	Tactical Lecture exercise (B) for Transversers.	
		11.15 A.M. to 12.0 (noon)	Officers - Corrected sights for draft.	
		12.0 (noon) to 12.30 p.m.	Care, cleaning and repairs for Drafts.	
		11.0 A.M. to 12.0 (noon)	Testing H.I. and ZERO for Range takers	
		12.0 (noon) to 12.30 p.m.	Care and cleaning of instrument for Range takers	
		2 p.m. to 4.0 p.m.	Sports.	
			Lieut C.W.R.BALL, M.C., assumed command of the Company vice Capt. J.E.PRICE. 2/Lieut B.E.RICHARDSON assumed duties of 2nd i/c vice Lieut C.W.R.BALL (A/O.C. Coy.)	J.E.Price Capt
			Capt. J.E.PRICE. granted leave to U.K. Pte CLIFFE proceeds to 1st Army Rest Camp. Pte NEWMAN proceeds to 93rd F.A. to attend an Water Master	J.E.Price Capt
	6.		Training continued with the following programme:-	
			ALL PARTIES	
		9.0 A.M.	Company Parade in marching order thou packs.	
		9.0 A.M. to 9.45 A.M.	Physical Training (Also N.C.Os)	
		OFFICERS and N.C. Os - 9.15 A.M.	Notes on Ante-Aircraft Sights.	

Army Form C. 2118.

WAR DIARY
or
INTELLIGENCE SUMMARY.
(Erase heading not required.)

Instructions regarding War Diaries and Intelligence Summaries are contained in F. S. Regs., Part II. and the Staff Manual respectively. Title pages will be prepared in manuscript.

Place	Date	Hour	Summary of Events and Information	Remarks and references to Appendices
In the Field.	June 6.		**TRAINED MEN.**	
		10.0 am to 11.0 am.	Use of traversing and elevating dials.	
		11.15 am to 12.30 pm.	Limber drill.	
		2.0 pm to 4.0 pm.	Overhead fire drill.	
			DRAFT.	
		10.0 am to 11.0 am.	Repairs and adjustments.	
		11.15 am to 12.0 noon.	Drill — Traversing.	
		12.0 noon to 12.30 pm.	Belt filling by hand.	
		2.0 pm to 4.0 pm.	Range. Traversing fire.	
			RANGE-TAKERS.	
		10.0 am to 12 noon.	Use of maps and an aid to a study of ground and range taking.	
		12.0 noon to 12.30 pm.	Cleaning instruments.	
		2.0 pm to 4.0 pm.	Ammunition carrying from cover.	9th L/Cpl.
	7th.		Training continued with the following programme :—	
		9.0 am.	Company Parade on fatigue duties with rifles.	
			TRAINED MEN.	
		10 am to 11.15 am.	Limber drill.	
		11.30 am to 12.30 pm.	Revolver drill.	
		2.0 pm to 3.0 pm.	Overhead fire drill.	
		3.0 pm to 4.0 pm.	Box Respirator and P.H. Helmet drill.	9th L/Cpl.

A5834 Wt.W4973/M687 750,000 8/16 D.D.& L. Ltd. Forms/C.2118/13.

Army Form C. 2118.

WAR DIARY
of
INTELLIGENCE SUMMARY.
(Erase heading not required.)

Place	Date	Hour	Summary of Events and Information	Remarks and references to Appendices
In the Field	June 7.		DRAFT.	
		10.0 a.m. to 11.0 a.m.	Drill. Searching.	
		11.15 a.m. to 12.0 noon	Semaphore drill.	
		12.0 noon to 12.30 p.m	Box Respirator Drill.	
		2.0 p.m. to 4.0 p.m.	Range. Searching fire.	
			RANGE-TAKERS	
		10.0 a.m. to 12.30 p.m.	Range work in attack including stalking by gun non-present.	
		2.0 p.m. to 4.0 p.m.	Advanced ranging and Range cards.	
			Pte WISE – Rejoined from BASE DEPOT.	
			Pte BARLOW. Returned from 1st ARMY REST CAMP.	
	8.		Training continued with the following programme:-	
		9.0 a.m. to 10.0 a.m.	Physical Training.	
		10.0 a.m. to 12.0 noon	Baths.	
		12.0 noon to 12.30 p.m.	Box Respirator Drill.	
		2.0 p.m. to 4.0 p.m.	Section and Transport Competitions.	
			Lieut BALL with 2/Lieuts BOTHWELL, BALL and MARSLAND proceed to reconnoitre line to be taken over. Details of relief arranged.	

A5834 Wt. W4973/M687 750,000 8/16 D. D. & L. Ltd. Forms/C.2118/13.

Army Form C. 2118.

WAR DIARY
INTELLIGENCE SUMMARY.
(Erase heading not required.)

Instructions regarding War Diaries and Intelligence Summaries are contained in F.S. Regs., Part II. and the Staff Manual respectively. Title pages will be prepared in manuscript.

Place	Date	Hour	Summary of Events and Information	Remarks and references to Appendices
In the Field	June 9.		Training continued with the following programme:— 9.0 a.m. to 12.30 p.m. Training and Section competitions. 2.0 p.m. to 4.0 p.m. Overhauling all equipment. Lieut. BALL and 2/Lt. MARSLAND visited Coy. H.Q. of 223rd M.G. Coy. Details of relief finally arranged. Leave being in progress. Five men despatched on leave. 2/Lt. RICHARDSON, Cpl. WOOD and Pte. HAGUE proceed to M.G.C. School.	J.S.¹ Cpl. C
	10.		Preparing Guns and equipment in readiness to proceed with line on night 11th/12th. Temp Lt. WILSON, J.H. 2/5 CHESHIRE REGT. (T.F.) attd. 94th M.G. Coy, awarded M.C.	J.S.¹ Cpl.
	11.	4.30 a.m.	Reveillé. During the night 11th/12th that was a heavy thunderstorm and the rain continued far into the morning. It was proposed to commence the march out ROCLINCOURT at 6.30 a.m., but on account of the rain it was postponed until 9.15 a.m. Final preparations made. At 7.30 p.m. the Company marched to rendezvous of guides (see Operation Order No. 20, Appendix I) and 300 x between Sections. Operation Order 20/Appendix	J.S.¹ Cpl. Appendix I

Army Form C. 2118.

WAR DIARY
of
INTELLIGENCE SUMMARY.
(Erase heading not required.)

Instructions regarding War Diaries and Intelligence Summaries are contained in F. S. Regs., Part II. and the Staff Manual respectively. Title pages will be prepared in manuscript.

Place	Date	Hour	Summary of Events and Information	Remarks and references to Appendices
In the Field	June 11.		I) attached relate to this relief. C.O. visited BDE. H.D. QTRS. before proceeding to Coy Hd. Qrs.	
	12	3.45 a.m.	Relief complete. C.O. visited guns nos. 1, 2, 3 and 4 starting at 8.30 a.m. and arriving back at 1 p.m. At 10 p.m visited Section Hd Qrs of guns 9, 10, 11 and 12 and visited guns nos 5 and 6. Reached Coy Hd Qrs at 2 a.m. 13th.	
	13th.		C.O. visited guns nos 7 and 8. 2/Lt MARSLAND reported at Coy Hd Qrs.	
	14th		C.O. and 2/Lt MARSLAND visited gun positions nos 1, 2, 3, 4, 7 and 8. The day was exceedingly quiet. There was scarcely any enemy shelling and no sniping. The plans, as far as machine guns were concerned, for the attack on CADORNA TRENCH were submitted to the G.O.C. 94th INF. BDE. 1/2 "B" SECTION relieves 1/2 "D" SECTION at position nos 7 and 8. Orders for same – Appendix II	J.C.Off.

Army Form C. 2118.

WAR DIARY
or
INTELLIGENCE SUMMARY.
(Erase heading not required.)

Instructions regarding War Diaries and Intelligence Summaries are contained in F. S. Regs., Part II. and the Staff Manual respectively. Title pages will be prepared in manuscript.

Place	Date	Hour	Summary of Events and Information	Remarks and references to Appendices
In the Field	June 14th		Company relief on night 15/16th received (See Operation Orders 19.21. (Appendix II)).	
	15th		Situation very quiet. C.O. visited guns Nos 9, 10, 11 and 12 in the evening.	
	16th		Capt. PRICE on return from leave assumed command of the Coy.	
	17th		C.O. visited advanced Coy H.Q. on the line and Bde Hd Qrs and arranged that he should come into the line on the 18th inst. Orders for 15th M.G. Coy to relieve guns Nos 5 and 6 in EARL TRENCH received. On proceeding to 15th Bde Hd Qrs the BDE MAJOR seemed to know nothing about the matter and O.C. 15th M.G. Coy could not be found. Arrangements for relief were continued on a message which was left in the hands of O.C. 13th M.G. Coy (being relieved by 15th M.G. Coy on night 16th/17th inst)	Yes Sir
		12.10 a.m.	Orders that whole of these two guns would be relieved on night 17th/18th inst instead of 16th/17th inst were received.	

Army Form C. 2118.

WAR DIARY
or
INTELLIGENCE SUMMARY.
(Erase heading not required.)

Instructions regarding War Diaries and Intelligence Summaries are contained in F. S. Regs., Part II. and the Staff Manual respectively. Title pages will be prepared in manuscript.

Place	Date	Hour	Summary of Events and Information	Remarks and references to Appendices
In the Field	June 18th	10 pm	C.O. reached Coy HQrs to take over command in the line. During the evening he visited gun positions Nos. 1, 2, 3, 4, 7 and 8. No 15 M.G. Coy relieved No. 5 and 6 commencing at 10.15 pm. During night 17 & 18 pm Coy HQrs received about 12 77 m.m. shells.	
	19th	2.0 pm	C.O. attended conference at Bde HQrs. Coy HQrs shelled with 15 c.m. shells. Operation Order No. 22 issued (see Appendix VII) for the relief of the Coy by the 192nd M.G. Coy. Relief commenced at 11.0 pm and completed without incident by 4.30 am 20th inst. Coy when relieved moved by sections to billets at ST CATHERINE.	Appendix VII
	20th		Coy overhauling guns and equipment.	
	21st	9.0 am	Coy resume overhauling of kit. Sections inspected by 2nd i/c for deficiencies. C.O. attends conference at Bde HQrs.	
		Afternoon	Sections move out carrying stones to practise ground for rehearse attack.	

A5834 Wt. W4973 M687 750,000 8/16 D. D. & L. Ltd. Forms/C.2118/13.

Army Form C. 2118.

WAR DIARY
INTELLIGENCE SUMMARY
(Erase heading not required.)

Instructions regarding War Diaries and Intelligence Summaries are contained in F. S. Regs., Part II. and the Staff Manual respectively. Title pages will be prepared in manuscript.

Place	Date	Hour	Summary of Events and Information	Remarks and references to Appendices
In the Field	June 22nd	7.45AM	Company move out to practice ground for continued rehearsal of attack	
		5.30pm	C.O. attends conference at Bde Bn HQ	
	23rd	7.45am	Company parade for movement to practice ground for Brigade rehearsal	
		5.30pm	C.O. attends conference at Bde HQ	
	24th	8.15am	Company parade for continued rehearsal of Bde attack	
		5.30pm	C.O. attends conference at Bde HQ	
			Lieut DURRANT and 27570 Pte BIRD return from Transport Course.	
			Leave being in progress & not interrupted on leave	
	25th	10.30am	C.O. holds conference with Section Officers to discuss impending attack	
			Company prepare guns and equipment for movement to the line – Operation Order No 23 (See Appendix IV) issued for relief of section of 92nd M.G. Coy	Appendix IV
		3pm	Section Officers and Gun Commanders attend lecture on aerial photographs	
		8pm	35 O.Rs under Lt under 2/Lt BOTHWELL and Ball proceed to the line to reconnoitre dumps	

A6945 Wt. W14423/M1160 350,000 12/16 D. D. & L. Forms/C./2118/14.

Army Form C. 2118.

WAR DIARY
or
INTELLIGENCE SUMMARY.

(Erase heading not required.)

Instructions regarding War Diaries and Intelligence Summaries are contained in F. S. Regs., Part II. and the Staff Manual respectively. Title pages will be prepared in manuscript.

Place	Date	Hour	Summary of Events and Information	Remarks and references to Appendices
In the Field	June 25th		Ammunition and water.	
	26th	2noon	2Lieuts BOTHWELL and BALL rejoined, conference of Battalion commanders at Warluck.	
			They are attached for the attack.	
		2.30 pm	C.O. resumes conference with Section Officers. Operation Orders No 84 (see Appendix D) Appendix D	
			Have been previously circulated to all concerned.	
		8 pm	Company moving up to line in accordance with Operation Orders No 23. Rear	
			2nd Bn Ris reserve at ST CATHERINE.	
	27th	3.45 am	Relief complete without incident.	
		9.30 am	C.O. visits Bde HQ and afterwards proceeds to front line trenches where	
			positions are inspected and discussed with Section Officers returning at 2.30 pm.	
		5.30 pm	C.O. again visits front line to complete details of gun dispositions.	
		8.10 pm		
		10.0 pm	Guns detailed to Battalions were sent the bus and report to the respective	
			Battalion Commanders to whom attached.	
			During the day "A" Section performs Anti-Aircraft duties. 8 clean guns and equipment.	

A6945 Wt. W14422/M1160 350,000 12/16 D. D. & L. Forms/C./2118/14.

Army Form C. 2118.

WAR DIARY
INTELLIGENCE SUMMARY
(Erase heading not required.)

Instructions regarding War Diaries and Intelligence Summaries are contained in F. S. Regs., Part II. and the Staff Manual respectively. Title pages will be prepared in manuscript.

Place	Date	Hour	Summary of Events and Information	Remarks and references to Appendices
In the Field	June 27th		No 89719 Pte MITCHELL, E reported missing	
	28th	1.0 A.M.	"A" Section while performing carrying duties to the line received the following casualties:-	
			No 57149. Pte LEWIS, B. killed by shell fire	
			" 68208 " DUNNING, F.A. wounded by shell fire.	
		10.30 A.M.	C.O. attends BDE HD QRS.	
		Evening	Coy to take part in an attack delivered on CADORNA TRENCH (MAP REF: SHEET 51b C.14), the assaulting Battalions being those of the 94th BDE. Employment of Coy was as follows:- Five were allotted to the attack, to move forward with the attacking troops to consolidate the positions taken.	
			Six guns were disposed in defensive positions to cover the withdrawal in case of failure.	J.G.[?]
			Five guns in reserve in hands of Coy Commander.	
			Guns allotted to the attack were distributed as follows:-	
			One each to the Right Battalion, Right Centre Battalion and Left Battalion.	
			Two guns were allotted to the Left Centre Battalion.	

Army Form C. 2118.

WAR DIARY
or
INTELLIGENCE SUMMARY.

(Erase heading not required.)

Instructions regarding War Diaries and Intelligence Summaries are contained in F. S. Regs., Part II. and the Staff Manual respectively. Title pages will be prepared in manuscript.

Place	Date	Hour	Summary of Events and Information	Remarks and references to Appendices
In the Field	June 29th		The role of the guns were as follows:— Rifle pm, one gun at left centre and 2 guns with left Battalion to move forward after consolidation and occupy a bay from which to with right centre Battalion in reserve in trenches of Battalion commanders. One gun at left centre Battalion to go in with the last wave.	
			Gun teams were practised with carriers to assist the ammunition supply. Extreme care throughout was kept to all movement in quick time. Guns, equipment and ammunition carried as concealed as possible.	
			The three guns allotted for occupation of strong points were also up with of assaulting the position. All guns occupied position in shell holes in front of captured line and assisted the reconstruction of the trench.	
			Several targets was obtained by three out of the four guns and excellent work was done. The left gun obtained no targets. In three cases the left L.G gun was seen firing down a short length of old hill, proved in two cases of the L.G guns value fixed with them to be of great value in facilitating rapid opening of fire.	J.G.L
			The casualties received were slight and as follows:—Pte H.Lt V— Killed by shrapnel bullet, one	

WAR DIARY
INTELLIGENCE SUMMARY
(Erase heading not required.)

Army Form C. 2118.

Place	Date	Hour	Summary of Events and Information	Remarks and references to Appendices
In the Field	June 28th		2nd Lieut BOTHWELL and No.57491 Pte DISNEY, E. Kennedy Rifle butts. The chief points to remember are	
			1st Time and nature of Advance. This should upon such a manner as possible from the past. Commence after the study of aerial photographs and personal interviews with officers who had commenced of raiding parties.	
			2nd Butts & company kits. This was carried in such a manner according to the line of advance of the respective teams so as to be invisible as far as possible from the front. This saved the gunners from dangers who were fairly active. All the gun numbers carried short lengths of muskets belong to rounds on their ammunition pouches so as to ensure ammunition at hand in event of the gun. In all cases a short length was inserted in the gun which was kept loaded before the advance and this continued with the use of the light trigger enabled fire to be opened within 10 seconds of arrival at the position. Owing to the conditions under which the attack was delivered (rain and mud) guns were served with water-proof kits and carried in a trench bag both being wrapped	JCN Lt

A6945 Wt. W11422/M1160 350,000 12/16 D. D. & L. Forms/C./2118/14.

Army Form C. 2118.

WAR DIARY
of
INTELLIGENCE SUMMARY.
(Erase heading not required.)

Instructions regarding War Diaries and Intelligence Summaries are contained in F. S. Regs., Part II. and the Staff Manual respectively. Title pages will be prepared in manuscript.

Place	Date	Hour	Summary of Events and Information	Remarks and references to Appendices
In the Field	June 28th		as to facilitate their removal. The guns were thus clean and ready for use as usual in their positions.	
			3rd Value of training in use of broken ground. The necessity and value of such training was seen from the ready ease with which guns were mounted in shell holes under fire & then in all cases within 30 seconds of reaching the position.	
			4th Value of Forward Distance and Observation of Fire. In one case one gun mounted got a good sight and covered considerable damage at a range of about 600+ by firing at intervals, and observing the fire, short corrects & noted great effect.	
			5th Use of Carriers. To be effective, carriers seem to have a little preliminary training with the gun teams to enable them to understand exactly what is wanted in action. As a rule the carriers were not exposed to rifle being supplied, but poured upon the belts supports in the event.	
			6th Connection. Connection was a matter of between all guns and M. & C.C. by means of runners and buggers the procedure was as follows:- Every gun commander was supplied with a number of report cards (see appendix I. to Operation Order Nº 24). If runners were [illegible] sent to M. & C.C. the orderly sorters at every time intervals and extent	J. [signature]

A6945 Wt. W1442/M1160 350,000 12/16 D. D. & L. Forms/C./2118/14.

WAR DIARY
INTELLIGENCE SUMMARY
(Erase heading not required.)

Army Form C. 2118.

Place	Date	Hour	Summary of Events and Information	Remarks and references to Appendices
In the Field	June 28th		In the case of wiring the procedure was:- After the code for address, the number of the sentence in sentences, or the report card which was desired to transmit was inserted. Each pair having been previously given a number equal to the number of pair referred to. The most satisfactory method was that of numbers on the acceptance of the signal stations caused delay in transmission.	
	29th	1.30AM	Lieut CANT proceeds from the reserve firing to the line to command in the place of 2/Lieut BOTHWELL (wounded).	John Capt
		9.0AM	C.O. visits the new captured front line and arranges with the Section Officers improvements in the defence of the captured position	
		2.30pm	C.O. visits BDE HD QRS and reports result of visit to the line	
			Operation Order No 25 was issued for inter-Company relief	(Appendix VI.)
		11.0pm	On the acknowledgment of the line relief commenced and accepted without incident by 4.0 AM morning of 30th. Four days proceed to Railway Cutting and four remain in reserve at Coy H.d Qrs.	
			During the afternoon Lieut HOWARD accompanied by his servant N° 42421 Private	

WAR DIARY
or
INTELLIGENCE SUMMARY.
(Erase heading not required.)

Army Form C. 2118.

Instructions regarding War Diaries and Intelligence Summaries are contained in F. S. Regs., Part II. and the Staff Manual respectively. Title pages will be prepared in manuscript.

Place	Date	Hour	Summary of Events and Information	Remarks and references to Appendices
In the Field	June 29th		JOHNSTON, J. report to Coy HQ Res. The deserter was securely mounted by sheet for when within 300 yards of Coy HQ Res.	
			No. 28135 Serj PUGH, R and No. 35923 Sgt MOORE despatched to Rein Hd Qrs in order to proceed for course at the M.G. School at CAMIERS	
	30th	3.0 A.M.	The gun team under Cpl TRUEMAN received direct hits from a 77mm shell and the following casualties occurred:—	J Stone Lt
			No. 86140 Pte LILLEY, J. Killed.	
			" 25026 " STANSFIELD, J. "	
			" 17005 Cpl TRUEMAN, F. Wounded	
			" 10115 Pte MORRISON, W. "	
			" 35014 " SYKES, A. "	
			" 13010 " THOMPSON, D. "	
			Gun team was despatched from Coy HD Qrs to replace their casualties.	
			C.O. proceed to BDE HD QRS and afterwards visits the line and ascertains the gun position occupied by M.G. Coy on the left and arranges mutual co-operation	

A6945/Wt. W11422/M1160 350,000 12/16 D. D. & L. Forms/C/2118/14.

Army Form C. 2118.

WAR DIARY
INTELLIGENCE SUMMARY.
(Erase heading not required.)

Place	Date	Hour	Summary of Events and Information	Remarks and references to Appendices
In the Field	June 30th		Between Companies. Afterwards C.O. reconnoitred portion of the new line to be taken over by the 94th M.G. Coy.	
		11.0 pm	Four guns from Railway Cutting escorted the gun positions on the Post Line.	John Cy

Wt. W1442/M1160 350,000 12/16 D. D. & L. Forms/C/2118/14.

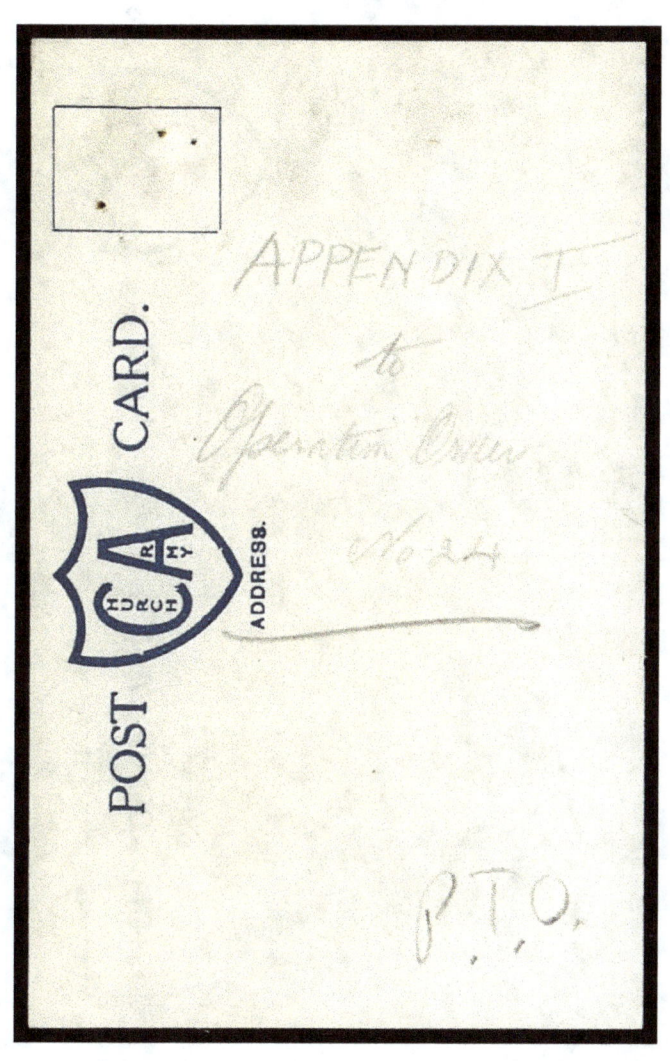

APPENDIX I
to
Operation Order
No 24

P.T.O.

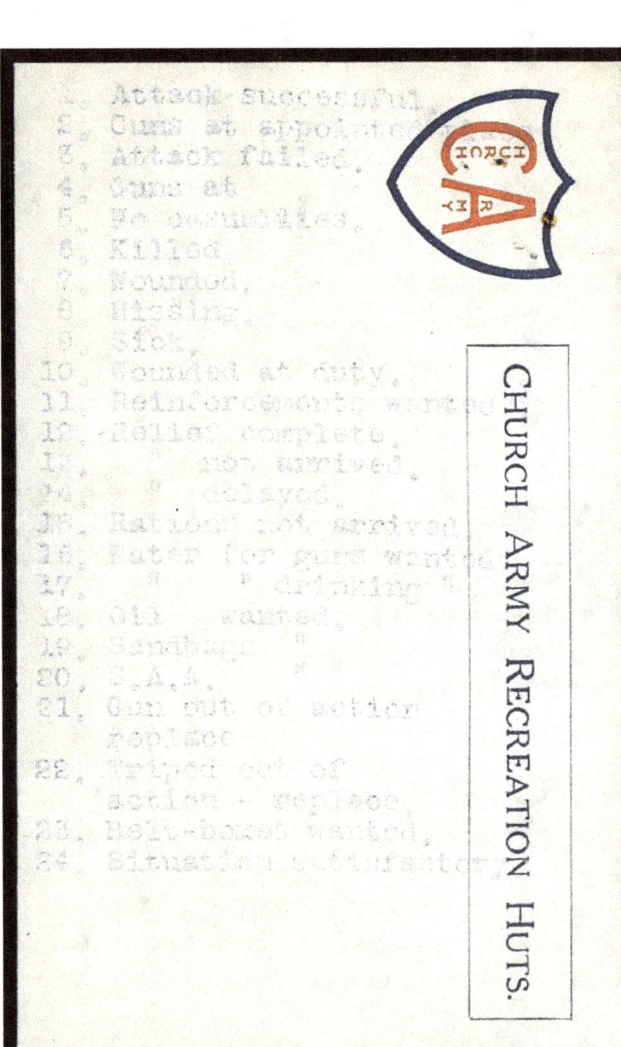

(APPENDIX I.)

SECRET   COPY No. 13

94th MACHINE GUN COMPANY, OPERATION ORDER NO.20.

Ref Map. 51 b N.W. 1/20,000.

1. The 94th Machine Gun Company will relieve the 223rd Machine Gun Company in the GAVRELLE sector, left sub-sector, on the night 11th/12th June.

2. The Company will move to transport lines on morning of 11th June, starting about 6-0.a.m.
Arrangements will be notified later.

3. The relief will be carried out according to attached relief table. A Guide from each gun-team to be relieved will be at last tree at B.25.d. 95.11 at 8.30.p.m. Each gun-team will know the number of the gun-team it is relieving.

4. The following will be taken over at gun positions :-
All belt boxes : Tripods at gun positions 1,2,3,4,5 & 6
Petrol Tins : All solidified alcohol.
Section officers will take over all trench maps and aeroplane photographs and gain all possible information.

5. One limber per section with guns and equipment will accompany sections to B.25.d.95.11. The transport officer will arrange with section officers direct.

6. Two signallers will arrive at Coy. Hd.Qrs. in the line to take over signal communication at 9.30.p.m. on 11th.

7. The rations for the 12th inst. will be carried under section arrangements. One filled petrol can per gun-team will be taken. In addition there will be six for Coy. Hd.Qrs.

8. Relief completed will be notified to Coy. Hd.Qrs. by runner from each officer. These runners will remain at Coy. Hd.Qrs.

9. When the relief is completed O.C. 94th M.G.Coy. will assume command of the machine guns in the sector. Coy. Hd.Qrs. will be in gun pits about B.28.a.5.5.

10. Acknowledge.

10th June 1917.

Issued at 4 pm 10/6/17

Randolph Tothill
2/Lieut.,
for O.C., 94th M.G.Coy.

Copies to:-
1. "A" Section.
2. "B" do
3. "C" do
4. "D" do
5. Transport Officer.
6. O.C. 94th M.G.Coy.
7. 94th Inf. Bde. (for Information.)
8. O.C. 223rd M.G.Coy.
9. C.Q.M.S.
10. C.S.M.
11. File.
12 & 13. War Diary.

94th MACHINE GUN COMPANY

Relief Table with Operation Order No. 20.

Date.	No. of gun post being relieved.	Map Ref. of gun Position.	Position being relieved by :-
Night	1.	C.19.c.70.30.	
	2.	C.19.c.30.50.	"C" Section.
9/10th	3.	B.24.d.95.70.	2/Lt. G.H.Ball.
	4.	B.24.d.30.70.	
June.	5.	B.18.d.0.0.	"D" Section less 2 gunteams
	6.	B.19.c.95.45.	2/Lt. J.R.Rothwell.
	7.	B.23.d.80.48.	"D" Section less 2 gunteams
	8.	B.23.d.70.48.	Sgt. Clark.
	9.	B.17.c.5.2.	
	10.	B.17.c.7.5.	"A" Section
	11.	B.23.a.70.58.	2/Lt. T.M.Philbin.
	12.	B.23.a.45.62.	
In reserve at Coy.Hd.Qrs.			"B" Section.

When marching to line 300 yards between Sections will be maintained.
From point B.23.d. 95.10. 4 minutes between gun-teams will be allowed.

9-6-17.

SECRET (APPENDIX II.) Copy No 7

94th Machine Gun Company
Operation Order No. 21

1. On the night 14th/15th ½ "B" Section will relieve ½ "D" Section in positions Nos 7 and 8. A Guide will be supplied by Coy H.Q. ½ "D" Section will return to Coy H.Q.

2. (a) On night 15th/16th the following relief will take place:—
   (1) ½ "D" Section at Coy H.Q. will relieve ½ "D" Section at positions 5 and 6. The relieved gun teams will proceed to positions Nos 7 and 8 and relieve ½ "B" Section. ½ "B" Section will then proceed to relieve ½ "C" Section (see para. 2 (a) (2) re guides).
   (2) "B" Section will relieve "C" Section at gun positions Nos 1, 2, 3 and 4.

   (b) Ref para. 2 (a) (1)
   Guides from positions 5 and 6 to report to Coy H.Q. before dawn on 15th. When relieved 2/Lt BOTHWELL will guide his two teams to positions Nos 7 and 8 proceeding via Coy H.Q. to pick up a guide if necessary.

   Ref para. 2 (a) (2)
   1 Guide from each gun team to be at Coy H.Q. before dawn on 15th inst. Two of these guides will be sent by Coy H.Q. to ½ "B" Section in positions 7 and 8.

3. The usual handing over certificates and receipts will be given and forwarded to Coy H.Q. by next ration party.

4. Relief complete will be notified to Coy H.Q. through Infantry Coy Signal Officer by code word "JACK".

5. All information and special maps relating to the positions will be handed over.

6. Guns tripods and all gun equipment will be handed over.

7. Acknowledge.

Issued at 9.15 pm
14-6-17
Copies to:—
No 1. 2/Lt PHILBIN
  2. 2/Lt BALL
  3. 2/Lt BOTHWELL
  4. 2/Lt MARSLAND
  5. C.S.M.
  6. File
  7. War Diary
  8. Sergt CLARK.

Reynold Marsland
2/Lieut for
O.C. 94th M.G. Coy.

SECRET

94th Machine Gun Coy

Instructions in connection with Operation Order No. 2?

1. RATIONS

Rations will be delivered as under on night 15th/16th.

(a) ½ 'D' Section proceeding to positions Nos 5 & 6 will carry their own rations.

(b) ½ 'B' Section proceeding [from Coy] Hd Qrs on night 15th/16th will take all rations of 'B' Section and will leave rations of other two ½ Sections at their Section Hd Qrs.

(c) Rations for ½ 'D' Section in positions Nos 7 & 8 will be arranged by Coy Hd Qrs.

(d) 'A' Section will draw their rations as usual.

2. WATER

(a) ½ 'D' Section proceeding to positions Nos 5 & 6 will take their own drinking water.

(b) ½ 'D' Section proceeding to positions Nos 7 & 8 will take their empty tins of water with them.

(c) ½ 'B' Section at Coy Hd Qrs will take water for whole of 'B' Section to WINDMILL sector, leaving 3 tins at Section Hd Qrs.

(d) On relief 'C' Section will bring out empty petrol cans.

(e) Water for ½ 'D' Section in positions Nos 7 & 8 will be arranged by Coy Hd Qrs.

(f) The one petrol can per gun position holding reserve water for gun must be left in the position in every case. These will be shown in handing over certificates.

Reginald Marslay? Lt
O C 94th M G Coy

SECRET. (APPENDIX III) Copy No. 9.

94th Machine Gun Company - Operation Order No. 22.

REF. MAP. GAVRELLE 1/20000
ROCLINCOURT 1/10000

1. The 94th M.G. Coy will be relieved by the 92nd M.G. Coy on night 19th/20th June.

2. For rendezvous of Guides see attached relief table.

3. Tripods, belts, ammunition boxes, one full petrol tin of water per gun, and one per Section Hd. Qtrs will be handed over in addition to trench stores.

4. Receipts for all stores handed over will be made out in triplicate, one copy being handed over to relieving gun team, two copies being sent to Coy Hd Qtrs as soon as possible after relief.

5. All information, range cards, aiming posts, maps, etc. will be handed over to relieving teams. Receipts in duplicate will be forwarded to Coy Hd. Qtrs.

6. After relief Section Officers will muster their Sections at ration dump, MAISON DE LA COTE, and dump guns and gun stores, leaving 1. N.C.O. and 2 men in charge. They will march their Sections independently to billets at ST CATHERINE Q.15 a 5.2. A Guide will meet them at foot of hill at junction of ST CATHERINE - ECURIE RD and ST CATHERINE - ANZIN RD.

7. Transport arrangements will be notified to transport Officer separately.

8. Relief complete without casualties will be notified to Coy Hd Qtrs by code word "BON". Signature of Officer and time. This message will be brought with trench store receipts as soon after relief as possible.

9. Acknowledge.

19.6.17
Issued at 1.30 a.m.

C.W.R.Ball.
Lieut for Capt.
Comdg 94th M.G. Coy.

Copy No 1 - A. Section
" " 2 - B. "
" " 3 - C. "
" " 4 - D. "
" " 5 - O.C.
" " 6 - LT. CANT.
" " 7 - C.Q.M.S.
" " 8 - 94th INF. BDE.
" " 9 - War Diary.
" " 10 - File.
" " 11 - Retained.
" " 12 - Retained.

9th Machine Gun Company
Relief Table in connection with Operation Order No 2

One ~~guide~~ per gun team
~~Guides to be at~~ u/p places
on night 19th/20th June.

GUN POSITION No:	MAP REF	SECTION	
1	C.19.c. 70.30	} B	B.29.d. 8.9 at 11 p.m.
2	C.19.c. 30.50		
3	B.24.a. 95.70		
4	B.24.a. 30.70		
7	B.23.d. 80.48	D Coy 2 Gun teams	Coy HD QTRS 10.0 p.m.
8	B.23.d. 70.48		
9	B.23.a. 70.35	} A	Coy HD QTRS 10.0 pm
10	B.23.a. 45.62		
11	B.17.c. 60.30		
12	B.17.c. 70.50		

Each guide will know the number of his gun position

19.6.17

E.W. Rtall Lieut
for O.C. 9th M.G. Coy

SECRET   (APPENDIX IV)   COPY No. 11.

94th Machine Gun Coy. Operation Order No. 23.

1. The 94th M.G. Coy. will move into the line on the night of 26th/27th June 1917.

2. Detachments will parade at Hd Qrs of 94th M.G. Coy. at 8.30 p.m. Dress: Fighting Order.

3. Command of teams
   Gun teams will be commanded as follows:—
   1 - 3   2/Lt MARSLAND.
   4 - 6   "   PHILBIN.
   7   Sgt THOMPSON.
   8   2/Lt BALL.
   9 & 10   "   BOTHWELL.
   11   Sgt CLARKE.
   12 - 16 Lt CANT.

4. Sections will move off under their own commanders, intervals of 200" being maintained. On arrival at Railway Bridge Sections will proceed to their rendezvous by gun teams taking the usual precautions for safety.

5. Disposition of teams
   Guides for 1, 3, 4 and 5 teams will be at Advanced Coy Hd Qrs at 10.15 p.m.
   These teams will proceed direct to their posts relieving 4 teams of the 92nd M.G. Coy.
   Belt boxes and tripods will be taken over and receipts given.
   No. 2 team will proceed to TYNE ALLEY and obtain from the gun position of 92 Coy. 1 Tripod and 14 Belt boxes. They will then proceed direct to the new post at S. WINDMILL.
   No. 6 team will proceed to TYNE ALLEY, obtain 1 Tripod and 14 Belt Boxes from 92nd Coy and proceed to new position in MARINE TRENCH.
   Nos 7 - 11 teams will proceed to entry at B 21. c. 7. 4.
   Gun commanders of these teams will then proceed to the line and locate their positions for occupation on night of 27th/28th June. They will on completion return to Coy.

Hd Qrs and report afterwards rejoining their teams in the battery.

No 12-16 teams will proceed to Coy Hd. Qrs. They will then act as carrying parties as required.

6. **Reports.**

O.C. teams 1-6 will send each a runner to Coy Hd Qrs to report relief and occupation of positions complete. Code used (No of guns) and Coy Code.

7. **Work.**

Gun commanders will immediately commence strengthening their positions, care being taken in the disposal of earth removed.

8. **Concealment.**

All ranks are warned of the necessity of avoiding all movement as far as possible by day. Particular care must be taken when moving along trenches which are not deep enough to wholly cover movement. Should hostile Aeroplanes come over the line all ranks are warned against movement of any kind and against looking up.

9. **A.A. GUNS.**

2/Lt PHILBIN will mount the guns under his command for A.A. work by day and vigorous action is to be taken against any hostile planes appearing within range. Special emplacements will be constructed for this purpose. A.A. sights will be used.

10. Rear Coy Hd Qrs will remain at ST CATHERINES pending further orders.

A.W.R.Ball Lieut
for O.C. 94th Machine Gun Coy

26-6-17
Issued at 11.30 a.m.
Copy No 1 2/Lt MARSLAND
         2 "   PHILBIN
         3 "   BALL
         4 LT CANT
         5 2/LT BOTHWELL
         6 O.C. 94th M.G. Coy
         7 LT BALL CWR
         8 SGT CLARK
         9 " THOMPSON
        10 FILE
      11 & 12 War Diary

SECRET (Appendix V)   COPY NO. 11

94th Machine Gun Coy. Operation Order No. 24.

REF MAP 51.G.N.W

Objective.

1. The XIII Corps will attack the enemy trenches on the front from the WINDMILL at C.19.c.9.4. to about B.12.d.5.7.

2. The objective for the 31st Division are the WINDMILL TRENCH from C.19.c.95.65. to C.19.d.4.9., TRENCH at C.19.b.7.0. CADORNA TRENCH at C.19.c.4.95., CADORNA TRENCH & its junction with WOOD ALLEY, WOOD ALLEY from its junction with CADORNA TRENCH to OPPY —— TRENCH.

The 94th Bde. is detailed to carry out the attack on the objective of the 31st Div.

3. *MACHINE GUNS.*

The Machine Guns of the 94th M.G. Coy. will take part in the attack and will be disposed of as follows:-

1 gun under 2/Lt THOMPSON assigned to Rt RIGHT BATT?
1   "   "   BALL   R. CENTRE
2 guns "   "   BOTTOMLEY   LEFT CENTRE
1 gun   "   "   CLARKE   LEFT BATT?

These guns will at once follow the advance of the O.P.C. to the trenches to which allotted and will cross immediately afterwards on the English. The primary role of this gun will be to assist in the consolidation of the line when taken.

These guns will move from the CUTTING at C.20.a.9.0. by Y night and practice by them the way to... by... will obtain work park enough to protect to their posts. Tripods will be obtained at C.19.d. ... All guns will be in position by 11 p.m. on Y night.

Rations will be issued to these before moving off according to instructions issued separately to Gun Commanders.

Defence Gun.

4. The guns of the 94th M.G. Coy. not taking the attack will remain in their present positions. These guns have full defence the whole front in the event of the attack being unsuccessful. When the position is gained they will act as support guns except those in the WINDMILL who ... will ... preserve their role of front line guns.

The O.C. the guns at WINDMILL will be prepared to assist the attack by covering the front of the RIGHT BATTN and protecting its flanks should the situation demand it otherwise fire will not be opened.

Work of the M.Gs.

5. The guns of the 92nd and 93rd M.G. Coys. together with the guns of the 2nd M.G. Squadron will assist by firing on targets as follows:—

Group	No. of Guns	Location	Targets	Units
A	6	B14 c 7.3	C.19 b.50 — C.19 b.5,7	92 M.G.Coy
B	4	B.29 a.3668	Tramd junction at C.13 c.65.57	" "
C	4	B.29 a 7.8	C.13 a.85.40 — C.13 a.9.0	" "
D	4	M.Coy	C.13 a.45.70 — C.19 b.5,0	93 M.G.Coy
E	4	Front line	On and behind enemy front line Rouex Loop to GAVRELLE-FRESNES road M 18.4,3	
F	4	B.29 a.1.5	C.19 a.50.75 — C.19 d.70.45	2 M.G. Squad.
G	4	B.30 a	C.20 c.10.15 — C.20 c.65.85	" "
H	4	B.30 c	C.20 c.4.75 — C.20 a.0,1	" "

These guns will open fire as follows:—

At ZERO all guns open on targets indicated above until ZERO + 40 minutes.

After ZERO + 40 minutes fire will be opened at irregular intervals on targets from 5-30 minutes every 2 day and through Z/Z+1 night.

On S.O.S. being given all guns open fire.

RESERVE GUNS

6. The remaining four guns of the 93rd M.G.Coy will be in reserve at Coy H.Qrs.

7. **Reports.**

Reports will be sent through BATTN H.Q. to Bde to which guns are attached & in the case of guns not under BATTN Commanders through nearest report centre or direct messenger to Bde Commander. These should be rendered ½ hour after ZERO and hourly afterwards. Important information not able to be sent by telephone will be reported direct by runner.

8. **Consolidation**

After the position is taken the guns on the front line will subject to the approval of BATT? Commanders of the guns attached to them be laid on the following true bearings to enable a belt of fire to be produced along the front.

No 1 Gun 140° T.B.
" 2   "   80° T.B.
" 7   "   330° T.B.
" 9   "   125° T.B.
" 10   "   6° T.B.
" 11   "   30° T.B.

Guns in defensive line will retain their present lines of fire. No 6 Gun will lay on T.B. of 120°.

9. **Reconnaissance of line.**

All guns will continue to hold their positions once gained until the last. After consolidation the position will be strengthened and improved. Changes for any readjustment of the guns will be issued as required.

J.E. Price Capt
Lieut
O.C. 94th M.G. Coy.

21-6-17
Issued at 2.30 pm
Copy No 1. 2/Lt Marsland
       2.   " Philbin
       3.   " Ball
       4. Lt Gant
       5. 2/Lt Bothwell
       6. Lt Col. H.R. Ball M.C.
       7. O.C. 94th M.G. Coy.
       8. Sgt Clark
       9.   " Thompson
      10. File
      11.) War Diary
      12.)

SECRET.   (APPENDIX VI.)   COPY NO. 6

92nd Machine Gun Company. Operation Order No. 25.

1. Owing to the readjustment of the line the following inter-company relief will take place.

2. Distribution.

(a) A SECTION under Lt CANT will relieve the four gun teams in the new front line. These posts are numbered from Right to Left as follows 2, 3, 4, 5.

No 1 post will be at the WINDMILL. Guides for these teams will report to Coy HD QRS at dusk.

(b) Sergt KENNEDYS team will leave their belt boxes, tripod and empty water cans at the dug-out at SECTION HD QRS. and taking their gun and spare parts will proceed to the WINDMILL and relieve No 1 Gun team, taking over tripods & belt boxes and obtaining receipts for the same.

This team will be accompanied by three men detailed by Coy HD QRS to assist the No 2 Gun team to carry out their kit. Lieut MARSLAND will make the necessary arrangements between 1 and 2 teams to enable as many of the latters belt boxes and all water tins to be withdrawn from the line. Any deficiency in the number of belt boxes held by Sergt THOMPSON should first be made good from this number. Surplus S.A.A above the 10000 per gun position should also be given to him.

Lieut MARSLAND will bring these two gun teams when relieved back to Coy HD QRS.

(c) The post now occupied by L/Cpl CLOUGH will be moved along RAILWAY TRENCH and a new position prepared on the West side of the road. This post will be known as No 6 and will be occupied by Cpl TRUEMAN and his team.

Arrangements will be made for this inter-relief by 2/Lt PHILBIN in such a manner as to avoid unnecessary carrying.

The post now occupied by Cpl TRUEMAN in RAILWAY TRENCH will be withdrawn and the stores removed to SECTION HD QRS until they can be removed from the line. Lieut CANT will replace any deficiencies in ammunition from this supply.

(d) The post at SECTION HD QRS will be known as No 7 post. L/Cpl CLOUGH and his team this post.

(e) The men on the post at SECTION HD QRS. will when relieved proceed to BARNSLEY TRENCH to Cpl HOLT and relieve the men of B. Section there.

(f) The men of B. SECTION now with Cpl HOLT will, when relieved, report to SECTION HD QRS. They will be required to carry up from there what kit they can to COY HD QRS. 2/Lt PHILBIN will arrange this.

The post in BARNSLEY TRENCH will be known as No 8 post

When all reliefs are complete 2/Lt BALL will assume command of Nos 1, 6, 7 and 8 Gun positions. 2/Lt PHILBIN with his orderly and servant will report to COY HD QRS

All Gun Commanders must ensure that as many water tins as possible are sent to COY HD QRS otherwise the supply of water cannot be maintained.

The guns will be laid for Night lines on the following TRUE BEARINGS pending arrangements with BDE on left for co-operation.

No 1 Gun - T B - 158°
" 2 "   "   135°
" 3 "   "   35°
" 4 "   "   128°
" 5 "   "   52°
" 6 "   "   0°
" 7 "   "   28°
" 8 "   "   130°

Section Officers will ensure that Range boards are prepared and order boards drawn for these new posts.

Issued 5.20 p.m
29-6-17
Copy No. 1/2 - O.C.
        3 - Lt CANT
        4 - 2/Lt PHILBIN
        5 - " MARSLAND
        6 & 7 " BALL
              WAR DIARY.

Confidential

Volume xix
Vol 15

War Diary.

94 Machine Gun Company.   31st Division

July 1917

Army Form C. 2118.

No. 94
MACHINE GUN
COMPANY.
No. Q.1/22.
Date 31/7/17

WAR DIARY
or
INTELLIGENCE SUMMARY.
(Erase heading not required.)

Instructions regarding War Diaries and Intelligence Summaries are contained in F. S. Regs., Part II. and the Staff Manual respectively. Title pages will be prepared in manuscript.

Place	Date	Hour	Summary of Events and Information	Remarks and references to Appendices
In the field	1/7/17	9 a.m.	Commanding Officer pays a visit to the four guns placed in reserve in the RED LINE. Selects new Aircraft positions and checks angles of Q.E. handed over.	
		2 p.m.	Visit from D.M.G.O. and D.M.G.O. 63rd Div. The latter remained to hand the line explained.	
			During the afternoon report received from the line that the gun at the WINDMILL had to change position owing to the Emplacement of WINDMILL - trenches & emplacement having been destroyed.	
		7/30 p.m.	Order from BDE. HD. QRs received directing four guns now at COY. HD. QRS. to occupy another position of the RED LINE and lines of fire laid out to place a barrage beyond the WINDMILL and on GAVRELLE - FRESNOY ROAD. These guns were in position, ammunition up and wire to BDE. HD. QRS to that effect despatched at 8.30 p.m.. COY. HD. QRS. and RED LINE heavily shelled with H.E. and shrapnel during this operation.	

J S Mc Cope

WAR DIARY
~~INTELLIGENCE~~ SUMMARY

(Erase heading not required.)

Army Form C. 2118.

Place	Date	Hour	Summary of Events and Information	Remarks and references to Appendices
(Continued)				
	1/7/17	11-00am	First Guard Store 2nd M.G. Squadron sent up as reserve in hands of M.G. Coy. Commander to replace those occupying the RED LINE.	JSL Cpt
			No. 28486 4/Cpl. WILLIS H. proceeds to Veterinary Hospital for course of instruction.	
In the field	2/7/17	4:45 am	Commanding Officer visits front line trenches and inspects all gun positions.	
		9:00 am	Maps showing defences of the line prepared and handed over to D.M.G.O. 63rd Div.	Appendix I.
			Operation Order No. 26 issued for the relief of the line by 92nd M.G. Coy.	
		5:00 pm	Orders received for the withdrawal of the 2nd M.G. Squadron who departed and rejoined their unit.	JSL Cpt
		11:30 pm	Relief of front line system commenced. One O.R. was intoxicated.	
	3/7/17	1:15 am	Completion of relief of front line system without incident.	
		3:20 am	Completion of relief in RED LINE without incident.	
		5:00 am	O.C. and H.Q. Q.R.S. staff departed from the line & moved to billets in ST. CATHERINE.	
		5:45 pm	Company moved back to rest billets at MAROEVIL, taking over same billets as occupied 23rd May to June 11th	JSL Cpt

A6945 Wt. W1427/M1160 350,000 12/16 D.D.&L. Forms/C/2118/14.

Army Form C. 2118.

WAR DIARY
or
INTELLIGENCE SUMMARY
(Erase heading not required.)

Place	Date	Hour	Summary of Events and Information	Remarks and references to Appendices
In the field	14/7/17		At MAROEUIL. The day spent in cleaning and overhauling of guns and gun gear, and cleaning and inspection of equipment and small kit. 1 O.R. reinforcement reported from A.H.J Depot. Lieut C.W.R. BALL M.C. proceeded to join 138 M.G. Coy. to take over duties as O.C. 138 M.G. COY.	JTU
do	5/7/17		The day was spent in completion of outreach of kit etc. Also repairing and cleaning of kilts. 2 O.R. reinforcements reported from Base Depot. 3 O.R's reported from course with 176th Tunnelling C.E. 2/Lt. R. MARSLAND & 3 N.C.Os reported to O.C. 63rd AA SECTION for course in AA work.	JTU
do	6/7/17		Training was carried out in accordance with detailed programmes by Company and Platoon staffs. 25023 PTE. SHEMELD E. was admitted to Field Ambulance suffering from wounds received two days previous. 2/Lt. G.N.B. WATKINS reported for duty from BASE DEPOT. 10 O.R. reinforcements arrived from BASE DEPOT.	JTU

John Capt

Army Form C. 2118.

WAR DIARY
or
INTELLIGENCE SUMMARY.
(Erase heading not required.)

Instructions regarding War Diaries and Intelligence Summaries are contained in F. S. Regs., Part II. and the Staff Manual respectively. Title pages will be prepared in manuscript.

Place	Date	Hour	Summary of Events and Information	Remarks and references to Appendices
In the field	7/7/17		Training was carried out including P.T. I.A. Gun Drill & Range Taking	JSP
do	8/7/17		Divine Services were held for all denominations. Cleaning & inspection of kits.	JSP
do	9/7/17		Rough ground drill. Gun Drill I.A. was carried out in the morning, and the afternoon was spent in Tactical Section Exercise. LT. J.S. WILSON M.C. joined from 95 M.G. Coy. for duty as second in command. LT. T. HOWARD was mentioned in SIR DOUGLAS HAIG'S despatch of 9th April 1917.	JSP
do	10/7/17	9 a.m. to 12 noon. 1 p.m. to 5 p.m.	Limber and Pack Drill. Company marched to A.C.R. for inspection of Box Respirators & passed through Gas Chamber. C.O. attended demonstration of aeroplanes at AUCHIEL.	JSP
do	11/7/17	4 a.m. 8.30 p.m.	Company prepared to move. Company marched to NEUVILLE-ST-VAAST. where they were billeted for night. C.O. visited 3rd CANADIAN BGDE. HQRS. to arrange relief of 3rd M.G. Coy.	JSP
do	12/7/17		Company clean guns & equipment. C.O. explains defence scheme of line to be taken over to the Section Officers & Operation Order No. 27.	See Appendix II J.S. Paul Capt.

Army Form C. 2118.

WAR DIARY
or
INTELLIGENCE SUMMARY

(Erase heading not required.)

Instructions regarding War Diaries and Intelligence Summaries are contained in F.S. Regs., Part II. and the Staff Manual respectively. Title pages will be prepared in manuscript.

Place	Date	Hour	Summary of Events and Information	Remarks and references to Appendices
In the field	12/7/17 (cont.)	9.0 p.m.	"A" & "B" Sections under LTS. CANT & HOWARD proceed to line in accordance with Operation Order No. 24.	JSP
	NIGHT 12 & 13 July.	1-4.45 a.m.	Relief completed without incident.	
do	13/7/17.	9.0 p.m.	REAR H.Q. move back to Transport Lines. "C" & "D" Sections under 2/LT: BALL & LT: RICHARDSON moved up to line to complete relief of 3rd CANADIAN M.G. COY.	JSP
do	14/7/17.	3.0 a.m.	Relief completed without incident. Guns on line work on improvement of positions. Guns in support lines carry out harassing fire during the night. Guns mounted for A.A. work in each that Guns in front line fired 100 rounds at an aeroplane passing low over trenches. During afternoon enemy lines. C.O. works to villages in defence of line. C.O. makes a reconnaissance of present defence of line from high ground behind. The following N.C.Os. & MEN awarded the military medal for gallantry in the field :- 27562 SGT. A. THOMPSON. 14656 A/CPL. W. HOLT. 10469 PTE. F. LOCK. 25023 PTE. E. SHEMELD. 46625 PTE. A. THOMPSON.	JSP
do	15/7/17.	10 a.m. to 3.0 p.m.	Company in line continue to improve positions. C.O. visits the line. Receive visit from C.M.G.O. and D.M.G.O.	JSP

J. S. Price Capt

WAR DIARY
or
INTELLIGENCE SUMMARY
(Erase heading not required.)

Army Form C. 2118.

Instructions regarding War Diaries and Intelligence Summaries are contained in F. S. Regs., Part II. and the Staff Manual respectively. Title pages will be prepared in manuscript.

Place	Date	Hour	Summary of Events and Information	Remarks and references to Appendices
In the field	15/7/17		The guns in the line work on improving positions.	J.L.P
	NIGHT 16/17 July 17		Guns in Support line carry out harassing fire on the following target:- U13c 20.30. and Ronsoy Road U13.b.2.c. Rounds fired 1750. "D" Section relieves "A" Section in the line. 3 O.R's proceed on special leave to U.K.	
do.	17/7/17		Company in the line carries on the work of improving emplacements & trenches. The guns on A.A. duty engaged several hostile aircraft. C.O. visited guns and gun positions.	J.L.P
		2pm— 4pm	C.O. and D.M.C.O. go round gun positions. During this tour a gun belonging to the 13th COY. in the sector on the right was discovered firing away to protect and smoke. 2 N.C.O's rejoin from BASE DEPOT.	
do.	18/7/17		Team at BRISTOL construct a new position in C.P.R. TRENCH. C.O. of 93rd M.G.COY. spent day in line with C.O. Arrangements made for relief.	J.L.P
do.	19/7/17.		Company in the line construct new works, and continue the improvement of positions. Operation Order No.28 issued for relief of Company by 93rd M.G.COY. 1 O.R. proceeds on leave to U.K.	Appendix III
do.	20/7/17.		Work on line continues. Two new positions made during night of 19/20 in CANADA TRENCH to complete the main line of defence. A.A. guns engage hostile patrols during the day. 5 O.Rs reinforcements from BASE DEPOT.	
do.	NIGHT 20/21st July.		93rd M.G.COY. relieve 9th M.G.COY. in the line. Guide for allotment went astray thus delaying relief. All guns finally relieved, and relieved teams clear of Vimy Ridge by 11 pm approx.	J.L.P. Capt. MGC Corps

Army Form C. 2118.

WAR DIARY
or
INTELLIGENCE SUMMARY.
(Erase heading not required.)

Instructions regarding War Diaries and Intelligence Summaries are contained in F. S. Regs., Part II. and the Staff Manual respectively. Title pages will be prepared in manuscript.

Place	Date	Hour	Summary of Events and Information	Remarks and references to Appendices
In the Field	MONT 20th July (Cont)			
do.	21/7/17		Company move from Transport Lines to the billets at MONT-ST-ELOY. The afternoon was spent in cleaning guns and overhauling kit. 2 O.R.s proceeded on leave to U.K.	JSL
"	22/7/17		The day was spent in the generals cleaning up of kits, and generally an easy day for the men.	JSL
"	23/7/17		The day was spent in the repairing of equipment and complete overhauling of guns.	JSL
do	24/7/17		Training was carried out including :- P.T. Gun Drill, S.A. Rapid Firing and the use of Elevating & Traversing Drill. Range Takers also arrived out a special programme with reference Object. Range Takers also arrived out a special programme. 6 O.R.s proceed on leave to W.H. Baths were attention in afternoon.	JSL
do	25/7/17		Three sections were practised in Application and Grouping on range at La Motte Staden when use of range practices in use of Elementary Discovery and elevating dial, & use of ground, S.A. (Handgrenades) and other training was carried out.	JSL

JSMci Capt

Army Form C. 2118.

WAR DIARY
or
INTELLIGENCE SUMMARY
(Erase heading not required.)

Place	Date	Hour	Summary of Events and Information	Remarks and references to Appendices
In the Field	26/7/17.		During the day training was carried out including:- O.S. fired laying. Immediate Action and Revolver Drill. In the afternoon three Sections carried out Tactical Section Exercises on the high ground W. of La Motte Farm, and another Section was practiced in Application and Grouping on range at La Motte Farm.	JSP
- do -	27/7/17.		Training was carried out including:- O.S., Lewis Drill. Immediate Action and Revolver Drill. During the afternoon Tactical Exercises were carried out on the high ground W. of LA MOTTE FARM. Seven O.R.s were granted leave to N.Z.H. Four O.R.s reinforcements arrived from BASE DEPÔT.	JSP
- do -	28/7/17.		Indirect Fire Drill Company Drill, Tactical Section Exercises, Lewis Drill, and a lecture to N.C.O.s were included in the days training.	JSP
- do -	29/7/17.		Divine Services were arranged for all denominations. There were heavy thunderstorms during the morning.	JSP
- do -	30/7/17.		The days training was occupied by:- use of Traversing & Elevating Dials, Lecture by Section Officers on French Standing Orders, Immediate Action in Prone Position. Identification of objects by means of Range Card. Study of ground and judging distance and Overhead Fire Drill. Three other ranks were granted leave to U.K.	JSP

Army Form C. 2118.

WAR DIARY
or
INTELLIGENCE SUMMARY
(Erase heading not required.)

Place	Date	Hour	Summary of Events and Information	Remarks and references to Appendices
In the Field	31/1/17		The days training included:- Company Drill, Limber Drill, Overhead Fire Drill. Indirect Fire Drill (Watson's Method). Immediate action in prone position and cleaning and filling Belts.	JSR

J S McCope
Comdg. 91st Machine Gun Coy.

SECRET.   Appendix I

94th Machine Gun Company, Operation Order No. 26.
****

1. **INFORMATION.**
    The 92nd Machine Gun Company will relieve the 94th Machine Gun Company in the GAVRELLE – OPPY sector on the night 2/3rd July.

2. **HANDING OVER LIST.**
    All belt boxes and tripods will be handed over, together with one petrol tin of water and all trench stores, the usual receipts being obtained.

3. **RELIEFS.**
    The guns in that portion of the RED LINE under 2/Lt. MARSLAND will be relieved at 5.p.m. 2/Lt. MARSLAND will on completion of relief despatch his Section by teams at ten minutes interval along OUSE ALLEY, and move to the RAILWAY CUTTING DUMP along the West side of the railway embankment, every precaution to be taken to avoid attracting attention to the movement of their teams.
    On arrival at the cutting, guns and kit will be left there at the dump under the charge of an Orderly detailed by COMPANY HEADQUARTERS for the purpose. Teams will then move independently to Company Billets at ST.CATHERINE.

4. **GUIDES.**
    Guides for the remaining gun teams will report at COMPANY HEADQUARTERS at 10-30.p.m. to conduct the new teams in to their positions.

5. **REPORTS.**
    Section Officers and gun team commanders will report independently at COMPANY HEADQUARTERS on completion of relief, and without any delay will then move their teams direct to the RAILWAY CUTTING and leave guns and kit under the charge of the party detailed. Teams will then move by their commanders independently to billets at ST.CATHERINE.

6. **TRANSPORT.**
    A light tractor will be at the RAILWAY CUTTING at 3-30.a.m. when the guns and kit will be loaded up and the tractor return to ST.CATHERINE. The loading party will return on the tractor.

                                    Captain,
                                    Commanding 94th M.G.Coy.

SECRET.   Appendix II   COPY NO:- 10.

94th Machine Gun Company, Operation Order No. 27.

****

Map Refs. Sheets 51 b. N.W. 1/20,000.
36 c. S.W. "

1. INFORMATION. The 94th M.G.Coy. will relieve the 3rd Canadian M.G.Coy. in the ACHEVILLE section of the VIMY sector on night 12/13 July & 13/14 July 1917.

2. DISPOSITION. "A" Section under Lieut. CANT will relieve the guns of the 3rd Canadian M.G.Coy. at the following positions :- ALDERSHOT, ANESBURY, ANDOVER, AVON, on night 12/13th July Section Headquarters will be at ALDERSHOT T.24.c 45.XX.15.
"B" Section under Lieut. Howard will relieve the guns at the following positions on night 12/13th July. BRIGHTON, BASINGSTOKE, BULFORD, ABERGELE.
Section Headquarters will be at ANGLESEY T.22,d,65.70.

3. TIME TABLE AND ORDER OF MARCH.
The Transport Officer will arrange for a limber to be in NEUVILLE ST. VAAST at A.9.a.3.9. at 9 p.m. on night 12/13th July. Guns, water and rations will be loaded up at this point. When loaded the limber with "A" and "B" Sections will move to cross roads at LES TILLEULS (A.11 a.9.9.) to arrive at 9-45 p.m. At this point a mounted guide of the 3rd Canadian Machine Gun Company will meet the column and conduct it to the ration dump at T. 27.d. 9.8. where guides will meet the teams and conduct them to their respective positions. Sections and limbers will each move at 100 yards interval and 20 yards between gun teams. Limbers to lead followed by "A" then "B" Sections.
On arrival at Ration Dump "B" Section will halt 100 yards short of the limber and await until "A" Section have moved off before unloading. All unloading to be done in silence and as quickly as possible.
Lieut. DURRANT and Sgt. COLLINS will both proceed with the limber on this occasion to enable the route to be identified.

4. HANDING OVER STORES.
All tripods, belt-boxes, maps and petrol tins will be taken over by the relieving teams and receipts given.
Completion of relief will be notified to Coy. Hd. Qrs. by the Officers relieved of the 3rd Canadian M.G.Coy.

5. LINES OF FIRE. Lines of fire and programme for firing will be taken over from the commanders of the sections being relieved.

6. RELIEF OF SUPPORT & RESERVE LINES.
"C" Section under 2/Lt.BALL will relieve the guns in the support lines on the night 13/14 July at the following positions :-
AYR, BUSHEY, BRISTOL, BALLINCOLLIG.
"D" Section under 2/Lt. RICHARDSON will relieve the guns in Brigade Reserve at Bde. Hd. Qrs. on night 13/14 July.

7. TIME TABLE. The limber will be at the same place and time as detailed in para 3. On reaching the cross roads at LES TILLEULS, "D" Section will be met by a guide who will conduct them to the teams to be relieved. Hd. Qrs. of "D" Section will be at Coy. Hd. Qrs.
"C" Section and the limber will proceed by the route reconnoitred on the night of 12/13 to the ration dump where guides will meet them to conduct the gun teams to their respective positions.
Tripods, belt-boxes, maps and reserve rations will be taken over by the relieving teams and receipts given. Relief complete will be reported to Coy. H.Q. by Code.

8. COMMUNICATION. N.C.O. in charge of signallers will detail two signallers with a telephone to accompany Lieut. HOWARD, and two signallers with a telephone and exchange board to accompany 2/Lt. BALL.

Lieut. CANT will communicate with Coy. H.Q. via Battalion H.Q. at T.29.b.2.1.

Situation reports, firing report, ammunition return and work report of previous 24 hours up to 6-0.p.m. each night will be despatched by ration carriers to ration dump.

These will be brought back by the Officer or N.C.O. in charge of limber who will be met by an orderly at the cross roads at LES TILLEULS. This orderly will collect reports and bring them to Coy. Hd.Qrs.

Important information and casualties will be despatched at once to Coy. Hd.Qrs either by runner or sent on telephone in code. No such information is to be despatched " in clear ".

9. IMPROVEMENTS OF POSITIONS. Section Officers will take the necessary steps to improve their positions and will send into Coy. Hd. Qrs any suggestions for the best method of utilizing the shaft positions of the new gun positions at the dug-outs.

Night lines will be carefully laid out in accordance with the defence scheme explained by Coy. Commanders.

Special care will be taken that safety limits are preserved with the guns carrying out the firing programme.

10. A.A.WORK.

Lieut. CANT will detail one gun for A.A.Work.
  "   HOWARD "   "   two   "   "   "
2/Lt. BALL   "   "   one   "   "   "
Lieut. RICHARDSON "   "   one   "   "   "

11. Acknowledge.

Issued at :-
    12th July 1917.

                                                    Captain,
                                              Comdg. 94th M.G.Coy.

Copy No. 1 to Lieut. Cant.
         2 "   "   Howard.
         3 "   2/Lt. Ball.
         4 "   Lieut. Richardson.
         5 "   T.O.
         6 "   2nd in command.
         7 "   O.C., 3rd Canadian M.G.Coy.
         8 "   C.O.
     9 & 10 "   War Diary.
        11 "   File.

Operation Order No. 28. Appendix III

1. RELIEF.

The 94th Machine Gun Company will be relieved in the Acheville Sector on the night of the 20/21st July by the 93rd Machine Gun Company.

2. TIMES OF RELIEF.

Two guides from Headquarters will be detailed to meet the 93rd M.G. Coy. with its limbers at the Les Tilleuls cross roads at 10-0 p.m. These guides will take the limbers and Company to the ration dump, taking care not to move too fast so as to cause units to straggle.

Section Officers in the line will each detail one guide to be at the ration dump at 10-45 p.m. These guides will each conduct the gun teams to their respective guns.

3. HANDING OVER.

Belt boxes and tripods will be handed over to the relieving teams, receipts being obtained and a duplicate given to the relieving team. Gun commanders are warned of the importance of these handing over slips being correct, and will be held responsible for any inaccuracy which occurs. The post will be cleansed and in a sanitary condition, and a certificate to this effect will be inserted at the foot of the handing over slips, and signed by the gun commander taking over. On conclusion of relief gun teams will move direct under their gun commanders to the ration dump, and will leave there their guns and kit, and one man from each team to remain in charge, this man loading up the limbers on their arrival. The remainder of the team under the gun commander will then move back to Company Headquarters, which are by the Brigade Headquarters at THELUS CAVES, the gun commander reporting personally to O.C. Company, and handing in to O.C. Company his handing over list. Two guides will be at the ration dump to conduct "B" & "C" Section back to Company Headquarters. Gun teams after reporting will then move to the Transport Lines, and there await the remainder of the Company. Section Officers in the line will report personally to O.C. Company at Company Headquarters on conclusion of their relief.

1.

4. **TRANSPORT.**

The Transport Officer will detail two limbers. First limber will detach its rear portion on the road close to Company Headquarters. The front portion then going on to the line and to be at the ration dump at 12-30 a.m. This half limber will bring back the three guns of "C" Section now at "Bristol", Bushey and Ballincollig. On return it will pick up the hind portion of the limber at Company Headquarters, which will contain the guns of "A" Section. Headquarter stores being distributed between the front and rear portions, it will then move direct to the Transport Lines.

The second limber will go direct to the line, and will be at the ration dump at 2-0 a.m. This limber will bring back the guns of "B" & "D" Sections, including the one gun of "C" Section now at Ayr. The limbers must be clear of Vimy Ridge before day-break. The Second-in-command will arrange for a meal to be ready at the Transport Lines on arrival of the gun teams.

At 10-0 a.m. the Company will move off to Rest Billets at Le Pendu Camp (Map reference 51c NE. 1/20,000 F.1 A58.

Transport Lines for the moment will remain where they are, subsequent orders may be issued regarding the movement of the Transport Lines to the Company.

The Second-in-command will make the necessary arrangements on the 20th for taking over the billets for the Company, and arrange for baths and clean clothes for the afternoon of the 21st if it can be arranged.

J E Prie Cope
O.C. 94th M.G. Coy.

20/7/17.

Confidential

Volume xx
Vol 16

War Diary.

94th Machine Gun Company.   31st. Division

August 1917.

Army Form C. 2118.

WAR DIARY
or
INTELLIGENCE SUMMARY.
(Erase heading not required)

Instructions regarding War Diaries and Intelligence Summaries are contained in F.S. Regs., Part II. and the Staff Manual respectively. Title pages will be prepared in manuscript.

Place	Date	Hour	Summary of Events and Information	Remarks and references to Appendices
In the Field	1/8/17		The Company clean guns, belts and ammunition in preparation for going into the line. Three other ranks were granted leave to U.K.	
In the Field	2/8/17	10 a.m. 9.30 p.m.	The Company pack limbers and go to baths etc before moving to the line. Operation Order No. 29 issued for the relief of the 93rd Machine Gun Company in Right Sector of Divisional Front. Company Parade and march to the line. Relief Commenced.	Appendix I
	NIGHT 2/3rd/8/17	1.30 a.m.	Relief completed without incident	
In the Field	3/8/17 NIGHT 3rd/4th		Company at line repair trenches, overhaul kit taken over and reconstruct the emplacements. Guns at AYR, ANGLESEY & ABERGELE fired for harassing fire on the following targets:- ACASIA TRENCH U18A CROSS ROADS at U18A H.O. ROAD 3° R & L of CROSS ROAD at U18A H.O. Rounds fired 2,150. Result unknown.	

Army Form C. 2118.

WAR DIARY
or
INTELLIGENCE SUMMARY.
(Erase heading not required.)

Instructions regarding War Diaries and Intelligence Summaries are contained in F. S. Regs., Part II. and the Staff Manual respectively. Title pages will be prepared in manuscript.

Place	Date	Hour	Summary of Events and Information	Remarks and references to Appendices
In the Field	4/8/17		All positions improved, continued ammunition received, repaired emplacements. ANGLESEY received a few 77mm shells about 9.30.a.m. and 4.30 p.m. Slight harassing machine gun fire during the night 4/5th. 3 O.R.'s granted leave to U.K.	[sig]
In the Field	5/8/17		Situation generally quiet. Teams continue work of improving emplacements, constructing new emplacements, clearing and improving trenches in vicinity of positions. No. 86491 Pte ROBINSON H. was accidentally shot at 9.0.a.m. by 24998 L/CPL. THILWIND W, when the latter was cleaning a revolver. A little hostile aerial activity about 6.20 p.m. One machine about 3000 ft a/c fired at (50 rounds)	[sig]
	NIGHT 5 & 6 Aug.		S.O.S. Sent up from Dickson on Right, all guns stand to. Gas alarm given. No casualties to gun teams.	
In the Field	6/8/17		Situation generally quiet. Teams in line continue daily work as the improvement of the posts. Guns detailed for A.A. work open fire on hostile planes during the afternoon.	[sig]

Army Form C. 2118.

WAR DIARY
or
INTELLIGENCE SUMMARY.
(Erase heading not required.)

Instructions regarding War Diaries and Intelligence Summaries are contained in F. S. Regs., Part II. and the Staff Manual respectively. Title pages will be prepared in manuscript.

Place	Date	Hour	Summary of Events and Information	Remarks and references to Appendices
In the Field	7/8/17		Situation generally quiet during the day. Posts in vicinity of ABERGELE + ANGLESEY fired on with long range rifle (M.G. fire?). Three bursts of a few minutes duration each delivered between 10.0 p.m. and 12 midnight.	July/
	Night 7 & 8 Aug/17		Guns at ANGLESEY + BRIGHTON engaged in harassing fire. ANGLESEY fired at road at T.12.d.4.1. Searching and Traversing at different times between 10.0 p.m. 4.2 a.m. Rounds fired 1500. BRIGHTON fired at T.24.v.95.85. Traversing 2° R.92.L. and searched inf. 2°. 1000 Rounds fired.	
In The Field	8/8/17		Situation generally quiet. Gun teams in the line continue to improve positions.	July/
	Night 8/9/ Aug/17		Six guns cooperated with the Divisional Artillery & 94th + 97 M.B. in a combined shoot on enemy's front & support lines. See Operation Order No. 30. (Appendix II) Two O.R's granted leave to U.K.	November II
In The Field	9/8/17		Company continued work on line on repair of trenches and construction of emplacements. Situation quiet generally.	July/

Army Form C. 2118.

WAR DIARY
—or—
INTELLIGENCE=SUMMARY.
(Erase heading not required.)

Instructions regarding War Diaries and Intelligence Summaries are contained in F. S. Regs., Part II. and the Staff Manual respectively. Title pages will be prepared in manuscript.

Place	Date	Hour	Summary of Events and Information	Remarks and references to Appendices
In The Field	10/8/17		Work in line continued. Situation quiet. Two O.R's granted leave to U.K.	
In The Field	11/8/17		Work in line continued. Situation quiet. One O.R. reinforcement from BASE DEPÔT.	
In The Field	12/8/17		Work in line continued. Situation quiet generally. Great aerial activity by hostile planes during the day. At 2-50 p.m. gun on A.A. work at BDE. H.Q. fired a belt at an "Albatros" machine, and is supposed to have winged it. This machine was brought down 5 minutes afterwards by one of our "Nieuport" machines. No. 34818 Pte. LEWIS E. wounded by M.G. bullet (Self-inflicted)	
In the Field	13/8/17		CAPTAIN J.E.PRICE left for 1st Army Conference. LIEUT. J.S.WILSON M.C. took over command. Visited line and explained Operation Order No.31 to all officers. Work started at ANGLESEY etc. (See O.O.No.31) Emplacements being built for the combined shoot. Situation extremely quiet. No. 28143 PTE DUFFY R & No. 34498 H/CPL. THIRLWIND W. with all witnesses detailed to attend Court Martial. Wiring continued round posts. Two O.R's granted leave to U.K.	APPENDIX III.

WAR DIARY
or
INTELLIGENCE SUMMARY.

(Erase heading not required.)

Army Form C. 2118.

Instructions regarding War Diaries and Intelligence Summaries are contained in F. S. Regs., Part II. and the Staff Manual respectively. Title pages will be prepared in manuscript.

Place	Date	Hour	Summary of Events and Information	Remarks and references to Appendices
In the Field	14/8/17		Very quiet all day, decrease in artillery activity. Court martial of two cases, all witnesses return. Work continued on the positions for barrage work. One hostile plane came well over our lines at about 10,000 ft. but was afterwards driven off by A.A. fire. Circled about 8.0 p.m. LIEUT. HOWARD after tea weather broke down about 8.0 p.m. Three guns of 'B' Section go forward and take up positions at BRISTOL in accordance with Operation Order No. 31.	
In the Field	15/8/17		Weather fair but showery. About 10.30 a.m. Brigade issued orders that Company Relief must take place on night of 15/8/16 instead of 16/8/17. Thus cancelling Operation Order No. 31. Operation Order No. 32 issued, and arrangements made for relief. Situation quiet. Our artillery active on LENS. Relief started about 9.0 p.m. Relief completed by 2.0 a.m. 1 O.R. killed. 1 O.R. wounded. 2 O.R's granted leave to U.K. Company marched from line to Transport Lines	Appendix IV
	NIGHT 15/16 Aug/17			
In the Field	16/8/17		Company marched from Transport Lines to rest billets at MONT ST-ELOY. Day spent in baths and cleaning up. 1 O.R. rejoined from No. 22 J.C.C.S. Pte DUFFY sentenced as 90 days F.P. No 1 & 40 Pr THILWIND sentenced to 60 day F.P. No 1 by F.G.C.M.	
In the Field	17/8/17		The day was spent in kit inspection, cleaning up of Limbers etc, and also in fatigue party in erecting Horse Standings. Company Train LIEUT. DURRANT granted leave to U.K.	

Army Form C. 2118.

WAR DIARY
or
INTELLIGENCE SUMMARY
(Erase heading not required.)

Instructions regarding War Diaries and Intelligence Summaries are contained in F. S. Regs., Part II. and the Staff Manual respectively. Title pages will be prepared in manuscript.

Place	Date	Hour	Summary of Events and Information	Remarks and references to Appendices
In the Field.	18/8/17.		The day's training included Reveille Drill and Inspection. In the afternoon recreational training and sports were carried out. 5 O.R's left for BASE DEPOT as inefficient. 3 O.R's reinforcements from BASE DEPOT	[signature]
In the Field	19/8/17.		Voluntary Church Parades were held. The day's training programme included Physical Training, Care and cleaning of guns, Gun Drill, Immediate Action and Box Respirator Drill. 2 O.R's granted leave to UK. CAPT. PRICE returned from Conference.	[signature]
In the Field	20/8/17.		The day's training programme included, Physical Training, Gun Drill, Grouping practice on the range, Revolver drill on range, and Limber Drill.	[signature]
In the Field	21/8/17.		The day's training programme included, Physical Training, Immediate Action (Blindfolded and with Box Respirator), Indirect Fire Drill, Squad Drill, Tactical exercises Respirator Drill. 1 O.R. rejoined from No. 6 C.C.S.	[signature]
In the Field	22/8/17.		The day was spent in, Physical Training, Rapid Laying and aiming, Use of clinometer, Sight test and sights, Stoppages (setting and rectifying), and firing Grouping practices and Revolver drill on range. Experiments were also carried out with Belt box carriers on Range. A night march wearing box respirators was also carried out.	[signature]

Army Form C. 2118.

WAR DIARY
or
INTELLIGENCE SUMMARY.
(Erase heading not required.)

Instructions regarding War Diaries and Intelligence Summaries are contained in F. S. Regs., Part II. and the Staff Manual respectively. Title pages will be prepared in manuscript.

Place	Date	Hour	Summary of Events and Information	Remarks and references to Appendices
In the Field.	23/9/17		The programme for the day included, Physical Training, Pack Saddlery, Gun Drill, Squad Drill, Tactical Exercise, Respirator Drill, 2 O.R's granted leave to U.K. LIEUT J.F. WILSON took over command of the company during the absence of CAPT. J.F. PRICE acting D.M.G.O. M.C.	JW/W
In the Field	24/9/17		During the day the Company was divided into two working parties. One party being detailed to repair the Stopbutt on the range and the other party to proceed with the erection of Winter Horse Standings. 1 O.R transferred to No. 166 Machine Gun Coy. 1 O.R. evacuated to No 42 nd C.C.S.	JW/W
In the Field	25/9/17		The days training programme included, Physical Training, Lecture on French Standing Orders, Pack Saddlery, Visual Training Sights, Setting & Laying from Horse position and a lecture on A.A Sights and types of aeroplanes. 1 O.R. granted leave to U.K.	JW/W
In the Field.	26/9/17		Church Parades for all denominations were voluntary. The training programme included Physical Training, Lecture on care and cleaning of Guns, Gun Drill, Immediate Action, Hit Inspector and Respirator Drill.	JW/W

Army Form C. 2118.

WAR DIARY
or
INTELLIGENCE SUMMARY.

(Erase heading not required.)

Instructions regarding War Diaries and Intelligence Summaries are contained in F. S. Regs., Part II. and the Staff Manual respectively. Title pages will be prepared in manuscript.

Place	Date	Hour	Summary of Events and Information	Remarks and references to Appendices
In the Field	27/8/17		Lieut. J.S. WILSON M.C. went into line to make arrangements with O.C. 93rd Machine Gun Company for relief. Operation Order No. 33 issued. Company training programme included Physical Training, Tunnel Belt filling and repairing, Tactical Exercises and Stoppages in Gun Positions. During the afternoon the Company had baths.	Appendix V July
In the Field	28/8/17	6-30 p.m. NIGHT 28/29.	The day was spent in packing limbers and preparing for the line. At 6-30 p.m. the Company moved to LA TARGETTE by light railway. Relief started at 8.4.5. Relief completed at ??. No important incident.	July
In the Field	29/8/17		During the day Company cleaned and strengthened the trenches and positions.	July
In the Field	30/8/17	2 a.m. & 4 a.m.	The guns at BRIGHTON, BASINGSTOKE, ABERGELE, ANGLESEY & BUSHEY carried out a shoot on targets given by B.H.Q. All guns were screened and 5,000 rounds fired. There was no retaliation from hostile artillery. Results unobserved. During the day all positions and trenches in vicinity of positions were cleaned and strengthened.	July

Army Form C. 2118.

WAR DIARY
or
INTELLIGENCE SUMMARY.
(Erase heading not required.)

Instructions regarding War Diaries and Intelligence Summaries are contained in F. S. Regs., Part II. and the Staff Manual respectively. Title pages will be prepared in manuscript.

Place	Date	Hour	Summary of Events and Information	Remarks and references to Appendices
In the Field	3/8/17	2 a.m.	A shoot was carried out by us on targets detailed, 2,000 rounds being fired. Result unobserved.	Sully
		3.45 a.m.	At 3.45 a.m. "S.O.S." call was received by BUSHEY & ANGLESEY, who sent to along by runner to the other guns. Barrage was put up very quickly after, & maintained until 4.50 a.m. All guns repaired fire until S.O.S. call was received, and a total of 21,450 rounds fired. Retaliation until Results unobserved. During the day the Company were occupied by revetting trenches and positions, also relaying trench boards and improving latrines.	J.W.Whelan lt M.G. Corps O/C 96 M.G. Coy

APPENDIX I

SECRET.

94th Machine Gun Company, Operation Order No. 29.

****

1. **INFORMATION.**
   The 94th Machine Gun Company will relieve the 93rd Machine Gun Company in the Right Sector (ACHEVILLE FRONT) on night 2/3rd August 1917.

2. **RELIEFS.**
   The Positions in the Sector will be relieved by the following Sections:-
   ALDERSHOT, AMESBURY - One sub-section of "C" under 2/Lt. Ball.
   SUPPORT LINE.
   AYR, ANGLESEY, ABERGELE, BULFORD, by "A" Section under Lieut. Cant.
   BASINGSTOKE, BRIGHTON by the remaining sub-section of "C"
   2/Lt. Watkins will assume command of the sub-section of "C" in the SUPPORT LINE, and will also take command of BULFORD instead of Lieut. Cant.
   RESERVE LINE.
   BIRMINGHAM, BUSHEY, BALLINCOLLIG and BALMAIN by "D" Section under Lieut. Richardson.
   BRIGADE RESERVE.
   "B" Section under Lieut. Howard and 2/Lt. Philbin. This Section will mount one gun at BRISTOL and will hold one gun ready to move to any position in the line if required. The remaining two guns will be in reserve at the COMPANY HEADQUARTERS.

3. **COMPANY HEADQUARTERS.** will be at BRISTOL. Section Headquarters will be as follows:-
   "C" At ALDERSHOT.
   "A" At ANGLESEY.
   "D" At BUSHEY.
   "B" At BRISTOL.
   2/Lt. Watkins at BRIGHTON.

4. **GUIDES.**
   Guides will be arranged for to meet the teams at the Ration Dump.

5. **KIT.**
   Tripods and belt boxes will be taken over from the teams being relieved. Section Officers will arrange to take in all other kit required.

6. **TIME-TABLE OF MARCH.**
   The Company will parade in fighting order at 6-0.p.m. and will move to the line via NEUVILLE ST. VAAST and LES TILLEULS. The cross-roads at LES TILLEULS will be passed at 9-30.p.m. Sections will move from NEUVILLE ST. VAAST TO LES TILLEULS with intervals of 200 yards between Sections. From LES TILLEULS to Ration Dump the movement forward will be by gun teams and 100 yards between Sections.
   Order of march will be as in paragraph 2.
   On arrival of leading teams at Ration Dump, teams will halt on the ground they are on and will only move up as the preceding team moves away from the limber.

7. **TRANSPORT**
   The Transport Officer will detail two S.A.A. limbers

to take forward the kit. These limbers will report to COMPANY HEADQUARTERS in billets at 5-30.p.m.

        The Transport Officer will send with these limber all available petrol cans to enable the water supply for the next day to be taken in with the teams.

        Animals for the fighting limbers and watercart will be sent at the same time, and these will then move direct to the Transport Lines.

8. RATIONS AND WATER.
        The Officers in commands will make the necessary arrangements for rations and water to go forward with the teams. He will also arrange for the subsequent removal to the Transport Lines of all stores.

9. RELIEF COMPLETE.
        To be sent to COMPANY HEADQUARTERS by the Officer being relieved or by Runner.

10. WORK.
        All necessary work to be put in hand at once after taking over. Section Officers are reminded that gun teams are responsible for the care and maintainence of the trench in which the gun position is situated for a distance of 20 yards on either side.

11. ACKNOWLEDGE.

                                                  a/Lieut ~~Captain~~,
                                        Commanding 94th M.G.Coy.

APPENDIX II

94th M.G. Coy. Operation Order 30
Secret
Copy No 6 War Diary

Map Ref. Fred Hill 1:10000

1. **Operation** — A combined shoot will take place on the enemy position in T 24 b & d & U 19 c in which the Divisional Artillery, 94th M.G. Coy. & Stokes T.M.B. will take part on the night 8/9th August.

2. **M Gun Work**
   Six guns of the 94th M.G. Coy will take part in the shoot. Three guns under Lt Coad will take up positions as follows. T 23 a; 15, 00 T 23 c 10, 60, T 23 c 00, 28.

   Three guns under 2Lt Watkins will take up position as follows. T 29 a, 10, 66, T 29 a 08, 00 T 29 c 10, 70

   Guns will be laid on the bearings & with Q.E. as below

Gun position	Grid Bearing	Range to Target	Q.E. used	Range & F.T.		Clearance required		Clearance given		Target
				Nearer	Farthest	Yds		Yds		
T 23 a 15, 00	102°30'	2150	4°47'	400	1550	11	39	31.7	64	U
T 23 c 10, 60	95°	2100	4°30'	800	1500	17	37	52.3	59	19 C
T 23 c 00 28	92°	2150	4°47'	850	1550	18	39	59.5	69.3	30,20
T 29 a 10, 66	87°	2100	4°30'	800	1500	17	37	52.3	59	to
T 29 a 08, 00	78°30'	2200	5°4'	500	1500	11	37	40.7	73.7	38,00
T 29 c 10, 70	74°30'	2300	5°43'	500	1400	11	34	46.3	91	

All guns will traverse 2° R. & L. of Zeroline & will search 1° up.

3. **Rate of fire** — All guns will fire 1 belt in the 1st minute. Afterwards the rate will be reduced to about 55 rounds per minute for the remainder of the time of firing.

4. **Zero** — Zero will be at 2.30 am & fire will be maintained until Zero + 15 minutes. Zero will be taken from the Artillery.

5. **S.O.S. Lines** — All guns will have S.O.S. lines laid on from the positions detailed above so that they can switch on if required.

6. **Acknowledge.**

Copies issued to Clor concerned
9.30 pm 8/8/17

J E Price Capt
OC 94th

APPENDIX III   COPY No. 11

No. 94 M.G. Coy. Operation Order No. 31.

SECRET.   Map Ref. (Special map of Acheville Sector)

1. INFORMATION.

The 31st Division will carry out a combined shoot on the enemy's position on a date to be notified later, in which the Special Coy R.E (E Coy.) 31st Div. Artillery and the 31st Div. Machine Guns will take part.

2. 94th M.G. COY'S TASK.

The 94th M.G. Coy. will occupy positions and engage targets using the elevation & direction according to the following table:

No. of Guns	Coordinate of Gun Position	Guns to Occupy the Positions	Officer to Command the Guns	Co-ordinate of Targets to Engage	Q.E. in Degrees & Minutes	Direction Grid Bearings	Traverse	Search Up
1A	T28d 9,4	BRIGHTON	2/Lt. WATKINS	T24b 95,82	7° 6'	53°	2° on each side of Direction LINE.	1° 30'
1	T28b 90,15	BASINGSTOKE		T24b 47,55	5° 10'	56°		2° -
2B	T28b 95,48	BRISTOL & 1 GUN of "B" from RESERVE	LIEUT. HOWARD 2/Lt. PHILBIN	T18c 90.30	3° 50'	50°		2° -
2C	T28b 20.90	BALLINCOLLIG & BALHAM	OFFICER DETAILED BY D.M.G.O.	T18c 84.73	5° 29'	51°		1° - 30'
2D	T22d 10,20	BIRMINGHAM & BUSHEY	LT. RICHARDSON	T18a 58.60	6° 10'	45°		2° -
2E	T22d 90,40	BULFORD & ABERGELE	OFFICER DETAILED BY D.M.G.O	T18d 85.86	5° 38'	43°		2° -
2F	T22d 80,40	1 Sub. Section of "B" FROM RESERVE	2/Lt. PHILBIN	T18b 61.02	5° 20'	58°		—
2G	T22b 8,1	ANGLESEY & AYR	LIEUT. CANT	T24d 87.92	4° 16'	93°		2° -
1H	T29b 40,54	AMESBURY	2/Lt BALL	V19c 31.94	2° 15'	62°		2° -

3. All guns will be in position and ready to fire by 10-0 p.m. on Z day.

4. RATE OF FIRE.

At zero + 5 minutes all guns will open intense fire and will continue until each gun has expended 10 belts of ammunition.

5. The Officer commanding each Sub. Section will check the Q.E & direction before firing commences & will be responsible that these are maintained correctly throughout.

6. The flash of all guns will be ~~corrected~~ concealed by the use of canvas screens.

7. Condensers will be attached and spare water will be taken with each gun.

8. On completion of operations, all guns will be returned to their original positions & relaid on their S.O.S lines & expended belts refilled. Guns to be cleaned at once before relaying on S.O.S lines.

9. A report on the firing will be submitted to COMPANY H.Qrs. with the morning reports.

10. Officers will arrange for the collection & return of fired cases to COMPANY dump at COMPANY H.Q.

11. Please acknowledge.

Issued at 3.0 p.m. 13/9/17.

[signature]
Lieut. for
O.C. 94th M.G.Coy.

COPIES TO.
1. O.C. Company
2. 2/in Command
3. Lieut. Richardson
4. " Howard
5. " Cant.
6. 2/Lieut. Ball
7. 2/Lieut. Watkins
8} To Officers detailed
9} by D.M.G.O.
10. D.M.G.O.
11} War Diary
12}
13. File.

APPENDIX IV

SECRET. No. 94 M.G. Coy. Operation Order No 32.

Copy no 11

1. INFORMATION.
The 94th M.G. COMPANY will be relieved by the 93rd M.G. COMPANY in the Right Sector to-night the 15/16th.

2. GUIDES. for all guns will be at BRISTOL by 9-45 p.m. One guide will be detailed by H.Q at 9.0 p.m. to meet the 93rd COMPANY and convey them down trench to BRISTOL

3. All tripods, ammunition, belt boxes. S.A.A. bombs. very pistols, very lights and reserve supply of water will be handed over on relief and signed receipts obtained for same. These signed receipts to be handed in at ADVANCED H.Q.

4. LIEUT. HOWARD will hand over ADVANCED COY. H.Q to O.C. No. 93 COMPANY, and get any receipts from him.

5. Signallers will hand over positions but no telephones to the in-coming Company

6. TRANSPORT. (a) One limber will be available for "B" & "D" SECTIONS and will report to LIEUT. HOWARD at BRISTOL at 10-30 p.m.

(b) One limber will be available for "A" & "C" SECTIONS and will report to LIEUT. CANT at BULFORD at 11-0 p.m.

(c) "B" SECTION will supply brakesman for "(a)", "A" SECTION will supply one brakesman for "(b)"

7. All guns emplacements & vicinity to be handed over scrupulously clean.

8. All co-ordinates, bearings & Q.E's to be handed over by Officers.

9. All new gun positions, aiming posts for barrage positions to be handed over.

LIEUT. CANT   6 positions
  " RICHARDSON 4   "
2/LT. PHILBIN   2   "
LIEUT. HOWARD   2   "
2/LT. BALL   1   "

10. Each Section as it comes out will report relief completed at THELUS CAVE and then march independently to TRANSPORT LINES where a

OPERATION ORDER NO. 32.
SHEET 2.   COPY No. 11

hot meal will be served. A guide will be detailed from H.Q. to conduct ADVANCED H.Q. & 2/LT. BALL to COMPANY H.Q.

11. ACKNOWLEDGE.

                                                     Lieut.
                                      a/O.C. 94th M.G.COY.

COPIES TO

1. O.C. COMPANY.
2. LIEUT. HOWARD
3. LIEUT. DURRANT.
4.   "   RICHARDSON.
5.   "   CANT
6. 2/LT. WATKINS
7.   "   BALL
8.   "   PHILBIN.
9. D.M.G.O.
10. O.C. 93rd COMPANY.
11. } WAR
12. } DIARY.
13. FILE.

APPENDIX V

Copy No. 10

SECRET.

94th Machine Gun Company, Operation Order No. 33.

****

1. **INFORMATION.**
   The 94th Machine Gun Company will relieve the 93rd Machine Gun Company in the Right Sector (ACHEVILLE FRONT) on the night 28th/29th August 1917.

2. **RELIEFS.**
   The positions in the Sector will be relieved by the following Sections:-
   ALDERSHOT, AMESBURY - One Sub-Section of "B" under 2/Lt. W.H.Philbin.
   SUPPORT LINE.
   AYR, ANGLESEY, ABERGELE and BULFORD by "D" Section under Lieut.G.E Richardson.
   BASINGSTOKE and BRIGHTON by the remaining Sub-Section of "B".
   2/Lt. Watkins will assume command of the Sub-Section of "B" in the SUPPORT LINE, and will also take command of BULFORD.
   RESERVE LINE.
   BIRMINGHAM, BUSHEY, BALLINCOLLIG and BALMAIN by "A" Section under Lieut. Cant.
   BRIGADE RESERVE.
   "C" Section under 2/Lt. Ball. This Section will mount one gun at BRISTOL and will hold one gun ready to move to any position in the line if required.

3. **COMPANY HEADQUARTERS** will be at THELUS CAVES, Section Headquarters will be as follow:-
   "B" AT ALDERSHOT.
   "D" At ANGLESEY.
   "A" At BUSHEY.
   "C" At BRISTOL.
   2/Lt. Watkins at BRIGHTON.

4. **GUIDES.**
   Guides will be arranged to meet the teams at BRISTOL.

5. **KIT.**
   Tripods and belt boxes will be taken over from the teams being relieved. Section Officers will arrange to take in all other kit required.

6. **TIME-TABLE OF MARCH.**
   The Company will parade in Fighting Order ready to move off at 6-0 p.m. The Cross-roads at LA TARGETTE to be passed at 8-0 p.m. Sections will proceed to BRISTOL under Sections Officers, keeping a distance of 200 yards between each Section.
   Order of March will be as in paragraph 2.

7. **TRANSPORT.**
   The Transport Officer will detail two S.A.A. limbers to take forward the kit. These limbers will report to COMPANY HEADQUARTERS in billets at 5-30 p.m.
   The Transport Officer will send with these limbers all available petrol cans to enable the water supply for the next day to be taken in with the teams.
   Animals for the fighting limbers and watercart will be sent at the same time, and these will then move direct to the Transport lines.
   One limber will also be sent for Headquarters gear.

8. **RATIONS AND WATER.**
   The 2nd-in-Command will make the necessary arrangements for rations and water to go forward with the teams.
   The C.Q.M.S. will arrange for subsequent removal to the Transport Lines of all stores.

-1-

9. **RELIEF COMPLETE.**
   To be sent to COMPANY HEADQUARTERS by the Officer being relieved or by Runner.

10. **WORK.**
    All necessary work to be put in hand at once after taking over. Section Officers are reminded that gun teams are responsible for the care and maintainence of the trench in which the gun position is situated for a distance of 20 yards on either side.

11. **HANDING OVER SLIPS.**
    All handing-over slips to be at COMPANY HEADQUARTERS on morning after relief.

12. Special care has to be taken in Storage of Trench Stores.

13. **ACKNOWLEDGE.**

                                            W.Wilson
                                            Lieut.
                                    A/O.C. 94th Machine Gun Company.

Copy No. 1. Lieut. J.S.Wilson, MC.
       2.   "   T.Howard.
       3.   "   A.M.Cant.
       4.   "   O.E.Richardson.
       5. Transport Officer.
       6. 2/Lt. G.H.S.Watkins.
       7.   "   C.H.Ball.
       8.   "   W.M.Philbin.
       9. D.M.O.O.
      10. War Diary.
      11.   "   "
      12. O.C. 93rd M.G.Coy.
      13. File.

Issued 28/8/17.

-2-

Confidential

Volume XX¹

Vol 17

War Diary.

31st Division.

94th Machine Gun Company

September 1917.

WAR DIARY or INTELLIGENCE SUMMARY

Army Form C. 2118.

Place	Date	Hour	Summary of Events and Information	Remarks and references to Appendices
In the Field	1/9/17		Company still in the line. LIEUT. WILSON goes round the line to make arrangements regarding further shoots.	J.E.P. Capt.
"	NIGHT 1/2 Sept 1917		A Shoot was carried out by the guns at ANGLESEY, ABERGELE, BRIGHTON & BASINGSTOKE. Targets engaged were Nos. 24A on DIV ORDER "SG" 13/66. 4000 rounds were fired, but results were unobserved.	J.E.P. Capt.
"	2/9/17		LIEUT. HOWARD went round the line to inspect the gun positions and the work done. 4 O.R's reinforcements arrived from Base Depot.	J.E.P. Capt.
"	NIGHT 2/3 Sept 1917		Another shoot was carried out by the guns at BALLINCOLLIG, BALHAM and BIRMINGHAM, on indirect fire targets. The guns at AYR and ANGLESEY engaged targets detailed on D.M.G.O/30/F. and 7,150 rounds were fired. A.A. gun at BIRMINGHAM fired 300 rounds on enemy aircraft.	J.E.P. Capt.
"	3/9/17		Work in line continued. CAPT. J.E. PRICE returned from D.H.Q. and takes over command of the Company. Operation Order No.34 issued for relief of seven guns by 15th CANADIAN M.G.C. One O.R. evacuated sick to 22 F.C.C.G. One O.R. granted leave to U.K.	Appendix J.E.P. Capt.
"	4/9/17		CAPT. J.E. PRICE visited the line. Work by the Company was carried out as usual.	J.E.P. Capt.

Army Form C. 2118.

WAR DIARY
or
INTELLIGENCE SUMMARY.
(Erase heading not required.)

Instructions regarding War Diaries and Intelligence Summaries are contained in F. S. Regs., Part II. and the Staff Manual respectively. Title pages will be prepared in manuscript.

Place	Date	Hour	Summary of Events and Information	Remarks and references to Appendices
In the field	NIGHT 4/5th Sept.	9.30pm 11.15pm	Relief of seven guns by 16th Canadian M.G. Coy. started. Relief completed without incident.	J.B.L Cpt
"	5/9/17		CAPT. J.E. PRICE goes out to 95th C.C.S. area and reviews gun positions. He also completes details for relief of the 95th Machine Gun Coy. Operation Order No. 35 issued. One O.R. evacuated to No 22 C.C.S.	Appendix IV J.B.L Cpt
"	6/9/17		Situation in line generally quiet. Work in trenches and emplacements continued. Trenches noted.	J.B.L Cpt
"	NIGHT 6/7th Sept.	8pm 11-32	Relief of 95th M.G. Company and inter company relief commenced. Relief completed without incident.	J.B.L Cpt
"	7/9/17		New gun positions inspected in line, general work in trench improvements. Two guns fired 2,500 rounds harassing fire during the night.	J.B.L Cpt
"	8/9/17		Actual trench work in line. Coulson at ARLEUX LOOP constantly shelled during the night. C.O. goes with D.M.G.O. to arrange new Defence Scheme.	J.B.L Cpt

Army Form C. 2118.

WAR DIARY
or
INTELLIGENCE SUMMARY.
(Erase heading not required.)

Instructions regarding War Diaries and Intelligence
Summaries are contained in F. S. Regs., Part II.
and the Staff Manual respectively. Title pages
will be prepared in manuscript.

Place	Date	Hour	Summary of Events and Information	Remarks and references to Appendices
In the field	9/9/17		Situation generally quiet except around ARLEUX LOOP. All posts looked at and emplacement and usual trench repairs. Emplacements prepared for combined shoot and conjunction with gas projectors. 90,000 rounds of S.A.A. carried to new positions during the night. Enemy air aircraft too high to engage. Operation Order No 36 issued for combined shoot.	J.T.L. Cpt Appendix IV
In the field	10/9/17		Situation quiet generally. O.C. 243 M.G. Coy taken round the line to see positions for relief. Order for relief by 243rd M.G. Coy received. Operation Order No. 34 issued to carry this out. One O.R. granted leave to U.K.	J.T.L. Cpt Appendix V
In the field	11/9/17	10 p.m.	Situation quiet generally. Usual cleaning and repairing of trenches carried out.	J.T.L. Cpt
	11/12 Sept 17	Night 8.0 pm to 1-30am	Relief by 243rd M.G. Coy started. Relief completed without incident. Company now back by sections to jeff SPRINGVALE CAMP.	J.T.L. Cpt

Army Form C. 2118.

WAR DIARY
or
INTELLIGENCE SUMMARY
(Erase heading not required.)

Place	Date	Hour	Summary of Events and Information	Remarks and references to Appendices
In the Field	12/9/17		After a short rest the Company had baths and the rest of the day was spent in the general cleaning up of gun kit and personal kit.	JSL CyR
"	13/9/17		During the morning Section Officers inspected the Section personal kit. A party was also detailed for work on the Winter Horse Standings. The C.O. gave the Section Officers a lecture on Barrage Drill, and the remainder of the morning was spent on the continuation of the cleaning of kit and ammunition etc. 5 O.R. reinforcements arrived from Base Depôt.	JSL CyR
"	14/9/17		The training programme for the day included :- Infantry Drill, Physical Drill, Gun Drill, Immediate Action, and Belt-filling competition. The afternoon was devoted to Recreational Training. During the morning a party was detailed for the work on the erection of Winter Horse Standings.	JSL CyR
"	15/9/17		During the morning all Iron Rations, Steel Helmets, Box Respirators and P.H. Helmets were inspected. The training programme included Infantry Drill, Immediate Action, Rapid Laying and use of Reference Objects, and cleaning guns and ammunition.	JSL CyR

WAR DIARY
or
INTELLIGENCE SUMMARY.
(Erase heading not required.)

Army Form C. 2118.

Place	Date	Hour	Summary of Events and Information	Remarks and references to Appendices
In the field	16/9/17		Church Service for all denominations were arranged for the morning and the time not occupied by Church Service was spent in cleaning guns and equipment. During the afternoon the Company moved from Gwynoak Camp to Ecuke West Camp. 1 O.R. joined from U.K.	JSP / Cpe
-do-	17/9/17		The training carried out during the day included Infantry Drill, Barrage Drill, Belt-filling, Rapid aiming and elevating drill. A party had details for work on Winter Horse Standings. LIEUTS. HOWARD & CANT and 2/LT. BALL proceeded to 31st DIVNL. ARTILLERY for course of instruction. One O.R. reinforcement joined from No. 22 C.C.S.	JSP / Cpe
-do-	18/9/17		For the day 3 O. and 23 O.Rs were granted leave to BETHUNE, into ceeding by motor bus. The remainder of the Company were detailed to work on Winter Horse Standings.	JSP / Cpe
-do-	19/9/17		The days training programme included Infantry Drill & Barrage Drill. A party was also detailed for work on Winter Horse Standings.	JSP / Cpe
-do-	20/9/17		The day was occupied by Company Drill, Belt-filling by hand and machine, Barrage Drill, Explanation of Barrage Chart and Barrage fire and use of Lingfling micro. LIEUTS. HOWARD & CANT & 2/LT. BALL returned from 3rd DIVNL. ARTILLERY.	JSP / Cpe

Army Form C. 2118.

WAR DIARY
or
INTELLIGENCE SUMMARY.
(Erase heading not required.)

Instructions regarding War Diaries and Intelligence Summaries are contained in F. S. Regs., Part II. and the Staff Manual respectively. Title pages will be prepared in manuscript.

Place	Date	Hour	Summary of Events and Information	Remarks and references to Appendices
In the field	21/9/17		The starting programme for the day included Company Drill, Construction of Shell hole machine Gun Emplacements and Jerkin Pack work. One O.R. was evacuated to No 42 C.C.S.	JRP Cpr
-do-	22/9/17		The day was spent in the completion and also a full inspection of work on Shell hole emplacements, and also a full inspection of the work. Baths were also provided for the Company. CAPT. J.E PRICE visited O.C. 243 M.G.Coy and made arrangements for relief.	JRP Cpr
-do-	23/9/17		Church Service for all denominations were arranged for the morning. Operation Order No 38 for relief of 243 M.G.Coy issued. See Appendix I. Afternoon all kit was packed ready for going in the line.	JRP Cpr
		5.30 pm	Company Parade in Fighting Order and move to line One O.R. granted leave to U.K.	JRP Cpr

Army Form C. 2118.

WAR DIARY
or
INTELLIGENCE SUMMARY.
(Erase heading not required.)

Instructions regarding War Diaries and Intelligence Summaries are contained in F. S. Regs., Part II. and the Staff Manual respectively. Title pages will be prepared in manuscript.

Place	Date	Hour	Summary of Events and Information	Remarks and references to Appendices
In the Field	NIGHT 23/24 Sept	4.30pm 11.0pm	Relief of 243rd M.G.Coy on the FRESNOY-ACHEVILLE SECTOR commenced. Relief completed. Situation generally quiet. Hostile M.G. active against ARLEUX LOOP.	JFLCoy
-do-	24/9/17		Situation generally quiet. Our Machine Guns engaged enemy aeroplanes during the day. 1 O.R. leaves for UK as candidate for Commission. 2 O.R. evacuated to 22nd C.C.S.	JFCoy
-do-	NIGHT 24/25 Sept		Hostile Trench Mortar fired into vicinity of ALDERSHOT Gun teams prepared alternative positions for co-operation in gas projection	JFLCoy
-do-	25/9/17		Company work on improvement of trench and emplacements. Anti-aircraft machine Guns active against hostile air craft. Enemy shelled heavily MONTREAL TRENCH in vicinity of new Gun positions. One O.R. struck off our strength and attached to XIII Corps School.	JFLCoy

Army Form C. 2118.

WAR DIARY
or
INTELLIGENCE SUMMARY.
(Erase heading not required.)

Instructions regarding War Diaries and Intelligence Summaries are contained in F.S. Regs., Part II. and the Staff Manual respectively. Title pages will be prepared in manuscript.

Place	Date	Hour	Summary of Events and Information	Remarks and references to Appendices
In the Field.	NIGHT 25/26 Sept.		Our machine guns fired on specially selected targets during the night. 3,000 rounds were fired.	J.S.L. Cpt.
-do-	26/9/17		Company continue the usual work in the trenches. Hostile aircraft engaged during the day.	J.S.L. Cpt.
-do-	NIGHT 26/9/17		Usual harassing fire on enemy approaches and tracks. Rounds fired 5,000. Enemy M.G. located by its flash, and shooted out of action.	J.S.L. Cpt.
-do-	27/9/17		1st usual report. Work on line during day and anti-aircraft work.	J.S.L. Cpt.
-do-	NIGHT 27/28 Sept.		Our Machine Guns engaged special targets. Rounds fired 20,000. Four guns made into a battery and moved up to O.C. Battalion in front line who directed fire on various object as required. This worked splendidly. One French mortar and one machine gun being silenced in this way.	J.S.L. Cpt.
-do-	28/9/17.		Usual repair work in line. Situation generally quiet. Enemy registered on TRIUMPH TRENCH by ALDERSHOT. Anti-aircraft gun fired 500 rounds.	J.K. Cpt.

Army Form C. 2118.

WAR DIARY
or
INTELLIGENCE SUMMARY
(Erase heading not required.)

Place	Date	Hour	Summary of Events and Information	Remarks and references to Appendices
In the field	29/9/17		Usual repair work in the line. Situation generally quiet.	[signature]
-do-	NIGHT 29/30 Sept.		Our guns engaged in harassing fire during the night, 5000 rounds were fired.	[signature]
-do-	30/9/17		Usual repair work in the line. Situation generally quiet.	[signature]
		noon	Enemy shelled gas Sector with gas shells 3 O.R's wounded gas.	[signature]

SECRET.

Appendix I

Copy No. 11

The 94th Machine Gun Company - Operation Order No. 54.

****

1. INFORMATION.

    Seven guns of the 94th Machine Gun Company, namely AYR, ANGLESEY, ABERGELE, BALLINCOLLIG, BALHAM, BUSHEY and BIRMINGHAM, will be relieved by the 15th Canadian Machine Gun Company on the Night 4th/5th September.

2. GUIDES.

    Guides for each of the above-mentioned gun teams will be at BRISTOL at 9-30 p.m. where they will conduct the gun teams to their respective positions. 2/Lt. G. H. Ball will be in charge of guides.

3. HANDING OVER.

    All maps except ~~FOOTHILL~~ FOOTHILL, Aiming Posts, S.O.S. Scheme, Defence Scheme, Belt Boxes, S.A.A., Very Lights, Bombs, and positions will be handed over and receipts obtained.

4. Gun teams when relieved will go to the positions as shewn in the following table.

    "A" Section to BRISTOL.
    AYR to BULFORD.
    ANGLESEY to BASINGSTOKE.
    ABERGELE to BRIGHTON.

5. 2/Lt. G.N.B.Watkins will arrange to draw "D" Sections' Rations. 2/Lt. G.H.Ball will take charge of "A" Sections' rations.

6. All empty petrol cans will be taken to BRISTOL. No Anti-Aircraft Mountings to be handed over.

7. All positions to be clean.

8. Handing-over slips to be sent on relief to 2/Lt.G.H.Ball, who will send them immediately to Company Headquarters.

9. Acknowledge.

                                          Captain,
Copies to:-   Commanding 94th Machine Gun Coy.
    1. O.C. Company.
    2. 2nd in-Command.
    3. Lieut. G.E.Richardson.
    4. Lieut. T. Howard.
    5. Lieut. A.M.Cant.
    6. 2/Lt. G.H.Ball.
    7. 2/Lt. G.N.B.Watkins.
    8. 2/Lt. W.M.Philbin.
    9. O.C. 15th Canadian M.G.Coy.
    10. D.M.G.O.
    11. War Diary.
    12. War Diary.
    13. File.

Appendix II

SECRET.   Copy No. 11

The 94th Machine Gun Company.

Operation Order No. 35.

==*=*=*=*=*=*=*=*

1. **INFORMATION.**

    Owing to certain readjustments of the line held by the Division, the following reliefs and readjustments will take place.

2. **RELIEFS.**

    The 94th Machine Gun Company will relieve certain guns of the 95th Machine Gun Company in the ARLEUX and SEVERN ALLEY (FRESNOY) SECTOR as follows:-

    "C" Section under 2/Lt. C.H.Ball will take over the following positions:- 1 A and 2 RED LINE, 2 & 3 in PINNER TRENCH.
    "A" Section under Lieut. A.M.Cant will take over Nos. 19, 19, 23 and 24.
    "D" Section under Lieut Howard will take over Brigade positions No. 7 and 8.

3. **INTER-COMPANY RELIEFS.**

    The following inter-Company relief will take place in consequence of moves in para. 2.

    1 Sub-Section of "D" Lieut. Richardson to relieve "B" Section at BASINGSTOKE and BRIGHTON.

    1 gun detached of "D" Section to relieve one gun detached of "C" Section at BRISTOL.

    The line BULFORD, BASINGSTOKE, BRIGHTON, BRISTOL will be commanded by Lt. Richardson with 2/Lt Watkins as Sub-Section Officer.

4. **RECONNAISSANCE OF POSITIONS.**

    Lieut. Cant and 2/Lt. Ball will report to COMPANY HEADQUARTERS 95th Machine Gun Company at 8-0 P.M. 5th inst. to be shewn over the portion of the line they will take over.

    Lieut. Howard will meet Lieut. Bristow, 95th M.G.Coy at junction of NEW HUDSON and BRANDON TRENCH at 10-0 a.m. 5th inst. to be shown the gun positions he will take over.

5. **TIME OF RELIEF.**

    All movements will be conducted at such a time as will permit the respective sections reaching their new positions at 8 p.m.

6. **TAKING OVER.**

    Belt boxes, water tins and the usual trench stores will be taken over and receipts given.

7. **FIRE ORDERS.**

    Fire orders and lines of fire will be taken over and carried out pending further orders.

    Completion of reliefs will be transmitted to COMPANY HEADQUARTERS by the quickest means available, using the Company Code.

8. **HEADQUARTERS.**

    COMPANY HEADQUARTERS will close at THELUS CAVE at 4 p.m. and will open at the NEW COMPANY HEADQUARTERS, No. 2 Gun position RED LINE at 6 p.m.

    Section Headquarters will be as follows:-
    "C" At COMPANY HEADQUARTERS.
    "D" At BRIGHTON.
    "A" To be notified later.
    "B" At Nos. 7 & 8 gun position (T 30 a 92.26.)

9. **WORK.**

    All necessary work to be put in hand immediately after taking over.

-1-

10. TRANSPORT.

Rations will be brought forward on two half limbers. That for "D" & "A" Sections will proceed up VANCOUVER ROAD and on to BULFORD and LEWIS DUMP. Rations for COMPANY HEADQUARTERS and "C" Section will be dumped at RED LINE. That for "A" Section at point where ARLEUX LOOP TRENCH crosses WILLERVAL-ARLEUX ROAD. Orderlies must be waiting at these points and limbers must not be delayed.

11. CORRECTIONS.

To para. 4 add "One man from each gun team will be conducted by the Section Officers orderlies to their new gun positions at 5-0 p.m. on 6th inst. These men will afterwards act as guides to the other teams."

12. ACKNOWLEDGE.

J.E.Price

Capt.
Commanding 94th Machine Gun Company.

Copies to:-
1. O.C. "A" Section.
2. O.C. "B" Section.
3. O.C. "C" Section.
4. O.C. "D" Section.
5. Transport Officer.
6. O.C.
7. 2nd in-Command.
8. O.C. 95th M.G.Coy.
9. D.M.G.O.
10. War Diary.
11. War Diary.
12. File.

SECRET Appendix III

94th M.G. Coy. Operation Order No 36.

No. 8 Copy

1. **Information.**
    Gas will be projected by the Special Coy R.E. from this Divisional front on a date and time to be notified later. Artillery and M. guns will co-operate by firing on selected areas in conjunction with the gas projection.

2. **M.G TASK** The guns of the 94th MG Coy will take part by firing on selected areas as shown in Fire Direction table attached. All guns will be in position and ready for action 1 hour before zero.

3. **FLASH SCREENS** will be used and Group Commanders will make the necessary arrangements for water supply and belt filling. One petrol tin full of water will be ready at each gun position.

4. **DEPRESSION STOPS** will be used and limits of traverse accurately fixed for each gun. Group commanders will check the laying of each gun before fire is opened.

5. On **COMPLETION** of **OPERATIONS**, guns will be moved back to their battle positions if degree of hostile visibility permits and relaid on S.O.S. Lines

6. **ALL REPORTS.** to be sent to Coy Hd.Qrs as soon as possible on conclusion of firing.

7. **CODE** The following code words

No 94 M.G. Coy. Operation Order No 36 Ctd.   (2)

7 (Ctd.) will be used.

Gas WILL be projected — WHITE
 "   WILL NOT "   — BLACK
WIND SUITABLE   — RED
 "   UNSUITABLE   — GREEN
PROJECTION POSTPONED   — YELLOW
GAS PROJECTED   — BLUE.

No references will be made to this matter on the TELEPHONE and the only reference to the operation will be by use of one of above colour references.

8/ SYNCHRONISATION. Watches will be synchronised by the watch brought to positions by 2/LT. BALL. NO synchronisation will be given or asked for on the TELEPHONE

9/ GROUP COMMANDERS will ensure that belts are refilled on conclusion of operations.

10/ ACKNOWLEDGE.

Issued at 7 p.m. 9/4/17.   J. Pine Capt.
                                        O.C. 94 M.G. Coy

Copies to. 1. LT. CANT
           2. " HOWARD
           3. " RICHARDSON
           4. 2/LT WATKINS
           5. " BALL
           6. O.C
           7. DMGO.
           8 & 9. WAR DIARY
           10. FILE.

FIRE DIRECTION TABLE. (ATTACHED)

No of Coop	No of GUNS	Co-ordinate gun Position	Co-ordinate of Target	RANGE	GRID BEARING	SEARCHING	TRAVERSING	GROUP COMMANDERS
1.	2.	T.29 c 2,3	T.18 c 8,7	2600	31°	10' DOWN for each 80' traverse	5° RIGHT & REVERSE	LT. CANT
		"	T.24 b 3,9	2600	41°	10' UP for each 80' traverse	5° LEFT " "	
2.	4. Left gun directing	DIRECTING GUN T.28 b 9,1, 20' interval between guns	T.18 c 6,0 to T.18 d 85,20	2700	L.G. 43° 45° 47° 48°30'	DEPRESS 30' at end of each 3° traverse. Repeat each time traversing is done to the RIGHT till 150' depression has been given	EACH gun 3° RIGHT & reverse, No searching to take place when traversing to the Left	2/LT BALL LT RICHARDSON
3.	2.	T.28 b.9.8	T.18 b.6.0	2400	R.G. 49° 46° 43'	DEPRESS 1° 20' for each Elevate 1 deg. traversed	R. Gun. 6° LEFT, L. Gun 6° RIGHT	LT WATKINS
4.	2.	T.29 d 1,6 B5 a 3.5,2.5	T.18 d 85,15 T.24 b 33,86	2200 2700	39° 36°	— —	2° LEFT & REVERSE 2° RIGHT " "	LT HOWARD CPL DONNING

Artillery will open zero plus 1 minute. M.G open as in table opposite

from zero	To zero	Rate of Fire
+5'	+10'	Intense
+10'	+20'	100 rds per minute (50 at commencement of each ½ minute)
+20'	+30'	50 " "
+30'	+60'	25 " "
+60'	+90'	No firing
+90'	+95'	Intense
+95'	+120'	50 rds per minute.

Appendix IV

94th M.G Coy Operation Order No 37

Copy No 11.

1) INFORMATION

The 94th M.G. Coy will be relieved by the 43rd M.G Coy on the night of Sept 11/12, 1917.

2) ARRANGEMENTS FOR RELIEF

A guide will be detailed by Coy Hd Qrs to meet the relieving Coy at a place to be decided between the Company Commanders. This guide will conduct the relief to Coy Hd Qrs. Guides from 'A' Section, (less guide from 4Cpl Harrold's team) will report at Coy Hd Qrs at 8 pm to conduct the relieving teams to their positions. Guides from B & D Sections + 1 guide from 4Cpl Harrold's team will report at BRISTOL at 8 pm. Guides will also be detailed to conduct relieving officers to respective Section Hd Qrs.

3) HANDING OVER

Tripods, belt boxes and all trench stores will be handed over and receipts obtained. Attention is directed to the unsatisfactory compilation of handing over slips and greater care must be taken in checking and recording. Signatures must be obtained from the relieving commanders for these stores. Section Officers will hand over maps, Operation Order No 36 if the subject of that order is still pending and carefully explain arrangements made.

94th M.G. Coy Operation Order No 37 (Ctd) 2

1/ INFORMATION.   Copy No 11

3/ CTD   LIEUT. CANT will arrange to hand over from the Hd Qrs at T 29 d 1,6 which will be the Hd Qrs of the officer who relieves him. LIEUT HOWARD will arrange to hand over his command from ALDERSHOT which will be the Hd Qrs of the officer commanding the front system of guns.

Work in progress and work to be put in hand will be explained and handed over, a copy being sent to Coy Hd Qrs by 5 p.m. 11th Sept 1917.

4/ NAMES OF GUN POSITIONS.

The posts now known by numbers will be given names as follows.

No 7 & 8 B.to Guns will be called AVON & ANDOVER
No 24 GUN (CPL HARROLD'S POSITION) will be called CARLISLE
" 23 "   (Sgt MOORE'S   ") "   "   "   CHESTER
" 19 "   (L/CPL SURGENOR'S   ") "   "   "   CREWE
" 18 "   (CPL DUNNING'S   ") "   "   "   CORK
" 8 "   (Sgt SPENCER'S   ") "   "   "   DOVER
" 4 "   (L/CPL CLOUGH'S   ") "   "   "   DEAL
" 1A "   (CPL HOLT'S   ") "   "   "   DURHAM
" 2 "   (L/CPL TAYLOR'S   ") "   "   "   DORSET

The names already given to other positions in the sector will be retained.

These names will be handed over to the relieving teams and their positions explained.

94th M.G. Coy. Operation Order No 37. CTD.   (3)

5/. TRANSPORT   Copy No 11

The T. Officer will detail a limber to be at BRIGHTON at 12MN. This limber will pick up all guns of D, B and the gun from CARLISLE. A limber will also be detailed to be at point on ALLEUX – WILLERVAL road opposite CORK (Cpl DOWNING's team) at 11 p.m to pick up A & C section and Hd Qrs stores. In the event of any relief being completed before arrival of limbers Section Officers will detail one man from each gun team to remain at the halting places of the limbers to load up his team's equipment. Limbers must on no account be kept waiting about. Section Officers will ensure that time is not lost in handing over.

One N.C.O per section will be detailed to see that limbers are correctly loaded. The party will then follow limber to camp at 100ˣ interval behind limber.

6/. MOVEMENT TO CAMP

On conclusion of relief Section Officers will conduct their sections back to camp at ECURIE WOOD, (d (A 21 d) detaching one N.C.O to report to Company Hd Qrs

94th M G Coy Operation Order No 37 CTD

6) CTD   Copy No 11
with the landing over ships.

7) ACKNOWLEDGE

                            [signature] Capt
                    O.C. 94th M.G. Coy

Copies to:

1. OC "A" Section
2. " "B" "
3. " "C" "
4. " "D" "
5. TRANSPORT OFFICER
6. 2nd IN COMMAND
7. O.C. No 243 MG Coy
8. DMGO
9. OC COY
10. } WAR DIARY
11. }
12. FILE

SECRET.   Copy No. 10

Appendix IV.

94th MACHINE GUN COMPANY, OPERATION ORDER No.58.

1. **INFORMATION.**

    The 94th Machine Gun Company will relieve the 243rd Machine Gun Company in the ACHEVILLE-FRESNOY Sector on night 23/24th September 1917.

2. **DISTRIBUTION IN THE LINE.**

    "D" Section under Lieut. RICHARDSON will relieve the guns at ALDERSHOT, AMESBURY, AVON and ANDOVER.
    "C" Section under 2/Lt. BARR BALL will relieve the guns at CARLISLE, CHESTER, CREWE and CORK.
    "B" Section under Lieut. HOWARD and 2/Lt. PHILBIN will relieve the guns at BULFORD, BASINGSTOKE, BRIGHTON and BRISTOL.
    "A" Section under Lieut. CANT will relieve the guns at DEAL, DOVER, DURHAM and DORSET.
    2/Lt. WATKINS will assist the O.C. at COMPANY HEADQUARTERS.
    Section Headquarters will be at ALDERSHOT, CARLISLE, BRIGHTON and DORSET.
    COMPANY HEADQUARTERS will be at DORSET.

3. **ORDER OF MARCH.**

    The Company will parade in Fighting Order at 5-30 p.m. and move to the line. Lieut. CANT and 2/Lt. BALL will proceed to the line during the afternoon and take over the tactical dispositions of their Sections.
    Tripods and belt boxes will be taken over in the line. Sections will pack guns and kit into two limbers.
    Section Officers will arrange the packing so that the guns for the front system will be in the fore portion of one limber, and guns of "C" Section in fore portion of limber for the Southern route. Two belt-filling machines to be taken (one each by "A" & "C").

4. **OPERATION AND WORK ORDERS.**

    O.C. Sections will take over the firing programmes, operation orders, and work programmes of the Section being relieved. The Brigadier is anxious that the Company should construct their trenches to certain standard measurements. These dimensions will be issued to Section Officers as soon as they are received.

5. **REPORTS.**

    Relief completed will be sent to COMPANY HEADQUARTERS by the quickest means available.
    Posts where telephones are installed may report by Company Code.

6. **SIGNAL COMMUNICATION.**

    N.C.O. in charge of Signallers will detail Signallers to BRIGHTON and CARLISLE.

7. **ACKNOWLEDGE.**

    Copies to:-

    1 - O.C. "A" Section.
    2 - O.C. "B" Section.
    3 - O.C. "C" Section.
    4 - O.C. "D" Section.
    5 - O.C. Company.
    6 - Transport Officer.
    7 - 2nd in Command.
    8 - O.C. 243 M.G.Coy.
    9 - D.M.G.O.
    10.- War Diary.
    11.- War Diary.
    12.- File.

                                                    Captain,
                                        Comdg. 94th Machine Gun Company.

Confidential

Volume XXII
Vol 18

War Diary.

9th Machine Gun Coy. 31st Division.

October 1917.

Army Form C. 2118.

WAR DIARY
or
INTELLIGENCE SUMMARY.
(Erase heading not required.)

Instructions regarding War Diaries and Intelligence Summaries are contained in F. S. Regs., Part II. and the Staff Manual respectively. Title pages will be prepared in manuscript.

Place	Date	Hour	Summary of Events and Information	Remarks and references to Appendices
In the field	1/10/17		Situation quiet. Hostile Machine Gun from the direction of ACHEVILLE was rather quiet. ARLEUX was shelled in the afternoon with 5.9's. We fired 9,000 rounds on selected targets. A hostile Trench Mortar was engaged at the request of Infantry and was subsequently silenced.	RWD
-do-	2/10/17		Situation quiet. During the day we engaged enemy aircraft and in all 2,500 rounds were fired. In conjunction with Artillery a harassing shoot was carried out from dusk until midnight on tracks, consolidated shell holes, Trench Mortars etc. a total of 6,000 rounds being fired. 1 O.R. reinforcement arrived from A.H.T.D.	RWD
-do-	3/10/17	9.30pm	Situation quiet generally. RED LINE in vicinity of Battery about B11 a 5.3. was slightly shelled. Gas was projected in ENEMY's system. Enemy signals were double green lights followed by double red, shortly afterwards this was changed to yellow flares. Our machine guns in battery positions at B11 c 26 26 and T 29 e 10.14 fired in conjunction with gas projection between 9-35 p.m. and 10-30 p.m.	RWD

Army Form C. 2118.

WAR DIARY
or
INTELLIGENCE SUMMARY.
(Erase heading not required.)

Instructions regarding War Diaries and Intelligence Summaries are contained in F. S. Regs., Part II. and the Staff Manual respectively. Title pages will be prepared in manuscript.

Place	Date	Hour	Summary of Events and Information	Remarks and references to Appendices
In the Field	3/10/17	4.45pm	Enemy retaliated by shelling out front line. Heavy artillery from LENS direction appeared to barrage WINNIPEG ROAD.	Appendix I RWD
		10.0pm	Enemy fired a number of gas shells. During the day projectors we fired a total of 27,500 rounds. One OR reinforcement arrived from No. 22 C.C.S. Question Order No. 39 issued for raid on Enemy trenches	
-do-	4/10/17		Situation quiet. A few 4.2's were fired on ARLEUX-FRESNOY road near BRITANNIA TRENCH during the day. Trench mortar and machine gun O activity on the part of the enemy was very small during the day. The was considerable artillery activity on the left Sector. Indirect firing was carried out from T29c 10.53 on targets at T24a 95.95, T24 b 9.3, T24 b 35.65. The total number of rounds fired being 5,250. Capt. J.F.PRICE left for UK and LIEUT. J.S. WILSON took over command of the company. CAPT. F. BAILEY M.C. arrived from No.151 M.G.COMPANY to take over command of company. 1 OR transfered from No 151 M.G.Coy. M.C. R.L.	RWD
-do-	5/10/17	11.30pm	Situation during the night was quiet. During the day WILLERVAL was occasionally shelled by guns of heavy calibre. Enemy planes fire was turned back by our fire about 6.0pm (Rounds fired +50). At the request of O.C. 124 y9 F.Regt. battery at T29c No.53 engaged	RWD

Army Form C. 2118.

WAR DIARY
or
INTELLIGENCE SUMMARY.
(Erase heading not required.)

Instructions regarding War Diaries and Intelligence Summaries are contained in F. S. Regs., Part II. and the Staff Manual respectively. Title pages will be prepared in manuscript.

Place	Date	Hour	Summary of Events and Information	Remarks and references to Appendices
In the Field	5/10/17 (Cont)		T.24.b.35.65 (Rounds fired 1502). As a result the enemy T.M. ceased fire.	RWD
In the Field	6/10/17.		Situation during the day was very quiet. Enemy artillery action was normal.	
	NIGHT 6/7th (Cont.17)		In accordance with Operation Order No. 39 the raid on enemy tactical was attempted. All guns were in position and ready to fire on their targets at 9 P.M. At 10.0 P.M. artillery opened out and all guns at once fired. Our fire slowly slackened off as artillery ceased fire all guns stood to until 12.29 a.m. when our artillery laid a barrage on the enemys lines and then intense fire was opened. Stoppages were fust and a total of 56,000 rounds were fired. Enemy retaliation was slight, only Trench Mortars firing.	RWD
In the field.	7/10/17.		Situation during the day was quiet. VILLERVAL was shelled also our forward positions. Operation Order No. 40. for relief by 243rd Machine Gun Company issued.	Appendices II RWD

Army Form C. 2118.

WAR DIARY
or
INTELLIGENCE SUMMARY
(Erase heading not required.)

Instructions regarding War Diaries and Intelligence Summaries are contained in F.S. Regs., Part II. and the Staff Manual respectively. Title pages will be prepared in manuscript.

Place	Date	Hour	Summary of Events and Information	Remarks and references to Appendices
In the Field	NIGHT 7/8th 4/10/17	4.30 P.M. Oct. M. 11.0 P.M.	Relief started. Relief completed without incident. Section move back to rest billets in ECURIE WOOD CAMP.	RWP
In the Field	8/10/17		The day was spent in cleaning guns kit and personal kit. During the morning the Company had baths. A party was also detailed for work on Winter Horse Standings. One OR was granted leave to U.K.	RWP
-do-	9/10/17		The training programme for the day included, Kit Inspection, Continuation of cleaning guns & kit etc., and a party was detailed for work on Winter Horse Standings. One OR was granted leave to U.K.	RWP
-do-	10/10/17		The day was spent in, Infantry Drill, Armourer's Inspection, and Recreational Training. Work was also carried out on the Winter Horse Standings. 2/Lt. G.H. BALL left for course on Camouflage work. Two ORs granted leave to U.K.	RWP
-do-	11/10/17		The morning's programme included Infantry Drill, and work on Winter Horse Standings. The programme for the afternoon consisted of Recreational Training	RWP

Army Form C. 2118.

WAR DIARY
or
~~INTELLIGENCE SUMMARY~~

(Erase heading not required.)

Instructions regarding War Diaries and Intelligence Summaries are contained in F. S. Regs., Part II. and the Staff Manual respectively. Title pages will be prepared in manuscript.

Place	Date	Hour	Summary of Events and Information	Remarks and references to Appendices
In the Field.	12/10/17		The days training programme included :- Infantry Drill, Physical Training, Barrage Drill and Immediate Action wearing small Box Respirators. Two O.R's were granted leave to U.K.	RWP
- do -	13/10/17		The training for the day included Infantry Training, Cleaning of Guns, Immediate Action, use of HILL-JACKSON anti-aircraft sights, and use of elevating dials. Two O.R's were granted leave to U.K.	RWP
- do -	14/10/17		Divine Service were arranged for all denominations. The time not occupied by Church Service was spent in the cleaning of guns and work on Winter Horse Standings. One O.R. granted leave to U.K	RWP
- do -	15/10/17		The day was occupied by Infantry Drill, Gun Cleaning Barrage Drill and Recreational Training. Two Sections were detailed for work on Winter Horse Standings. One O.R. left for U.K. as candidate for Commission. 2/Lt. G.H. BALL returned from Course.	RWP

Army Form C. 2118.

WAR DIARY
or
INTELLIGENCE SUMMARY.
(Erase heading not required.)

Instructions regarding War Diaries and Intelligence Summaries are contained in F. S. Regs., Part II. and the Staff Manual respectively. Title pages will be prepared in manuscript.

Place	Date	Hour	Summary of Events and Information	Remarks and references to Appendices
In the Field	16/10/17		Fourteen O.R's were attached from the various Battalions of the Division. 2 O.R's left for U.K for Special Course of Instruction. The programme for the days' training included Kit Inspection, Infantry Training, Barrage Drill, and C.O's inspection of guns and kit. Work was also carried out on the Winter Horse Standings. The afternoon was spent in Recreational Training.	RWP
In the Field	17/10/17		Training was carried out including Limber Cleaning, Barrage Drill, Route march (Fighting Order), and Recreational Training. "D" Section and all attached men proceeded to the line for the purpose of digging Battery positions.	RWP
-do-	18/10/17		The days training programme included Limber Cleaning, Physical Training, Barrage Drill and Recreational Training. One Section worked on Winter Horse Standings. One O.R. was evacuated sick to No. 42 C.C.S. Operation Order No. 41 issued for relief of 243rd Machine Gun Company in the line.	Appendix VI RWP

Army Form C. 2118.

WAR DIARY
or
INTELLIGENCE SUMMARY.
(Erase heading not required.)

Instructions regarding War Diaries and Intelligence Summaries are contained in F. S. Regs., Part II. and the Staff Manual respectively. Title pages will be prepared in manuscript.

Place	Date	Hour	Summary of Events and Information	Remarks and references to Appendices
In the Field	19/10/17.		The days training included :- Infantry Drill, Barrage Drill, Overhauling belts and gun kit, and recreational training. A party of eleven men was detailed for work on Winter Horse Standings.	RWD
-do-	20/10/17.		During the morning the Company was paid, and both were arranged Six OR's reinforcements arrive from Base Depot. In the afternoon all kit was packed in limbers prior to moving off to the line.	RWD
		4.30 p.m.	Company paraded in Fighting Order and move off to relieve 243rd M.G. Coy.	
		10-30	Relief complete without incident	
-do-	NIGHT 20/21st Oct 1917.		There was a certain amount of Trench Mortar activity by the enemy on our front line during the hours of darkness. Several Gas shells we fired on L1 Sector at 10.0 pm and rattles were sounded.	RWD
		12.25 am	"Gas alert" cancelled and quiet during the rest of the night	

Army Form C. 2118.

WAR DIARY
or
INTELLIGENCE SUMMARY.
(Erase heading not required.)

Instructions regarding War Diaries and Intelligence Summaries are contained in F. S. Regs., Part II. and the Staff Manual respectively. Title pages will be prepared in manuscript.

Place	Date	Hour	Summary of Events and Information	Remarks and references to Appendices
In the Field	21/10/17		During the day the enemy shelled our front system of trenches and also ARLEUX. Our artillery was very active against the enemy's forward trenches, which were heavily shelled from 3 pm to 5 pm.	RWD
		11-30pm	Was fired 2,000 rounds on selected target. One I.O.R. evacuated to No. 2 C.C.S.	
-do-	22/10/17		The situation during the day was very quiet.	RWD
		6.15pm	In accordance with Brigade Orders gas was projected on enemy's positions in FRESNOY PARK. Our guns co-operated with artillery and a total of 9,450 rounds were fired. Results were unobserved, but there was no retaliation by the enemy.	
-do-	23/10/17		Situation very quiet. Enemy again shelled ARLEUX. Company in the line work on the general repair and improvement of positions and trenches.	RWD
-do-	24/10/17		During the day aerial activity was very great. One of our artillery machines was driven down and crashed. Enemy artillery was very active on all parts of the sector.	RWD

Army Form C. 2118.

WAR DIARY
or
INTELLIGENCE SUMMARY.
(Erase heading not required.)

Instructions regarding War Diaries and Intelligence Summaries are contained in F. S. Regs., Part II. and the Staff Manual respectively. Title pages will be prepared in manuscript.

Place	Date	Hour	Summary of Events and Information	Remarks and references to Appendices
In the field	24/10/17 (Cont)	4.30 p.m.	There was a very heavy shelling of our forward positions. During the day we fired a total of 3,000 rounds at enemy aircraft.	AMD
- do -	25/10/17		Situation very quiet. Slight enemy trench mortar activity on our forward positions. Hostile machine gun fire below normal.	AMD
		11-0 p.m. to 11-20 p.m.	Our artillery opened an intense bombardment on the enemy front line N. of MERICOURT.	
		7-0 p.m. to 12.	We fired 4,750 rounds on selected targets.	
- do -	26/10/17		Situation comparatively quiet with the exception of our forward positions being shelled at intervals during the day. Gas alert was received at 9.0 p.m. Artillery activity was normal.	AMD
- do -	27/10/17		Artillery activity on both sides was above normal. Aerial activity was also above normal and many air fights took place. All enemy machines within range were engaged, and a total of 4,800 were fired at aircraft alone. There was heavy shelling of our back areas. WILLERVAL receiving much attention	AMD

(A7092) Wt. W12359/M1293. 750,000. 1/17. D.D. & L., Ltd. Forms/C.2118-14

Army Form C. 2118.

WAR DIARY
or
INTELLIGENCE SUMMARY.
(Erase heading not required.)

Instructions regarding War Diaries and Intelligence Summaries are contained in F. S. Regs., Part II. and the Staff Manual respectively. Title pages will be prepared in manuscript.

Place	Date	Hour	Summary of Events and Information	Remarks and references to Appendices
In the Field	27/9/17	11 p.m.	We fired 3,000 rounds on selected targets, ~~results unobserved~~ during night	RMD
In the Field	28/9/17		Both artilleries were fairly active during the day. Our forward positions at ACTON & ASTON were lightly shelled. TRIUMPH TRENCH was shelled by enemy trench mortars at about 10.0 a.m. & 6 p.m. There was the usual enemy machine gun fire.	RMD
-do-	29/9/17.		Situation very quiet. All hostile aircraft were engaged by our guns, and a total of 1,800 were fired. During the early part of the night 2,000 rounds were fired on specially selected targets. Results unobserved.	RMD
-do-	30/9/17.		Situation very quiet. In accordance with arrangements in co-operation with the artillery in hurricane shoots on V.19.a. during night a total of 5,500 rounds were fired. Small effects were unobserved. There was no retaliation by the enemy.	RMD
-do-	31/9/17.		Enemy artillery was very active during the day. About noon Brigade forward lines were shelled for about two hours. WINNIPEG ROAD seemed to be the centre of activity. There was the usual machine gun fire during the night. Aerial activity was above normal during the day.	RMD RM Barker Capt

SECRET   Appendix I
        94th M.G. Coy Operation Order No. 39.   Copy No 8
Map Ref. Foothill 1/20,000.   2/10/17

1. INFORMATION   A Coy of the 12 York. Regt will raid the enemy's posts at T.24.d.40.35 & T.24.d.40.55 on the night of the 5/6 October. Gaps will be cut in the enemy's wire at about T.24.d.4,4 & T.24.d.40,65 by means of Bangalore Torpedoes.
   The divisional artillery will co-operate by forming a standing barrage on the following trenches and trench junctions.

   2, 18 prs on TAMARISK TRENCH from T.30.b.72,72 to U.25.a.16,86.
   1 battery on U.25.a.16,86 to U.19.c.10.50.
   1 "   " U.19.c.10.50 to T.24.b.75,00.
   4 guns. " T.24.b.75,00 to T.24.d.46,91
   4.5 how's. on T.24.b.27,08 ; T.24.b.55,00
              T.24.d.85,20   T.24.d.55,00
              T.30.b.55,44.

2. M.G. ACTION
   The 94th M.G. Coy will assist by placing barrages as follows.
   B. Section under LIEUT HOWARD will place a barrage from T.24.b.2,1 to T.24.b.35,23 (2 guns) and from T.24.b.40,28 to T.24.b.40,40 (2 guns).
   C. SECTION (+ ½ SECTION of A) under 2/LT BALL will place a standing barrage on FRESNOY TRENCH from U.19.c.10,62 to U.25.a.12,95.
   flank. A. SECTION (less ½ SECTION) under LT. CANT will place a standing barrage from T.24.d.60,00 to T.24.d.85,20.
   Section Officers will arrange to work out all calculations and send them in to Coy HQrs to be checked as early as possible.
   New barrels will be used and special precautions taken to secure accuracy of fire.

3. RATES OF FIRE
   Zero to Zero + 4 minutes = INTENSE (about 350 rds per gun per minute).
   +4m. "   +10   "   — NORMAL (250 rds per 2 guns per min)
   +10 " "   +15   "   — RAPID   (250 rds per gun per min)
   +15 " "   +30   "   — INTENSE
   +20 " "   +30   "   — NORMAL
   +30.   CEASE FIRE.

4. SIGNAL COMMUNICATIONS
   Arrangements will be made to connect Coy HQ with the nearest F.A. Battery by wire. 2/LT BALL will arrange

SECRET   94 M.G. Coy. Operation Order. No. Ct.1   Copy No. 8

4. Ctd

for signallers to be at his H.Q. to plug in direct from Coy Hd Qrs to his battery. LIEUT HOWARD will arrange a line to tee off the main battery line to his battery. LT. CANT will be in touch with H.Q. 15 by RUNNER.

In the event of the signal communications breaking down all guns will take the cue from hearing LT CANT'S guns. Normally all firing will cease at Zero + 30 mins, but if more fire is required orders will be communicated as above described.

5/ ZERO.

The following arrangements are being made for ZERO. The approximate time will be 9.30 p.m. The actual time will be fixed by O.C. 170 Bde R.F.A on his receiving the message in code from the front line that all is ready. The artillery will fire a salvo at ZERO and this will be the signal for the M. Guns and T.M'S to open fire.

6/ CODE

The following code will be used in connection with this operation

```
ALL READY    —   RATIONS CORRECT.
ZERO         —   BLACKMAIL.
9 p.m        —   P.
```

SECRET   94 M.G. Coy. Operation Order. No.   Copy No 8

6 CTD

     10 p.m   —   Q
     11 p.m   —   R
     12 M.N.   —   S,

Minutes will be given in clear. Therefore for example ZERO 10.30 p.m will be sent BLACKMAIL Q .30.

7. **SYNCHRONISATION**

Section officers will send a representative to Coy Hd Qrs at 8 p.m to synchronise watches.

8. **REPORTS**

Brief report on conclusion of operations to be sent immediately to Coy HQ. for transmission to Bde HQ. A further written report to be sent in with morning report.

9. **ACKNOWLEDGE**

ISSUED AT 12 NOON   [signature] Capt.
     3/10/17.   OC. 94 M.G Coy.

Copies to.
No 1.   O.C
   2   LT. CANT
   3   LT HOWARD
   4   2/LT BALL
   5   LT RICHARDSON
   6   DM GO.
   7   OC. 12 YcL REGT
   8 & 9. WAR DIARY.   ✓
   10.   FILE,

Appendix II

SECRET.   94th M.G. Coy Operation Order No 40

M.R.
Maroeuil. 1/20,000.

1. INFORMATION.

The 94th M.G. Coy. will be relieved in the Left Bde. Sector by the 243rd M.G. Coy in the afternoon of the 7th October 1917.

2. GUIDES

Guides for all gun positions will be at Coy. Hd. Qrs. at 4.45 p.m on the afternoon of the 7th October 1917 to conduct relieving gun teams to their respective positions.

3. RELIEVING.

All guns will be relieved at the discretion of the Section Officers involved.

4. HANDING OVER.

All trench stores, order boards, S.O.S. lines, defence line, work programmes, tripods and belt boxes will be handed over and receipts taken. Also R.E. material. German belt boxes will be brought out. Handing over slips will be made up, signed, and handed in to Coy. Hd. Qrs. on completion of relief.

5. TRANSPORT.

Two limbers at BRIGHTON and one limber at HEAD QUARTERS will be available for taking out guns and kit. All guns being taken out will be stored at BRIGHTON and COY. HD. QRS. until these limbers arrive.

6. MOVEMENT.

Sections will move out under own arrangements to ECURIE CAMP

7. ACKNOWLEDGE

Issued at 6.A.M. 7/10/17.

for O.C. 94th M.G.Coy. LIEUT.

COPIES TO.
1. O.C. COY. ✓
2. 2/IN COMMAND
3. TRANSPORT OFFICER
4. LIEUT. CANT
5. LIEUT HOWARD
6. 2/LIEUT BALL
7. 2/LT WATKINS
8. D.M.G.O
9. O.C 243rd M.G.C.
10. } WAR DIARY
11. }
12. FILE

Appendix III

Copy No. 11

SECRET.

94th MACHINE GUN COMPANY.

OPERATION ORDER No. 41.

1. **INFORMATION.**

    The 94th Machine Gun Company will relieve the 243rd Machine Gun Company in the line on the night 20/21st October 1917.

DISTRIBUTION.

2. "A" Section will relieve the guns of the 243rd Machine Gun Company situated in the front system. Guides for this Section to be at BARNSTAPLE dug-out at 4-30 p.m.

3. "B" Section will relieve the Section in the AVELUX group, guides to be at BARNSTAPLE at 4-30 p.m.

4. "C" Section will relieve the Section in support. Guides to be at BRIGHTON dug-out at 4-0 p.m.

5. "D" Section will relieve the Section in reserve at CARDIFF HEADQUARTERS. The guns etc. will be brought up by limber at 6-0 p.m. to CARDIFF HEADQUARTERS.
Personnel of Section, together with attached men will be at CARDIFF dug-out at 4-0 p.m.

6. **TAKING OVER.**

    All belt-boxes, tripods, water cans, maps and gas appliances etc. will be taken over and receipts given.

7. **HEADQUARTERS.**

    "A" Section Headquarters will be at BARNSTAPLE.
    "B" Section Headquarters will be at BARNSTAPLE.
    "C" Section Headquarters will be at BRIGHTON.
    "D" Section Headquarters will be at CARDIFF.
    COMPANY HEADQUARTERS will be at CARDIFF.

8. **TRANSPORT.**

    The Transport Officer will detail one limber per Section and one for Company Headquarters to take kit etc. into the line.

9. **RELIEF COMPLETE.**

    Relief complete will be notified to COMPANY HEADQUARTERS by the quickest means available. All stations where telephones are installed will use the Company Code.

10. **HUTS.**

    All huts will be left thoroughly clean, Section Sergeants be held responsible.

11. **ACKNOWLEDGE.**

    Copies to 1 - O.C. Company.
    2 - 2nd in Command.
    3 - Transport Officer.
    4 - O.C. "A" Section.
    5 - O.C. "B" Section.
    6 - O.C. "C" Section.
    7 - O.C. "D" Section.
    8 - D.H.Q.
    9 - O.C. 243 M.G.Coy.
    10 - War Diary.
    11 - War Diary.
    12 - File.

R.M.Barley

.... Capt,
Comdg. 94th Machine Gun Company.

Issued - 4-0 p.m. 19/10/17.

Confidential

Volume XXIII
Vol 19

War Diary.

94th Machine Gun Company. 31st Division

November 1917.

Army Form C. 2118.

WAR DIARY
or
INTELLIGENCE SUMMARY

(Erase heading not required.)

Instructions regarding War Diaries and Intelligence Summaries are contained in F. S. Regs., Part II. and the Staff Manual respectively. Title pages will be prepared in manuscript.

Place	Date	Hour	Summary of Events and Information	Remarks and references to Appendices
In the Line.	1/11/17		Company still in the line (ACHEVILLE SECTOR). Situation very quiet and nothing of special interest reported. Operation Order No. 42 issued for	Appendix I
		5-30pm	relief by 243rd M.G. Coy. Relief started.	RW.
		8-30pm	Relief complete without incident. 4 O.R's reinforcements arrived from BASE DEPÔT	
-do-	2/11/17		Company in rest at ECURIE WOOD CAMP. The general cleaning of personal kit and gun kit was carried out during the day. One OR leaves for U.K. as candidate for commission. One OR granted leave to U.K.	RW
-do-	3/11/17		The training for the day included a thorough inspection of front Rations, Small Kit, Clothing and Gun gear. Company paid out. A report was rendered on the condition of all pistols and guns were inspected by Armourer Sergeant.	RW
-do-	4/11/17		During the day Services were arranged for all denominations. Recreational training was carried out during the afternoon. 10 OR's attached to Company from the various Battalions in the Brigade	RW

Army Form C. 2118.

WAR DIARY
or
INTELLIGENCE SUMMARY.
(Erase heading not required.)

Place	Date	Hour	Summary of Events and Information	Remarks and references to Appendices
5/5/5/2 In the Field	5/11/17		All sections were engaged in cleaning belts and ammunition. Operation Order No. 43. issued for Company to proceed to the line (less one sub-section of "D" and attached men.)	Appendix II NWB
		2.0pm	Sections detailed move off to the line. Four ORs transferred from No. 141 M.G. Coy.	NWB
-do-	6/11/17		Remainder of Company make full preparations for the line. All attached men parade for instructional purposes. One OR rejoins from No. 58 C.C.S.	NWB
-do-	7/11/17		Remainder of Company proceed to the line. Reports from the line state situation very quiet. The work on the line - improvement of Battery positions	NWB
-do-	8/11/17	12 noon	Situation unchanged. Infantry of the line, ascertained by Royal Engineers raided enemy front line. Our guns opened out a flank and creeping barrage. Raid was successful and 21 prisoners were taken.	NWB
		6.0 p.m	All guns withdrew and sections returned to Rest Billets at ECURIE WOOD CAMP.	

Army Form C. 2118.

WAR DIARY
or
INTELLIGENCE SUMMARY.
(Erase heading not required)

Instructions regarding War Diaries and Intelligence Summaries are contained in F. S. Regs., Part II. and the Staff Manual respectively. Title pages will be prepared in manuscript.

Place	Date	Hour	Summary of Events and Information	Remarks and references to Appendices
In the Field	9/11/17		The day was spent in cleaning guns and gun kit and rendering indents re deficiencies	Nil
-do-	10/11/17		The day was occupied by one section on Fatigue duties. A party was also detailed for work on Stables and the remainder of the Company had instruction in Stoppages and Immediate Action.	Nil
-do-	11/11/17		Church Services were arranged for all denominations. In the Afternoon Respirator Drill and Inspections were carried out.	Nil
-do-	12/11/17		The programme for the day included: Limber cleaning, Barrage Drill and Gun cleaning. A party was also detailed for work on the improvement of range. One OR evacuated to No 42 C.C.S.	Nil
-do-	13/11/17	5.30	All sections paraded at 9.0 am and made preparations for the Line. Operation Order No. 44 issued, for relief of 243rd Machine Gun Company in the ACHEVILLE SECTOR. Relief started.	Appendix III
		8.30	Relief complete. 3 ORs transferred to 243rd Coy.	Nil

Army Form C. 2118.

WAR DIARY
or
INTELLIGENCE SUMMARY.
(Erase heading not required.)

Instructions regarding War Diaries and Intelligence Summaries are contained in F.S. Regs., Part II. and the Staff Manual respectively. Title pages will be prepared in manuscript.

Place	Date	Hour	Summary of Events and Information	Remarks and references to Appendices
In the Line	14/4/17		Company in the line. Situation very quiet. During the night 8,000 rounds were fired on enemy tracks and trenches.	NIL
-do-	15/4/17		Situation still very quiet. During the night enemy shelled areas behind gun positions with gas shells. Enemy machine guns were fairly active during the night. A total of 6,500 rounds were fired on enemy tracks and trenches	NIL
-do-	16/4/17		Situation fairly quiet. Enemy artillery fairly active. About 10.15 am our guns engaged two enemy platoons 4,000 rounds were fired on enemy tracks and trenches during the night.	NIL
-do-	17/4/17		Enemy machine guns were very active during the night. Enemy replied to our hurricane bombardments on two occasions by shelling ARLEUX. Our artillery carried out three hurricane bombardments during the night. One OR wounded in action. One OR evacuated sick to No. 42 C.C.S.	NIL

Army Form C. 2118.

WAR DIARY
or
INTELLIGENCE SUMMARY.
(Erase heading not required.)

Instructions regarding War Diaries and Intelligence Summaries are contained in F.S. Regs., Part II. and the Staff Manual respectively. Title pages will be prepared in manuscript.

Place	Date	Hour	Summary of Events and Information	Remarks and references to Appendices
In the Field	18/11/17		Situation quiet. ARLEUX was shelled at intervals during the day. Enemy machine guns were not quite so active. Our artillery were fairly active during the night. LIEUT. G.F. RICHARDSON and SGT. DUNBAR proceeded on leave to U.K. Two ORs Reinforcements from Corps Base Depot.	MA
do	19/11/17		Enemy artillery fairly quiet. From 2pm to 3.9pm ARLEUX LOOP was shelled with 77mm. During the night we fired about 6,000 rounds on enemy communication trenches. One OR Leave to Base Depot	MA
do	20/11/17		At 4.30am our artillery opened out a 10 minute bombardment and in accordance with instructions as many guns as possible opened out. A total of 8,250 rounds being fired. Enemy's retaliation was slight and fairly scattered.	MA
do	21/11/17		Situation very quiet. In accordance with instructions from Brigade one sub section of B. and one subsector of C. together with to sections were transferred to the OPPY SECTOR and the remainder of the Company were relieved by guns of the Canadian troops. One OR rejoins from No.42 C.C.S. The guns relieved then withdrew to rest billets at ROBERTS CAMP	MA

Army Form C. 2118.

WAR DIARY
or
INTELLIGENCE SUMMARY.
(Erase heading not required.)

Instructions regarding War Diaries and Intelligence Summaries are contained in F. S. Regs., Part II. and the Staff Manual respectively. Title pages will be prepared in manuscript.

Place	Date	Hour	Summary of Events and Information	Remarks and references to Appendices
29th/17. In the Field	22/1/17		Situation in the line fairly quiet. Section in rest clear guns and kit. One OR granted leave to UK. One OR granted leave to UK. Usual night patrols.	AAA
-do-	23/1/17.		Situation reports from the line state that enemy artillery fairly active. Sections off in rest work on fatigue duties at Transport lines and during the afternoon Myrlven Gas drill and Respirator inspection. Three OR's granted leave to UK. Usual night patrols.	AAA
-do-	24/1/17.		Enemy artillery maintain the usual activity, but nothing special reported. Usual night patrols. Sections in rest continue Transport fatigue.	AAA
-do-	25/1/17.		Nothing of special importance reported. Fatigues at Transport Lines and camp carried out by the Section in rest. LIEUT. T. HOWARD granted leave to UK.	AAA
-do-	26/1/17.		Usual artillery activity reported from the line. Sections out in rest work on fatigues at Transport Lines. Night patrols. Two OR's granted Mess and rations allowance to UK.	AAA

Army Form C. 2118.

WAR DIARY
or
INTELLIGENCE SUMMARY.
(Erase heading not required.)

Instructions regarding War Diaries and Intelligence Summaries are contained in F. S. Regs., Part II. and the Staff Manual respectively. Title pages will be prepared in manuscript.

Place	Date	Hour	Summary of Events and Information	Remarks and references to Appendices
In the Field	27/11/17		Situation in the line unchanged, usual artillery activity. Sections out on rest continue on Transport Fatigues. Two OR's granted night leave	Nil
In the Field	28/11/17		Enemy artillery very active during the day. Sections out on rest continue Transport fatigue and during the afternoon have Gas Drill and Box Respirator inspection. Two OR's granted leave to UK. 2 pm Church Parade. Reg's for teams trained at night	Nil
-do-	29/11/17		Reports from the line state that enemy artillery very active during the whole day. Sections out on rest clean guns and limbers and continue Transport Fatigue. Three OR's granted leave to UK. Night firing teams trained.	Nil
-do-	30/11/17		Usual artillery activity by enemy. During the morning the Sections out on rest make preparations for the line. "A" and "C" Sections relieve "B" and "D". Three OR's granted leave to UK. Night firing teams trained.	Nil

R.W. Mulaey Capt.
O.C. No 94 M. G. COY.

Appendix I

SECRET.   Copy No. 10

94th MACHINE GUN COMPANY.

Operation Order No. 42.

Ref. HARDBUIL Map 1/20000.

1. The 243rd Machine Gun Company will relieve the 94th Machine Gun Company in the Left Brigade Sector on the night of 1/2 November 1917.

2. Guides for AYR, ANGLESEY, AB─ROPLE and BULFORD will be at BULFORD at 5-30 p.m.
   Guides for ALDERSHOT, AMESBURY, ACTON, ASTON, BARNSTAPLE, BOSTON and BURSLEM will be at CHALK MOUND at 5-30 p.m.
   Guides for BRIGHTON and BASINGSTOKE will be at BRIGHTON at 5-30 p.m.
   Guides for CHESTER, CORBY and CREWE will be at COMPANY HEADQUARTERS at 5-30 p.m.

3. All trench stores, tripods, belt boxes, anti-gas appliances, gas blankets, S.O.S.Lines, Defence Scheme, maps, work programmes and positions will be handed over and receipts obtained. Receipts to be forwarded to Orderly Room by Noon on the 2nd November 1917.

4. Company will move out as relieved, and will march by Sections to BOURIN WOOD CAMP.

5. A hot meal will be provided for them on their arrival.

6. TRANSPORT. (Time-table for limbers):
   8-0 p.m. One limber to be at CHALK MOUND for "A" Section.
   7-30 p.m. One limber for three teams of "C" Section to be at AB─ROPLE.
   7-0 p.m. One limber to be at BRIGHTON for two teams of "D" Section and one team of "C" Section.
   8-0 p.m. One limber for "B" Section to be at junction of WILLERVAL-ARLEUX ROAD and ARLEUX LOOP. This Limber will also pick up the teams from CREWE, CHESTER, and CORBY at the RED LINE.
   8-0 p.m. One limber for COMPANY HEADQUARTERS.

7. All positions must be handed over in a clean and sanitary condition.

8. Relief complete to be wired to COMPANY HEADQUARTERS by the Code word "SAND PLUGS".

9. ACKNOWLEDGE.

Copies to:-
1. - O.C. Company.
2. - 2nd in Command.
3. - Transport Officer.
4. - O.C. "A" Section.
5. - O.C. "B" Section.
6. - O.C. "C" Section.
7. - O.C. "D" Section.
8. - O.C. 243 M.G.Coy.
9. - D.M.G.O.
10. - War Diary.
11. - War Diary.
12. - File.

Capt.
Comdg. 94th Machine Gun Coy.

Appendix II

SECRET.   Copy No. 10

Operation Order No. 43.
94th Machine Gun Company.

1. **INFORMATION.** The Company will proceed into the line, less one sub-section of "D" and attached men.

2. **DISTRIBUTION.** "A" Section and two teams of "C" Section with tripods, "T" Bases and aiming posts to the gun positions.
"B" Section and two teams of "C" Section to the gun positions with the same kit as "A".
"D" Section less one sub-section to BARNSTAPLE.

3. **SIGNALLERS.** Signallers will report to CAPT. LEAH with telephones etc. at BRIGHTON.

4. **S.O.S. LINES.** The guns will have S.O.S. lines laid out, and will be ready by to-morrow morning the 7th.
Only two men per gun will be on duty during the day of the 7th.

5. **BARRAGE LINES.** On the night of the 7/8th barrage lines will be laid out and traversing stops arranged.

6. **TRANSPORT.** Three S.A.A. limbers will take up 216 belt boxes, "T" bases, and all kit for "A", "B" & "C" Sections.
Two fighting limbers will take up the 12 guns and tripods etc. to these positions.
One fighting limber will take up XX 2 guns, tripods and eight belt boxes per gun to BASINGSTOKE. One sub-section of "D" and their rations will accompany this limber.

7. **RATIONS.** Rations for "A", "B" & "C" Sections will be sent to BULFORD on one S.A.A. limber.

8. **ATTACHED MEN.** Sergeant COPE with 24 attached men will report at 4 o'clock to O's.C. "A" and "B" Sections to assist this party, and will return to camp at dawn.

9. **ACKNOWLEDGE.**

Copies to:—
1. O.C. Company.
2. 2nd in Command.
3. Transport Officer.
4. O.C. "A" Section.
5. O.C. "B" Section.
6. O.C. "C" Section.
7. O.C. "D" Section.
8. O.C. 243 M.G. Coy.
9. D.M.G.O.
✓ 10. War Diary.
11. War Diary.
12. File.

Capt.
Comdg. 94th M.G. Coy.

Issued 5/11/17

Appendix III

SECRET. Copy No. 10

94th MACHINE GUN COMPANY.

OPERATION ORDER No. 44.

1. The 94th Machine Gun Company will relieve the 243rd Machine Gun Company in the line on the 13/14th November 1917.

2. "C" Section will relieve the guns at ANDREW, ALDERSHOT, ACTON and ASTON. Guides for these positions to be at BARNSTAPLE at 5-30 p.m.

3. "D" Section will relieve the Section in the ARLEUX group, guides to be at BARNSTAPLE for ANESBURY and BARNSTAPLE positions at 5-30 p.m. Guides for BOSTON and BURNLEY will be at the junction of ARLEUX LOOP and WILLERVAL-ARLEUX ROAD at 5-30 p.m.

4. "A" Section will relieve the Section in the NEW BRUNSWICK area. Guides for ACE, ANGLESEY, ABERCILE and BULFORD to be at junction of SASKATCHEWAN ROAD and NEW BRUNSWICK trench at 5-30 p.m.

5. "B" Section will relieve the guns at BRIGHTON, BASINGSTOKE, CORTY and CHESTER.
   GUIDES for BRIGHTON and BASINGSTOKE will be at BRIGHTON at 5-30 p.m.
   Guides for CORTY and CHESTER will be at the junction of FLEURS TRENCH and WILLERVAL-ARLEUX ROAD at 5-30 p.m.

6. All belt-boxes, tripods, water cans, maps and Gas appliances etc, will be taken over and receipts given.

7. "A" Section Headquarters will be at ANGLESEY.
   "B" Section Headquarters will be at BRIGHTON.
   "C" Section Headquarters will be at BARNSTAPLE.
   "D" Section Headquarters will be at BARNSTAPLE.
   COMPANY HEADQUARTERS will be at CARDIFF.

8. The Transport Officer will detail the following limbers for kit etc.
   One limber for "C" Section.
   One limber for "A" Section.
   One limber for two guns of "D" and two guns of "B" for BARNSTAPLE and BRIGHTON.
   One limber for two guns of "D" and two guns of "B" which go to ARLEUX LOOP and FLEURS TRENCH.
   One limber for COMPANY HEADQUARTERS.

9. Relief complete will be notified to COMPANY HEADQUARTERS by the quickest means available. All stations where telephones are installed will use the Company Code.

10. All huts will be left thoroughly clean. Section Sergeants will be held responsible. 2/Lt. PILGRIM will hand over to 243 Company the Camp, belt-boxes, tripods etc., and take receipts.

11. ACKNOWLEDGE.

    Copies to 1 - O.C. Company.
              2 - 2nd in Command.
              3 - Transport Officer.
              4 - O.C. "A" Section.
              5 - O.C. "B" Section.
              6 - O.C. "C" Section.
              7 - O.C. "D" Section.
              8 - D.M.G.O.
              9 - O.C. 243 M.G. Company.
             ✓10 - War Diary.
              11 - War Diary.
              12 - File.

R. Manley .... Capt.
Comdg. 94th Machine Gun Company.

Issued at 10-0 a.m. 13/11/17.

CONFIDENTIAL.

WAR DIARY

OF

94TH MACHINE GUN COY.

from 1ST DEC 1917 TO 31ST DEC 1917

VOLUME XXIV

Vol 20

Army Form C. 2118.

WAR DIARY
or
INTELLIGENCE SUMMARY.
(Erase heading not required)

Place	Date	Hour	Summary of Events and Information	Remarks and references to Appendices
In the Field. OPPY·SECTOR	1/12/17		A & C Sections in the line. OPPY SECTOR. Situation fairly quiet. There was slight 900 shelling of the support area during the night. The R.E. Dump in BOYNE STREET receiving much attention. Enemy M.G. fire below normal. During the night our guns fired 10,000 rounds on enemy tracks and trenches. "B" & "C" Section at rest billets work on Transport Fatigue.	WM
—do—	2/12/17		Situation in the line quiet. There was slight shelling of BAILLEUL and R.E. DUMP with H.E. and Shrapnel, and at night with 900 shells. There were several direct hits on MARQUIS TRENCH. During the night a total of 10,000 rounds were fired into enemy areas. Sections in reserve continue Transport Fatigue.	WM
—do—	3/12/17		Situation quiet generally. Enemy shelled R.E. Dump behind MARQUIS T.R. with 77 m.ms. at intervals during the day. During darkness a total of 10,000 rounds were fired on enemy tracks running from C H C 25 22, to C H & D.6. Sections out on rest had Physical Training and work on Transport Fatigue. 2/LT. W.M. PHILBIN was admitted sick to Hospital.	WM
—do—	4/12/17		Situation quiet. Between 2 & 3 p.m. R.E. Dump. BOYNE ST. received attention. Enemy Machine Guns fairly active during the hours of darkness. 5,000 rounds were fired on enemy tracks during the night. Sections out on rest continue Transport Fatigue. 2/LT. W.M. PHILBIN evacuated to No.12 Stationary Hospital.	WM

WAR DIARY
or
INTELLIGENCE SUMMARY.
(Erase heading not required.)

Army Form C. 2118.

Instructions regarding War Diaries and Intelligence Summaries are contained in F. S. Regs., Part II. and the Staff Manual respectively. Title pages will be prepared in manuscript.

Place	Date	Hour	Summary of Events and Information	Remarks and references to Appendices
In the Field	5-12-17		Situation Quiet generally. The usual enemy shelling scattered generally over Bde Front. BARKIFUL received a fair amount of shelling during the night we fired 6,000 rounds on enemy tracks and Trenches. Sections out on rest work at Transport Lines cleaning limbers etc. 2 O.R's granted leave to UK	/M
-do-	6-12-17		Situation on the line quiet. Our guns fired 3,000 rounds on enemy lines during the night. Sections out on rest track limbers and make preparations for move.	/Ms
-do- MOUNT. ST ELOI	7-12-17		Sections in the line relieved by 168 M.G. Coy during the day. Relief completed without incident, and Sections moved back to MONT-ST-ELOY. During the morning the Sections out on rest moved off with Transport to DURHAM CAMP. MONT-ST-ELOY.	/MS
-do-	8-12-17		Company "Standing To" at MONT-ST-ELOY awaiting orders to further move. During the day guns and gun kit were cleaned and Respirator Inspection and Gas Drill carried out	/Mp
-do-	9-12-17		The training for the day consists of Kit Inspection, Inspection of Gas Parts, Gas Drill and inspection, Overhauling Belts and Physical training.	/Mp
-do-	10-12-17		No orders received re further move. The training carried out during the day instead Physical Training, Foot Drill, Barrage Drill and gun cleaning under Section Officers	/Mo

Army Form C. 2118.

WAR DIARY
or
INTELLIGENCE SUMMARY.
(Erase heading not required.)

Instructions regarding War Diaries and Intelligence Summaries are contained in F. S. Regs., Part II. and the Staff Manual respectively. Title pages will be prepared in manuscript.

Place	Date	Hour	Summary of Events and Information	Remarks and references to Appendices
In the Field	11-12-17		Company training. Programme for the day included Physical Training, Gas Drill, Barrage Drill and Immediate Action. LIEUT. T. HOWARD rejoined from leave. 2/LT. G.H. HOOD joined from BASE DEPOT	Nil
In the Field	12-12-17		No further orders received. The training carried out included P.T. Gas Drill Barrage Drill, Three Drill and Recreational Training. One OR granted leave to U.K. One OR evacuated to No. 23 C.C.S.	Nil
-do-	13-12-17		The training for the day consisted of P.T. Gas Drill Organisation of a Battery for advance and attack. 2/LT. G.H. BALL granted leave to U.K. Orders received from B.H.Q. to move to ST. CATHERINE. Operation Order No. 45 issued.	Appendix I
-do- ST. CATHERINE AREA.	14-12-17		A party of 15 O.R's under 2/LT. G.N.B. WATKINS were granted leave for the day to BETHUNE. The remainder of the Company marched from MONT-ST-ELOY to ST. CATHERINE, arriving at the new camp on the LENS - ARRAS ROAD about 12.30 p.m.	Nil
-do-	15-12-17		The training for the day included Tactical Schemes with Battalions, and the teams not engaged carried out Physical Training, Gun cleaning and overhauling &c.	Nil
-do-	16-12-17		Church Services were arranged as far as possible for all denominations and the remainder of the time was occupied in Gun cleaning and Physical Training, Arms Drill, Squad Drill, and Limber Cleaning. 4 OR's were evacuated to No. 42 C.C.S. Gas shell poison wounded.	Nil

Army Form C. 2118.

WAR DIARY
or
INTELLIGENCE SUMMARY.
(Erase heading not required.)

Instructions regarding War Diaries and Intelligence Summaries are contained in F. S. Regs., Part II. and the Staff Manual respectively. Title pages will be prepared in manuscript.

Place	Date	Hour	Summary of Events and Information	Remarks and references to Appendices
In the Field	17-12-17		The training for the day included P.T. Coy Drill and examination of applicants, Gun Drill. Immediate Action, Cleaning of guns and limbers. Three OR's were granted leave to U.K.	nil
-do-	18-12-17		The days training programme included Physical Training, Stoppages and Mechanism and a Barrage Practice. Operation Order No.44 issued for relief of 6th CANADIAN M.G. COY. ACHEVILLE FRONT (HUDSON POST SECTOR)	Appendix $\frac{1}{4}$ nil
ACHEVILLE SECTOR	19-12-17		During the morning the company park turnout, clean guns and make preparations for the line. Company moved into the line and relief completed without incident. During the night artillery on both sides was fairly active. Our Machine Guns fired a total of 400 rounds on enemy tracks. O.R. reinforcement arrived from Base Depot.	nil
-do-	20-12-17		Situation reports from the line give nothing of special interest during the day. During the night our Machine Guns maintained their usual harassing fire on enemy tracks and trenches. One OR evacuated to No. 42 C.C.S.	nil
-do-	21-12-17		Situation quiet. There was the usual enemy machine gun fire during the night. Our guns were also fairly active, firing a total of 4,000 rounds on enemy lines etc.	nil
-do-	22-12-17		Situation quiet. There was the usual artillery activity during the day and during the night our machine guns fired a total of 4,250. Green gas shells were reported at 85.a at 10.0pm. Enemy artillery were fairly active.	nil

WAR DIARY
INTELLIGENCE SUMMARY

Army Form C. 2118.

Place	Date	Hour	Summary of Events and Information	Remarks and references to Appendices
In The Field	22.12.17 (cont)		During the day on ARLEUX and SUGAR FACTORY ROAD and our trenches S.W. of OPPY WOOD. 1 O.R. rejoined from No.23 C.C.S.	NM
-do-	23.12.17		Our Artillery maintained the usual activity during the day. Enemy Machine Guns were fairly active. Hostile trench Mortars were active against our trenches in the vicinity of ANDREW. Precautions were taken against gas, but very little traces of any were reported. 2 O.R's evacuated to No.42 C.C.S.	NM
-do-	24.12.17		Artillery fairly quiet during the day, but there were continuous bursts of fire during the darkness up till midnight. Our Machine Guns were fairly active. During the night we fired 12,000 rounds, the chief targets being squares U.25 & 26. 2 O.R's evacuated to No.42 C.C.S.	NM
-do-	25.12.17		In accordance with programme from artillery, harassing fire was carried out at different times. Our Machine Guns co-operated where targets were within range. There was also a hurricane bombardment by medium French Mortars on enemy lines in FRESNOY at 12 noon. Enemy Artillery not particularly active during the day. There was little or no retaliation to our bombardment. A total of 6,500 rounds were fired during the night.	NM

WAR DIARY
or
INTELLIGENCE SUMMARY.

(Erase heading not required.)

Army Form C. 2118.

Place	Date	Hour	Summary of Events and Information	Remarks and references to Appendices
In the Field	26.2.17		Situation quiet generally. At all positions there was intermittent shelling on back areas during day. Usual hostile Machine Gun fire at night. Our guns fired 4000 rounds during the night on FLICKER TRENCH and ACHEVILLE MAZE. One enemy plane was engaged during the midday. 2 ORs granted leave to UK	NIL
In the Field	27.2.17		During the day enemy artillery fairly active on our front. Between 3.0 pm and 4.0 pm OAK ALLEY, ARLEUX LOOP and MANITOBA ROAD were shelled with 4" mnr and 4.2". There were five direct hits on OAK ALLEY and three on ARLEUX LOOP. The nights were quiet from our M.G. BATTERY position at T.29.d.4.9. we fired 5,000 rounds on 16 squares V.13.c and V.25.b during the night. 2 ORs granted leave to UK	NIL
-do-	28.2.17		Enemy planes were very active during the forenoon, several crossing our line, all of which were engaged. Fusilier section range. One Enemy Plane was seen to fall in Boche lines two parts of which were seen to fall in the vicinity of ANDRE?N position. At 8 pm shells were thrown at the vicinity of junction MONTON was shown to pieces by an enemy T.M. shell Operation Order No. 47 issued for relief by 243rd Machine Gun Company. 4,000 rounds were fired on FLICKER TRENCH during the night.	NIL Appendix III

Army Form C. 2118.

WAR DIARY
or
INTELLIGENCE SUMMARY.
(Erase heading not required.)

Instructions regarding War Diaries and Intelligence Summaries are contained in F. S. Regs., Part II. and the Staff Manual respectively. Title pages will be prepared in manuscript.

Place	Date	Hour	Summary of Events and Information	Remarks and references to Appendices
In the Field	29-12-17		Situation of in the line quiet during the day. Relief by 243 M.G.Coy. was completed without incident. On relief the Company moved back to ROBERTS CAMP in Divisional Reserve 2/Lt. W.M. PHILBIN rejoined from No 12 Stationary hospital. 2/Lt G.H. BALL rejoined from No 24.9 M.G.COY. One section in the line commanded by 2/Lt 2 Inf Bty	N/W
CURIE AREA	30-12-17		During the day the Company cleans guns and gun pits, and cleaning up generally after coming out the line	N/W
-do-	31-12-17		The training Programme for the day included Physical training, Cleaning, Inspection of guns by Armourer, Inspection of Prismatic Kits, and baths. During the afternoon the men had their Christmas dinner	N/W

W Rowles Capt.
O.C. NO 94 M.G. COY

Appendix I

OPERATION ORDER NO. 45.

94th MACHINE GUN COMPANY (Orders by CAPT. R.L.BAILEY M.C.).

1. Reveille 7-0 a.m.
   Breakfast 7-30 a.m.
   Parade 8-30 a.m.

2. Blankets will be rolled. One blanket per man will be carried on Section limbers. The second blanket will be handed in to Quartermaster Stores and rolled by 10's under Section arrangements.

3. Section Officers' valises will be carried on fighting limbers, and be on the limbers by 10-0 a.m.

4. All limbers will be packed by 10-0 a.m.

5. One limber will be detailed by Transport Officer for cooks stuff and rations, this will be ready to move off at 8-30 a.m. Transport dixies and Transport Cook will move with this limber.
   A billeting Party consisting of C.Q.M.S. and one man from each Section detailed by C.S.M. and a Lance Corporal from the Transport will move off with Cooks limber at 8-30 a.m. and will meet the Company at the Camp at 12 Noon.
   The billeting Officer will start at 9-0 a.m. and shew billeting party billets.

6. All kit not packed on limbers will be carried to the road near Canadian Bath House and a guard mounted over it, the C.S.M. will detail this guard. This dump will be moved by lorry. Limbers will make a second journey if no lorry available.

7. The Mess Cart will rpoceed at 10-0 a.m.

8. The Company will parade in full marching order at 10-30 a.m. in column of three's. The head of the column will be 200 yards South of White House. Limbers behind the respective Sections. Other limbers under Transport Officer will follow at 100 yards interval.

9. LIEUT. A. M. Cant and one sub-section of "A" will parade under his instructions. Rations to be carried by this party. Packs of this party will be handed in to Quartermaster Stores.

10. The following party is detailed to proceed to BETHUNE for Xmas shopping. 2/Lt. G.N.B.Watkins, one N.C.O. and two men per Section, Cpl. Brittain and one man from Transport. The lorry for this party leaves White House at 9-0 a.m. The kits of these men will be handed in to Quartermaster Stores. This party will carry their own rations.

Issued at 10-30 p.m. 13/12/17.

R.Bailey
Capt.
Comdg. 94th Machine Gun Company.

2/Lt. G.H.Hood and ten men detailed by C.S.M. will stay behind to clean up the camp and hand over to Town Major. These men will assist in packing lorry.

SECRET. 94th Machine Gun Company. *Appendix II*

Operation Order No. 46.

1. The Company will move into the line HUDSON POST SECTOR on 19/12/17.
2. "D" Section will take over 2 guns at ASTON, 1 at BRIGHTON and 1 at BRIXTON, Section Headquarters will be at BRIGHTON. "B" Section will take over 1 gun at AYR, 1 at BULFORD, 1 at ABERGELE & 1 at BASINGSTOKE, Section Headquarters will be at ANGLESEY. "A" Section will take over the 4 gun Battery Position in CANADA TRENCH. Company Headquarters will be at BUSHEY.
3. Guides for all guns will be at point where HUDSON C.T. crosses VANCOUVER Road at 4-30 p.m.
4. "D" Section limber will go first to BRIGHTON, and then on to BARNSTAPLE for ACTON and ASTON.
   "B" Section limber will go to ABERGELE DUMP.
   "A" Section limber will go BARNSTAPLE.
5. 10 Belt boxes per gun will be taken over at all positions except the Battery. Belt boxes will be taken up for the Battery. Tripods will be taken in also water for the guns. Guns will be filled (five pints) with ~~water~~ water and glycerine.
6. Transport and Stores will move to ECURIE WOOD lines.
7. "C" Section will remain at present camp to-day and will proceed by route march to CUBITT CAMP, NEUVILLE ST VAAST to-morrow. Fighting limbers and eight mules will be taken with Section.

R M Mailer
Capt.
Comdg. 94th Machine Gun Company.

Appendix III

SECRET.   94th MACHINE GUN COMPANY.   Copy No. 10
                        Operation Order No. 47.

1. The 94th Machine Gun Company will be relieved by the 243rd Machine
   Gun Company on 24th December 1917.
2. Guides for ANDREW, ALDERSHOT, AYR, ASHLEIGH, ARGYLLE, BULFORD, CANADA
   BATTERY 2 Guns, BASINGSTOKE, BRIGHTON and BRIXTON will be at junction
   of VANCOUVER ROAD and HUDSON TRENCH at 4-30 p.m.
3. Guides for ACTON, ASTON, BARNSTAPLE and BOSTON will be at junction of
   AULNUX LOOP and VILLERVAL-ARLEUX ROAD at 4-30 p.m.
4. Tripods and belt boxes will be handed over also gun water tins, all
   drinking water tins will be brought out.
5. "D" Section on relief will relieve a Section of 243rd M.G. Coy. at BRISTOL,
   and all men will be quickly made acquainted with the shell-hole positions
   held. 2Lieut. A.R.CANT will take charge of "D" Section.
6. One limber for two teams "A" at ACTON and ASTON and 2 teams of "B"
   at BOSTON and BARNSTAPLE and C/Lt. HAWKINS N.C. will be at junction
   of AULNUX LOOP and VILLERVAL- ARLEUX ROAD at 7-0 p.m.
7. Two limbers for the eight other guns, 2 of "A", 2 of "C" and 4 of "D"
   will be at junction of HUDSON TRENCH and VANCOUVER ROAD at 7-0 p.m.
8. One limber for COMPANY HEADQUARTERS will be at BRISTOL at 7-0 p.m.
9. Section Officers will report relief complete by telephone 2/Lieut. HOOD
   will report at BRISTOL HDQTRS.
10. The team at BRIXTON will report relief complete at COMPANY HEADQUARTERS.
11. The teams as at present grouped, ALDERSHOT CAMP, BARNSTAPLE
    CAMP, BRIGHTON CAMP including the team of "C" at BRIXTON, having
    packed their kit on limbers will move back to HOUETTE CAMP. Groups
    being in the communication trenches.
12. O.C's horse will be at BRISTOL HEADQUARTERS at 4-30 p.m.

Issued at 11-0 a.m. 22-12-17.   R.Bailey
                                                       Capt.
                                           Comdg. 94th Machine Gun Coy.

Copies to:-
1. to O.C. Company.
2. to O.C. "A" Section.
3. to O.C. "B" Section.
4. to O.C. "C" Section.
5. to O.C. "D" Section.
6. to Transport Officer.
7. to O.C. HQ A.C. Coy.
8. to D.A.O.C.
9. Orderly Rm.
10. War Diary.
11. War Diary.

— CONFIDENTIAL —

WAR DIARY

OF

94th MACHINE GUN COMPANY

from 1st JAN 1918 TO 31st JAN 1918.

VOLUME ~~XXV~~

Vol 21

WAR DIARY or INTELLIGENCE SUMMARY

Army Form C. 2118.

(Erase heading not required.)

Instructions regarding War Diaries and Intelligence Summaries are contained in F. S. Regs., Part II. and the Staff Manual respectively. Title pages will be prepared in manuscript.

Place	Date	Hour	Summary of Events and Information	Remarks and references to Appendices
In the Field	1/1/18		The Company still in Divisional Reserve at Roberts Camps. The days training programme included Physical Training, Route March, Kit Inspection, Gas Training, Gas Drill + G.O. Respirator Inspection.	
-do-	2/1/18		The days training programme consisted of Physical Training, Gas Drill and Respirator Inspection, Barrage Drill and Recreational Training.	
-do-	3/1/18		The programme for the day included Physical Training, Route March and test. "C" Section relieved "B" Section in the Line. During the latter part of the Company were carefully inspected and also a small party proceeded. 2/Lt G.M.G. WATKINS was granted leave to U.K.	
-do-	4/1/18		During the morning the training programme consisted of Physical Training and Bayonet, Grenade Drill, and Route march. "B" Section commenced Gas and Gun Test etc after carrying out of the line. "C" Section return from the Line.	
-do-	5/1/18		The training for the day consisted of:- Physical Training, Route March and Recreational Training. The men of "C" Section occupied the day in cleaning guns and personal kit. 3 O.R's granted leave to U.K.	
-do-	6/1/18		Church Parade was arranged for all Ranks. During the afternoon the Company paraded for Gas Instruction and walked through the 4 Gas Chamber at 3rd Bnd. Hd. Qrs.	
-do-	7/1/18		During the day the Company Training Programme consisted of Physical Training, Inspection of Box Respirators and Equipment. Band was also in use.	Passed H.

Army Form C. 2118.

WAR DIARY
or
INTELLIGENCE SUMMARY.
(Erase heading not required.)

Instructions regarding War Diaries and Intelligence Summaries are contained in F. S. Regs., Part II. and the Staff Manual respectively. Title pages will be prepared in manuscript.

Place	Date	Hour	Summary of Events and Information	Remarks and references to Appendices
In the Field	7-1-18 (cont)		Any round some of the huts thro. ORs were granted leave to U.K. Operation Order No 18 issued for relief of 243rd Machine Gun Company in the HUDSON POST SECTOR	Appendix VI
do	8-1-18		During the first parade hour of the morning the training consisted of physical training afterwards packing limbers and making preparations for the line. Company paraded in fighting order and move off to the line by sections. Relief started.	VII
	9.15pm			
	11.30pm		Relief completed (C/O in slight delay owing to one of our lorries breaking down. One OR injured. Item No. 49 CCS	
do	9-1-18		Nothing in the line situation very good and nothing of special interest reported. During the night our guns fired a total of 2000 rounds on enemy front line and communication trenches. CAPT. R.K. BAILEY MC granted leave to UK	VIII
do	10-1-18		Situation still very good. There was the usual artillery activity during the day and night. Our machine guns were firing S.O.S. intervals during the night & a total of 4250 rounds being fired on enemy back area trenches	IX
do	11-1-18		Reports from the line show nothing of special interest to report. The usual artillery activity on both sides. Machine guns during the day were active in consolidation of work. During the day our artillery were active on enemy batteries. We fired a total of 3500 rounds on enemy lines during the night.	X
do	12-1-18		During the morning the R.E. Dump in VANCOUVER ROAD was shelled at intervals. Attention was also paid to the batteries around WILLERVAL	XI

Army Form C. 2118.

WAR DIARY
or
INTELLIGENCE SUMMARY.
(Erase heading not required.)

Instructions regarding War Diaries and Intelligence Summaries are contained in F. S. Regs., Part II. and the Staff Manual respectively. Title pages will be prepared in manuscript.

Place	Date	Hour	Summary of Events and Information	Remarks and references to Appendices
In GHQ Shell	12-1-18 (Sep 6)		2nd FARBUS. Our Machine Guns fired 5,500 rounds during the night on enemy wire.	
-do-	13-1-18		Situation still quiet. The was again slight shelling of the Rd Bank on VANCOUVER ROAD. Our artillery were again between too and three per cent fired 5,800 rounds during the night. The chief target being enemy communication trenches	
-do-	14-1-18		During the day visibility was low, and the situation was very quiet. Our guns fired a total of 4,000 during the night. Our OP's. No movements formed from Sau Po pt. One OP evacuated to R.E.S.	
-do-	15-1-18		Reports from the Battns give nothing of special interest to report. Situation was very quiet and visibility low. Our guns fired 4,500 rounds the enemy were during the night. LIEUT. N.W. DURRANT 50th & CK's granted leave to U.K.	
-do-	16-1-18		Owing to the very bad state of the ground after the thaw operations work were practically nil. Enemy artillery were very quiet. 4,000 rounds or gun in enemy's wire during the night.	
-do-	17-1-18		Nothing of special interest reported during the night or day. Owing to trenches being bad in a very bad state during the night a good deal of enemys wire was the chief target of our fire, a total of 5,500 being fired on same.	
-do-	18-1-18		Situation very quiet. There was slight shelling of VANCOUVER RD. and VILLERVAL. Our artillery were fairly active during the afternoon. We fired	

(A7092) Wt. W12839/M1293. 750,650. 1/17. D.D. & L., Ltd. Forms/C.2118/14.

WAR DIARY
or
INTELLIGENCE SUMMARY

Army Form C. 2118.

Place	Date	Hour	Summary of Events and Information	Remarks and references to Appendices
In the Field	18-1-18 (cont'd)		3,800 rounds on guns on enemy wire. Operation Order No.49 issued for relief by 245th Machine Gun Company. Four ORs reinforcements joined from V Base Depot.	Appx. A/B
-do-	19-1-18		Situation still very quiet in the line. Enemy shelled our forward positions during the morning. Relief by 245th Machine Gun Company started.	
		5.0 pm		
		8.30 pm	Relief completed without incident. Company marched back by sections to ROBERTS CAMP in Divisional Reserve.	
-do-	20-1-18		Company cleaned all kit and equipment. 1 OR wounded during the arm. One OR evacuated to No.42 CCS.	
-do-	21-1-18		During the morning the Company Parade under Section Officers arrange- ment. By the Afternoon the Company parade for Baths. Two ORs proceeded leave to UK.	
-do-	22-1-18		The Morning of the day consisted of all ranks on full munitions order. Later two sections were engaged in cleaning Lewis Gun limbers, whilst two sections were Lewis gun self made practicey limbers.	
-do-	23-1-18		During the morning the Company Training Programme consisted of Physical Training and cleaning and personal training.	

Army Form C. 2118.

WAR DIARY
or
INTELLIGENCE SUMMARY.
(Erase heading not required.)

Instructions regarding War Diaries and Intelligence Summaries are contained in F. S. Regs., Part II. and the Staff Manual respectively. Title pages will be prepared in manuscript.

Place	Date	Hour	Summary of Events and Information	Remarks and references to Appendices
In the Field	24-1-18		During the morning all the N.C.O's of the Company were taken in Physical Training by the Brigade Gymnasium Instructor. The remainder of the Company consisted of Physical Training, Gun Drill and Squad Drill. The Company are still issued with other clothing.	
In the Field	25-1-18		The days training consisted of Physical Training, Gun Drill, Company Drill, and Gas Drill. The afternoon was spent in Recreational Training.	
-do-	26-1-18		The Company had Bombing Practice, Physical Training and Squad Drill during the morning. All N.C.O's had Voice Production and in the afternoon Squad Training.	
-do-	27-1-18		Church Service were arranged for all denominations for the day.	
-do-	28-1-18		The training programme for the day consisted of when Gun Drill, Physical Training, Instruction of gun test, immediate action and Range Training. Operation Order No. 50 issued for relief by 243rd Machine Gun Company on the line.	Appendix III
-do-	29-1-18	2.15 p.m. 4.30 p.m. 8.0 p.m.	Company make preparation for the line during the morning. Company paraded in fighting order and move off by Section. Relief stated. Relief completed without incident. Our guns fired 6,000 rounds on enemy communication trenches.	

(A7092). Wt. W18391/M1293. 750,000. 1/17. D. D. & L., Ltd. Forms/C.2118/14.

WAR DIARY
or
INTELLIGENCE SUMMARY.
(Erase heading not required.)

Army Form C. 2118.

Instructions regarding War Diaries and Intelligence Summaries are contained in F. S. Regs., Part II. and the Staff Manual respectively. Title pages will be prepared in manuscript.

Place	Date	Hour	Summary of Events and Information	Remarks and references to Appendices
In the Field	30th Jan 1918		Situation very quiet. There were hurricane bombardments of FRESNOY PARK and FRESNOY WOOD at intervals by our artillery. Enemy bombarded our front line between ALDERSHOT POSITION and ARLEUX being average active during the day, 450 rounds being fired at enemy platoons.	1/6
do	31-1-18		Situation during the day was very quiet. Our guns fired 700 rounds in scattered attempts during the day, taking advantage of weather conditions.	Appx 1/6

J. Stewart Lieut
for O.C. No. 94 M. G. COY.

SECRET.   *Appendix I*   Copy No. 10.

94th MACHINE GUN COMPANY.
OPERATION ORDER NO. 49.

1. The 94th Machine Gun Company will reliev the 243rd Machine Gun Company in the Letf Brigade Sector on January 9th 1918.

2. **GUIDES.**
   "C" Battery   )
   ½ "A" BRIXTON   ) To be at BRISTOL AT 5-0 p.m.
         BRISTOL   )

   ½ "A" BRIGHTON   ) To be at BRIGHTON at 5-15 p.m.
         BASINGSTOKE)

   ½ "B" ACTON   ) To be at CALK MOUND at 5-15 p.m.
         ASTON   )

   ½ "B" (ANDREW   )
         (ALDERSHOT   )
          AYR   ) To be at BULFORD at 5-15 p.m.
          ANGLESEY   )
          ABERGELE   )
          BULFORD.   )

3. **TRANSPORT.**
   One limber for "C" Section to BRISTOL.
   One limber for "D" Section to BULFORD.
   ½ "A" BRIGHTON   )
         BASINGSTOKE) One limber to BRIGHTON and thence to
   ½ "B" ACTON   )   CALK MOUND.
         ASTON   )
         BRISTOL   )
   ½ "A" BRIXTON   ) One limber to BRISTOL and thence
   ½ "B" ANDREW   )   to BULFORD.
         ALDERSHOT   )

4. **PARADE.**
   The Company will parade in Fighting Order at 2-15 p.m. ready to move at 2-30 p.m.

5. A G.S.Waggon will be available at 2-0 p.m. to transport all stores from ROBERTS CAMP to Transport Lines.

6. Lists of gun teams will be handed in to Orderly Room at 9-30 a.m. to-morrow by Section Officers.

7. **RATIONS.**
   All rations for the 9th inst. will be made up by C.Q.M.S. and packed on limbers by 1-30 p.m.

8. The Camp must be left in a clean and sanitary condition.

9. **TAKING OVER.**
   Tipods, belt-boxes, and all trench stores will be taken over in the line.
   S.O.S. Lines, Defence Scheme and maps will be taken over by Officers at their respective Headquarters.

10. **HEADQUARTERS:-** COMPANY HEADQUARTERS - BRISTOL.
    "A" Section - BRIGHTON.
    "B" Lieut. T. Howard - BRIGHTON.
    2/Lt. W.M.Philbin - ALDERSHOT.
    "C" Section - BRISTOL.
    "D" Section - ANGLESEY.

    Lieut. N.W.Durrant will hand over billets etc. at ROBERTS CAMP.

                        P.T.O.

11. SIGNALS.
There will be stations at BRIGHTON, ANGLESEY, and BRISTOL. Signallers will be detailed by CPL. BRITTAIN.

12. ACKNOWLEDGE.

R M Bailey
Lieut. for Capt.
Comdg. 94th Machine Gun Company.

Copies to:-
            No. 1 - Second-in-Command.
            No. 2 - Transport Officer.
            No. 3 - O.C. "A" Section.
            No. 4 - O.C. "B" Section.
            No. 5 - O.C. "C" Section.
            No. 6 - O.C. "D" Section.
            No. 7 - 2/Lt. W.M.Philbin.
            No. 8 - D.M.G.O.
            No. 9 - O.C. 243 M.G. Coy.
            ✓No.10 - War Diary.
            No.11 - War Diary.
            No.12 - File and C.Q.M.S.

SECRET.   *Appendix II*   Copy No. 10

94th MACHINE GUN COMPANY.
Operation Order No. 49.
By
LIEUT. J.S.WILSON M.C., COMMANDING 94th MACHINE GUN COMPANY.

1. **INFORMATION.** The 94th Machine Gun Company will be relieved in the LEFT Right Brigade Sector (HUDSON POST) on the 19th January 1918.

2. **GROUPS.**

    | ALDERSHOT) | 2/Lt. Ball | ASTON) | Lieut. A.H.Cant |
    | ALNWICK) | at | ACTON) | at |
    | ANDREW) | ALDERSHOT. | BRIGHTON) | BRIGHTON. |
    | | | BASINGSTOKE) | |

    | AYR) | | BRIXTON) | Lieut. T. ~~Heard~~ Howard |
    | ANGLESEY) | Lieut. Richardson | BRISTOL) | at BRISTOL |
    | ABERGELE) | at | BATTERY) | |
    | BULFORD) | ANGLESEY. | | |
    | BINGHAM) | | | |

3. **GUIDES.**
    For 2/Lt. G.H.Ball at LEVIS DUMP.
    For Lieut. A.H.Cant, 2 at BRIGHTON and 2 at CHALK MOUND.
    For Lieut. Richardson at junction of HUDSON C.T. and SASKATCHEWAN ROAD.
    For Lieut. Howard at BRISTOL.
    All guides to be at various dumps by 5-0 p.m.

4. **HANDING-OVER.** All tripods, belt boxes, trench stores, S.O.S. and Defence Lines, Barrage "A", work programme and R.E.Material will be handed over.
    N.B. All gum boots and water cans will be brought out, particular care must be taken regarding gum boots. A limber will be available for gum boots at BRISTOL, these can be carried out and dumped there. No trench stores will be handed over at ALNWICK and BINGHAM.

5. **POSITIONS.** All positions must be handed over as clean as conditions permit. All empty tins within twenty yards radius of guns to be buried. No empty cases or empty S.A.A.boxes to be left.

6. **TRANSPORT.** ~~One~~

    One half limber to LEVIS DUMP for ANDREW and ALDERSHOT.
    1. Rear half to be left at BRISTOL for BRISTOL and BRIXTON.

    2. One half limber to CHALK MOUND for ACTON and ASTON.
    Rear half to be left at BRIGHTON for BRIGHTON and BASINGSTOKE.

    3. One limber to HUDSON C.T. for AYR, ANGLESEY, ABERGELE and BULFORD.

    4. One limber to BRISTOL for BATTERY POSITION, BINGHAM and ALNWICK.

    5. One limber to BRISTOL for Headquarters.

    6. One limber to BRISTOL for gum boots. (Gas N.C.O. will be in charge of gum boots).

7. **BILLETS.** Sections will march back under Section Officers independently to ROBERTS CAMP, where a hot meal will be provided.

8. **TAKING-OVER.** 2/Lt. W.H.PHILBIN will arrange to take over ROBERTS CAMP, and will have a supply of fire wood for each hut.

9. **ACKNOWLEDGE.**
    Copies to:-
    1 to O.C. Company.
    2 to O.C. "A" Section.
    3 to O.C. "B" Section.
    4 to O.C. "C" Section.
    5 to O.C. "D" Section.
    6 to Transport Officer.
    7 to O.C. 243 M.G.Coy.
    8 to D.M.G.O.
    9 to File.
    10 to War Diary.
    11 to War Diary.

    Lieut.
    Comdg. 94th Machine Gun Coy.

SECRET.   Appendix III   Copy No. 9
                        94th MACHINE GUN COMPANY
                        OPERATION ORDER NO. 50.

1. The 94th Machine Gun Company will relieve the 243rd Machine Gun Company in the Left Brigade Sector on January 30th 1918.

2. GUIDES.   All guides to be at the respective dumps at 5-30 p.m.
   "D"   ALDERSHOT   )
         ALNWICK   ) To be at LEVIS DUMP. (Limber can be taken
         ANDREWS   )   to WINNIPEG ROAD.
         BINGHAM   )
   "C"   AYR   )
         ANGLESEY   ) To be at junction of HUDSON C.T. AND
         ABERGELE   )   SASKATCHEWAN ROAD.
         BULFORD   )
   "B"   BRIGHTON   ) To be at BRIGHTON.   BINGHAM will be under
         BASINGSTOKE)   -do-   the command of 2/Lt.
         ACTON   ) To be at CHALKMOUND.   G.H.Ball.
         ASTON   )   -do-
   "A"   BRIXTON   )
         BRISTOL   ) To be at BRISTOL.
         BATTERY POS.)

3. TRANSPORT.
   There will be one limber per Section and one for Company Headquarters, which will be at the dumps stated at 5-30 p.m. Care must be taken that the limbers do not cross the sky line in day-light.   All limbers will be loaded by 12 noon.
   A G.S. Wagon will be available at 2-0 p.m. to transport stores from ROBERTS CAMP to Transport Lines.

4. PARADE.
   The Company will parade at 2-15 p.m. ready to move off at 2-30 p.m.

5. Lists of gun teams will be handed in to Orderly Room by 9-0 a.m. by Section Officers.

6. RATIONS.
   All rations for the 30th inst. will be made up by C.Q.M.S. and packed on the respective limbers by 12 noon.

7. The Camp must be left in a clean and sanitary condition.

8. TAKING OVER.
   Tripods, Belt-boxes, and all trench stores will be taken over in the line. S.O.S. Lines, Defence Scheme and maps will be taken over by Officers at their respective Headquarters.
   The attention of all Officers is drawn to 94th Inf. Bde. G 6 dated 27-1-18. This letter can be seen in the Orderly Room.

9. HEADQUARTERS.
   COMPANY HEADQUARTERS - BRISTOL.
   Lieut. T. Howard - Transport Lines.
   "A" Section - BRISTOL.
   2/Lt. G.H.Hood - Bristol.
   "B" Section (2/Lt. Watkins) - Brighton.
   "C" Section (2/Lt. Ball) - ANGLESEY.
   "D" Section (Lieut. G.E.Richardson) ALDERSHOT.
   Lieut. T. Howard will hand over billets etc. at ROBERTS CAMP.

10. SIGNALS.
    There will be stations at ANGLESEY, ALDERSHOT, BRIGHTON and BRISTOL.

11. ACKNOWLEDGE.

                                              T. Howard Lieut.
                                              O.C. 94th Machine Gun Company.

Copies to:-
    No. 1 - O.C.Company.
    No. 2 - Transport Officer.
    Nor 3 - O.C. "A" Section.
    No. 4 - O.C. "B" Section.
    No. 5 - O.C. "C" Section.
    No. 6 - O.C. "D" Section.
    No. 7 - D.M.G.O.
    No. 8 - O.C. 243 M.G.Coy.
    ✓No. 9 - War Diary.
    No.10 - War Diary.
    No.11 - War Diary File.

CONFIDENTIAL

WAR DIARY
(ORIGINAL)
OF
94th Machine Gun Company

From 1st February 1918
To
28th February 1918

VOLUME 26

Army Form C. 2118.

WAR DIARY
or
INTELLIGENCE SUMMARY.
(Erase heading not required.)

Place	Date	Hour	Summary of Events and Information	Remarks and references to Appendices
In the Field.	1-2-18		Company still in the line (Left Brigade FRESNOY SECTOR) During the day the situation was quiet generally. There was only occasional fog firing during the day by Artillery on both sides. Activity increased at night, especially between 9.30 pm and 11.0 pm. There was slight hostile shelling and trench mortaring on front in vicinity of HUDSON POST. Hostile Machine Gun fire was below normal during the night. Occasional bursts were fired by our Machine Guns by day during the fog. For an experiment all but one gun was fired without check the day, night conditions were observed owing to fog. and guns were mounted and manned as per night orders. A total of 6,000 rounds were fired on enemy tracks and trenches during the day.	[signature]
In the Field	2-2-18.		During the day there was considerable aerial activity on both sides, with correspondingly increased A.A. fire. Several enemy aircraft attempted to cross our lines but were driven back. Our Machine Guns at AYR & BASINGSTOKE fired on two enemy planes which came within range at 1.30 am and 11.35am. coming from the direction of MERICOURT & ACHEVILLE, expenditure 600 rounds. Situation was fairly quiet until 1.0 pm. when there was considerable hostile gas shelling. This was scattered all over the sector. After mid-night the night was fairly quiet. Between 2-0 pm a 3.0 pm hostile trench mortars were active against our front line systems, especially in the vicinity of ANDREWS, many parts of the trench being	[signature]

Army Form C. 2118.

WAR DIARY
or
INTELLIGENCE SUMMARY.
(Erase heading not required.)

Place	Date	Hour	Summary of Events and Information	Remarks and references to Appendices
In the Field	2-2-18 (cont)		Mourn nw. Vice OR3 granted leave to U.K.	
-do-	3-2-18		Situation quiet generally. Enemy aircraft on both sides very active again. At 7.35 a.m. and 9.20 a.m. the enemy low ran out lines (5,890) from MERICOURT and turned immediately - 350 rounds being fired - no effect observed. During afternoon 6 enemy planes flew over our lines but were out of range. During the afternoon the enemy's shelling was very scattered, thus continued intermittently throughout the night. Artillery activity in the Divisional area on our right was very quiet. There was only slight hostile trench mortar activity on our immediate front. Hostile machine Gun fired occasional bursts on our support lines during the hours of darkness. We fired a total of 8,000 rounds on enemy ahead. One OR left for Special Signal Course at DUNSTABLE.	
-do-	4-2-18		During the 24 hours the situation was quiet. Shortly after 2 p.m. enemy aircraft activity increased. One enemy plane circled our lines coming from the direction of MERICOURT but was soon turned back by anti-aircraft fire. Our guns at BASINGSTOKE fired 250 rounds. 240 rounds were observed. Enemy bombarded WILLERVAL with gas shells at 8.0 p.m. and gas was blown into L2 Sector by the wind. The effect of this gas was felt at 8.15 p.m. about the vicinity of VANCOUVER ROAD. 2 ORs granted leave to U.K.	

Army Form C. 2118.

WAR DIARY
or
INTELLIGENCE SUMMARY.
(Erase heading not required.)

Instructions regarding War Diaries and Intelligence Summaries are contained in F. S. Regs., Part II. and the Staff Manual respectively. Title pages will be prepared in manuscript.

Place	Date	Hour	Summary of Events and Information	Remarks and references to Appendices
In the Field	5-2-18		In conjunction with artillery we carried out harassing fire at 10.15 p.m. and 11.0 p.m. firing on various enemy tracks and roads which were within range. In reply to this shoot the enemy only retaliated was small, with the exception of Trench Mortars which were very active where against our front line. No damage was done to our emplacements. A heavy bombardment was noticed on the front of the Corps on our left at about 10.0 p.m. Enemy shelled 21' Sector with gas shells at intervals during the night. One enemy aeroplane crossed our lines about 4.0 p.m. flying very high to be engaged by anti aircraft batteries. During the night machine guns by indirect and overhead fire, they above mentioned shot a total of 24000 rounds were fired.	[signature]
do	6-2-18		Situation fairly quiet, hostile artillery were active during the day Enemy machine guns were active during the hour of stand to but nothing of special interest was observed. A total of 10,500 rounds were fired during the night by enemy MG and Vickers.	[signature]
do	7-2-18		In consequence of Divisional Order No. 603/8 the situation was to be kept very quiet. No firing was done at enemy MG during the period except when AREUX was fired at intervals throughout the day and night. Enemy machine gun was inconsiderable their range of activity was fair, their harassing was by no means accurate. 2nd Lt O.R.E. Humfrymands joined from BASE DEPOT Officer Order No. 51 issued for relief of 248th Machine Gun Company.	[signature]

(A7092) Wt. W12839/M1293. 750,000. 1/17. D. D. & L., Ltd. Forms/C.2118.14

Army Form C. 2118.

WAR DIARY
or
INTELLIGENCE SUMMARY.
(Erase heading not required.)

Instructions regarding War Diaries and Intelligence Summaries are contained in F. S. Regs., Part II. and the Staff Manual respectively. Title pages will be prepared in manuscript.

Place	Date	Hour	Summary of Events and Information	Remarks and references to Appendices
In the Field.	8.2.18		During the day the situation was quiet. There was the usual aircraft activity on both sides. A few enemy planes were observed but were well out of range of machine gun fire. During the day the time was spent in making preparations for relief. LIEUT. A.M.GANT granted leave to UK.	[initials]
		5.30 pm	Relief commenced	
		6.10 pm	Relief completed without incident and Company marched back by sections to ROBERTS CAMP into Divisional Reserve. On arrival at ROBERTS CAMP the men were issued with a hot meal.	
-do-	9.2.18		During the morning the Company had baths, they also cleaned up all gun kits, ammunition and personal kit after coming out of the line. CAPT. R.L.BAILEY rejoined from leave.	[initials]
-do-	10.2.18		During the day Church Services were arranged for all denominations as follows:- 9.40 am Roman Catholics Parade. 10.30 am Church of England Parade. 10.30 am Non-Conformists Parade. During the afternoon there was an inspection of arms by the Commanding Officer. One O.R. was evacuated sick to No.142 C.C.S.	[initials]

Army Form C. 2118.

WAR DIARY
or
INTELLIGENCE SUMMARY.
(Erase heading not required.)

Instructions regarding War Diaries and Intelligence Summaries are contained in F. S. Regs., Part II. and the Staff Manual respectively. Title pages will be prepared in manuscript.

Place	Date	Hour	Summary of Events and Information	Remarks and references to Appendices
In the Field	10-2-18 (contd)		11 O.R's (attached) were returned to duty as "Not likely to become efficient Machine Gunners.	[sig]
-do-	11-2-18		The order for the day consisted of:-	[sig]
		9.0 am	C.O's Orderly Room	
		9.0am to 9.30 am	Parades under Section Officers	
		9.30 am to 10.0 am	Brigade & inspection in full marching order	
		10.15am to 12.30 pm	Shirt inspection	
		2.0 pm to 4.0 pm	Arm inspection by Armourer & cleaning of Arms parts	
-do-	12-2-18		The training Programme for the day consisted of:-	[sig]
		9.15 am to 10.0 am	Physical Training	
		10.15 am to 10.30 am	Company parade and inspection in full marching order	
		10.45 am to 12 Noon	Mechanism and stoppages	
		2.0 pm to 4.0 pm	Company Gas Inspection, Recreational Training and work on digging bomb sets.	
			One O.R. evacuated to No.42. C.C.S.	
-do-	13-2-18		During the day the following programme was carried out:-	[sig]
			One N.C.O. and two men per Section parade at 9 am for work at Transport Lines.	
		9.45 am	C.O. Orderly Room	

Army Form C. 2118.

WAR DIARY
or
INTELLIGENCE SUMMARY.
(Erase heading not required.)

Instructions regarding War Diaries and Intelligence Summaries are contained in F. S. Regs., Part II. and the Staff Manual respectively. Title pages will be prepared in manuscript.

Place	Date	Hour	Summary of Events and Information	Remarks and references to Appendices
In the Field	13.2.18 Cont		9.0 am to 9.45 am - Physical Training 10.0 am to 10.30 am - Company Parade & inspection in Fighting Order 10.30 am to 12.30 pm - Entrenching tools 2.0 pm to 4.0 pm - Recreational Training One OR granted leave to UK.	
-do-	14.2.18		The Training for the day carried out :- 7.45 am - EO's Orderly Room 9.0 am to 9.45 am. Physical Training 10.0 am to 12.30 pm Camp Fatigues A party 17 ORs. was detailed for work on Transport Lines after the Bayonet Training One OR granted leave to UK.	
-do-	15.2.18		The Training carried out during the day was as follows :- 7.45 am - EO's Orderly Room 9.0 am to 9.45 am. Physical Training 10.0 am to 10.30 am Company Parade in Fighting Order for EO's inspection. 10.30 am to 12.30 pm Gun-cleaning and Transport Fatigues 3.30 pm. 'E' Section proceeded to the line for work on Shell hole positions. One OR granted leave to UK. CAPT. R.L. BAILEY &. LIEUT. T. HOWARD proceeded to Small Arms School G.H.Q.	

Army Form C. 2118.

WAR DIARY
or
INTELLIGENCE SUMMARY.

(Erase heading not required.)

Instructions regarding War Diaries and Intelligence Summaries are contained in F. S. Regs., Part II. and the Staff Manual respectively. Title pages will be prepared in manuscript.

Place	Date	Hour	Summary of Events and Information	Remarks and references to Appendices
In the Field	15.2.18 (cont)		LIEUT. J.S. HUSON M.C. took over command of the company in the absence of CAPT. R.L. BAILEY M.C.	
-do-	16.2.18		During the morning the following training programme was carried out:- 7.45 am to 9.45 am C.O's orderly Room. 9.0 am to 9.45 am Physical Training. 10 am to 10.30 am Company parade & inspection in Fighting Order. 10.30 am to 12.30 pm Camp and Transport Fatigue. One O.R. granted leave to UK.	
-do-	17.2.18		Church Parade for all denominations were arranged for the morning:- The hours being 9.40 am Roman Catholic Parade. 10.0 am Church of England Parade. 10.30 am Non conformist Parade. A portion of the day was also spent in Camp Fatigue. One O.R. granted leave to UK.	
-do-	18.2.18		The morning of the day consisted of:- 9.0 am to 9.45 am Physical Training. N.C.O's - Communication Drill. 10 am to 10.30 am Company Parade and Inspection in Fighting Order.	

Army Form C. 2118.

WAR DIARY
or
INTELLIGENCE SUMMARY.
(Erase heading not required.)

Instructions regarding War Diaries and Intelligence Summaries are contained in F.S. Regs., Part II. and the Staff Manual respectively. Title pages will be prepared in manuscript.

Place	Date	Hour	Summary of Events and Information	Remarks and references to Appendices
In the Field	18.7.18 (cont)		10.45am to 12.30pm Use of Heliolamp & Lucasgong drill. 2.0 pm to 4.0 pm Recreational Training. Operation Order No.52 issued for relief of 93rd Machine Gun Company in Right Brigade Sector. One O.R. granted leave to UK.	Appendix I
Do.	19.7.18		During the morning the Company made final preparations for the relief.	
		3.0 pm	Company paraded in Fighting Order and move off to the line.	
		5.30 pm	Relief started.	
		8.45 pm	Relief completed without incident.	
		9.0 pm	Enemy laid down a very heavy barrage along and front line consisting of 5.9", 4.2", 77mm and light and medium trench mortars the following localities on the Brigade front:— BRITANNIA Trench, Right (J BRAND) Trench, SEVERN VALLEY, BLACKBURN ROAD, ARLEUX OAK POST, and ARLEUX LOOP SOUTH. A strong German raiding party followed close behind the barrage, and a party tried to rush out positions at ALTON. On this barrage being laid down all our guns opened fire immediately with intense fire on their S.O.S. lines and the S.O.S. signal was then sent up on our Brigade sector. This signal was afterwards received by wire, meanwhile the	

WAR DIARY or INTELLIGENCE SUMMARY

Army Form C. 2118.

Place	Date	Hour	Summary of Events and Information	Remarks and references to Appendices
In the Field	19-2-18		Guns kept up intense fire. The gun at ACTON POSTER was received soon after the opening of the enemy barrage and was consequently out of action. 2/Lt. G.H. BALL, who was in command of this post immediately withdrew his post to the dug out. As soon as the barrage lifted the Germans jumped into the trench, and threw two bombs down the dug out, but did no damage. 2/Lt. G.H. BALL with the remainder of his post rushed out and encountered the close and very hard fighting which took and eventually, after the assaulants with loss, much credit being due to the gallant leadership of 2/Lt. G.H. BALL. Our guns fired 29,000 rounds during the raid and from section shots every gun fired excellently, very few stoppages being reported. On return from the ACTON MG POST the enemy left 1 killed and 3 wounded in our hands.	
In the Field	20-2-18		Situation quiet after raid. The had scattered shelling by the enemy in the early hours of the morning, many shells falling in the vicinity of SAPPER DUMP. A few gas shells were also fired into VILLERVAL. Enemy Trench Mortars were active against our front line. Machine guns on both sides were active.	

WAR DIARY
or
INTELLIGENCE SUMMARY

Army Form C. 2118.

Place	Date	Hour	Summary of Events and Information	Remarks and references to Appendices
In the Field	21.7.18		Situation during the day # was very quiet. Shortly after noon a field gun registered on junction of OAK ALLEY and ARLEUX LOOP. There was no direct hit. One enemy plane was brought down at 2.0 p.m. in the direction of NEUVIREUIL. At 6.0 p.m. a large number of complete lights were sent up from enemy lines near ACHEVILLE. Enemy trench Mortars were quiet during the night. About a dozen gas shells were fired into ARLEUX. There was slight shelling of WILLERVAL - BAILLEUL Road. One O.R. granted leave to U.K.	
-do-	22.7.18		During the early hours of the morning ARLEUX WOOD was lightly shelled. At 3.0 p.m. burst fired at our position at CHESTER. The front areas of L2 Sector received attention from hostile light and medium trench mortars between 7.0 a.m. and 10.0 a.m. SAPPER DUMP was lightly shelled at 9.45 p.m. Enemy machine guns were fairly active during the hours of darkness. One O.R. granted leave to U.K.	
-do-	23.7.18		The front of L2 Sector was again shelled by light and medium trench mortars about 9.0 a.m. This morning at 8.0 a.m. about a dozen H.E. shells fell behind our ASHFIELD position. ARLEUX WOOD received slight	

Army Form C. 2118.

WAR DIARY
or
INTELLIGENCE SUMMARY.
(Erase heading not required.)

Instructions regarding War Diaries and Intelligence Summaries are contained in F. S. Regs., Part II. and the Staff Manual respectively. Title pages will be prepared in manuscript.

Place	Date	Hour	Summary of Events and Information	Remarks and references to Appendices
In the Field	23.2.19		attention, the action being chiefly H.E. Enemy Trench Mortars were active against our Left Brigade Sector. At 6.0 p.m. a few gas shells fell in the vicinity of ARLEUX ROAD. At 12 noon VANCOUVER ROAD was shelled with H.E. & Shrapnel. There was intermittent shelling around our positions CUMMINGS CROSSBY & CANT between 3.0 p.m. & 5.0 p.m. A great deal of individual movement was seen in C.7.b. v.d. Enemy aeroplane aircraft were active during the afternoon and we fired a total of 250 rounds into enemy aircraft. Gave to W.K.	
-do-	24.2.19		Our ALTON position was lightly shelled about noon. Few shells fell just in front & one on it. BLACKBURN gun Left. After 6 p.m. a few gas shells fell in the vicinity of SUGAR FACTORY ROAD. STATION WOOD was heavily shelled between 4.45 p.m. and 5.45 p.m. with H.E. About 10.30 p.m. several Trench Mortar shells fell on the ARLEUX ROAD near ALTON. Enemy machine guns fired occasional bursts during the night. Enemy Patrol were active during the afternoon and but were all put of range of M.G. fire like was individual movement was again observed in C.7.b.q.d. One O.R. granted leave to U.K.	

WAR DIARY
or
INTELLIGENCE SUMMARY.
(Erase heading not required.)

Army Form C. 2118.

Place	Date	Hour	Summary of Events and Information	Remarks and references to Appendices
In the Field	25-2-18		During the day the situation was quiet. There was only scattered shelling by the enemy, no special shots being observed. Our front wire fairly active. Movement was observed round BOIS VILAIN, and parties of about 20 men were seen moving about this area. Operations order No. 53 issued for relief by 93rd M.G. Col.	Initials Appendix III
In the Field	26-2-18		Green line reinforced. Situation fairly quiet. Went averaged activity. During the latter part of the day the time was spent making preparations for relief. Relieved by 93rd M.G. Coy. Relief completed at 8-30 p.m. the Company marched back to huts at Roberts Camp.	Initials

Army Form C. 2118.

WAR DIARY
or
INTELLIGENCE SUMMARY

(Erase heading not required.)

Instructions regarding War Diaries and Intelligence Summaries are contained in F. S. Regs., Part II. and the Staff Manual respectively. Title pages will be prepared in manuscript.

Place	Date	Hour	Summary of Events and Information	Remarks and references to Appendices
In the field	27.2.18		During the day the company cleaned up all gun Kit, ammunition, and personal Kit, after central out of the line, and made preparations for march to Laust and in the evening the company had baths. Two OR's granted leave to UK.	
-do-	28.2.18		The orders for the day consisted of :- 8.30 a.m. A party of 8 men reported to 6 A.M.S. for loading S.A.A. etc. The remainder of the company packing all limbers and had General clean up of mens huts and camp ready to march off at 1 P.M. 12.50 P.M. Company paraded ready to march off at 1 P.M. 2-30 P.M. Company arrived at F.38.F.6.6. BRUNEHAULT FARM Area. Two OR's granted leave to UK. One OR reinforcement from Base Depot.	Offs in movement Diary

[Signature]

Apen I. Operation orders by LIEUT J.S. WILSON M.C.
No 10   Commanding 94th M.G. Coy
                    Operation Order No. 51.

I. INFORMATION

The 94th M.G. Coy will be relieved in the line on the 8th inst by 243rd M.G. Coy.

II. GUIDES

| ANDREWS, ALDERSHOT, ALNWICK, BINGHAM, ALTON, ASTON | At Lewis dump | AYR, ANGLESEA, ABERGELE, BULFORD | At junction of Saskatchewan Road & HUDSON C.T. |
| BRIGHTON, BASINGSTOKE | At BRIGHTON | BRISTOL, BRIXTON, BRISTON POST | At BRISTOL |

All guides at 5:30 P.M.

III. HANDING OVER

All tripods, belt boxes, belt filling machines, trench stores (this includes ANTI TANK AMMN) S.O.S. lines, maps & instructions will be handed over. Positions and trench stores must be shown. All lines for a nucleus of 25 must be cleared. Any N.C.O failing to observe this order will be summarily dealt with.

IV. TRANSPORT

One limber for	ALDERSHOT, ALNWICK, ANDREWS, BINGHAM	At Winnipeg Road thence back to Lewis dump 8.0 P.M.
One limber for	ALTON, ASTON, BASINGSTOKE, BRIGHTON	At Winnipeg Road thence back to BRIGHTON via Saskatchewan Road. Limber to be at Winnipeg Road 7:45 P.M.
One limber for	AYR, ANGLESEA, ABERGELE, BULFORD	At junction of Saskatchewan Road & HUDSON C.T. 7.30 P.M.
One limber for	BRISTOL, BRIXTON, BATTERY	At BRISTOL 1.30 P.M.
One limber for	H.Q.	BRISTOL at 6.30 P.M.

Sections will march back personally conducted by section officers to ROBERTS CAMP where a hot meal will be provided for them.

CONTINUED

Second in Command will arrange to take over
Camp and arrange for the move.
Completion of relief will be noted to Bde HQ
by the code word SIGNS DEFINED AT ———

ACKNOWLEDGE

COPIES TO
1 O.C. A Section
2 O.C. B
3 O.C. C
4 O.C. D
5 —
6 2ND IN COMMAND
6 TRANSPORT OFFICER
7 D.M.G.O.
8 O.C. 243 M.G.Coy
9 —
10 WAR DIARY
11 FILE

Wilson Lieut.
O.C. N-94 M.G.Coy.

Appx 2

Operation Order No. 23.

1. **INFORMATION.**
The 24th Machine Gun Company will relieve the 63rd Machine Gun Company in the Right Brigade Sector on February 19th 1

2. **GUIDES.**
Guides for all guns will be at CASHIFF at 5-30 p.m.

3. **DISTRIBUTION.**

ALTON	}		BARNSTAPLE	}	
ASHFIELD	}	"C" Section.	BOLTON	}	"D" Section.
GARDINS	}		CHESTER	}	
CASHTOUS	}		COSTY	}	

CHESHIRE	}		BLACKBURN	}	
CROSSLEY	}	"A" Section.	BERKLEY	}	"B" Section.
CAMP	}		BURNLE	}	
CLAYTON	}		ASHLEY	}	

4. **HEADQUARTERS.**
"C" Section ALTON   "B" Section - BERKLEY.
"D" Section BARNSTAPLE.   "A" Section - CROSSLEY.
COMPANY HEADQUARTERS & CASHIFF.
The Company Sergeant Major will be in charge of CASHIFF & CASHIEL

5. **COMMUNICATION.**
Signal Stations for buzzing only will be at:-
BARNSTAPLE, BERKLEY, CROSSLEY, CASHIFF.
Two men per Section will be detailed to stay at Company Headquarters.

6. **TAKING OVER.**
All S.O.S lines, Battle lines, Trench Stores, Belt Boxes and tripods will be taken over, and receipts given.

7. **PARADE.**
The Company will parade at 5-0 p.m. and move off at 5-15 p.m.
Order of march "C" - "D" - "B" - "A".

8. **TRANSPORT.**
"D" Section - One limber to COSTY and CHESTER thence to junction of Arleux Loop and Willerval-Arleux Road.
"C" Section - One limber to CASHIFF, thence to ARLEUX.
"A" Section - One limber to junction of RED LINE and ARLEUX-WILLERVAL ROAD.
"B" Section - One limber as "A" Section.
Headquarters - One limber to CASHIFF.
All limbers will be at SUNKEN CAMP as soon as possible to be loaded. Limbers to be over Ridge as soon as possible and to their respective Dumps.

9. **DISTRIBUTION SLIPS.**
Distribution Slips will be in Orderly Room by 8-30 a.m. on the 19th Inst.

10. **SANITATION.**
BRIDGE CAMP will be vacated in a clean and sanitary condition.

11. **COMPLETION OF RELIEF.**
Relief complete will be wired to Company Headquarters by the code phrase "WATCH GLASS ARRIVED A" ....

12. **RATIONS.**
Ration Dumps for 20th inst. will be notified later.

13. **ACKNOWLEDGE.**

Copies to:- 1.- O.C. Company.
2.- Lieut. F.W.Durrant.
3.- Lieut. E.G.Richardson.
4.- Lieut. A.W.S.Watkins.
5.- 2/Lt. G.A.Hall.
6.- 2/Lt. J.W.Road.
7.- O.C. 23rd M.G.Coy.
8.- O.C. "C".
9.- O.C. "D".
10.- War Diary.
11.- War Diary.
12.- File.

Lieut.
O.C. 24th M.G.Coy.

SECRET. 94th Machine Gun Company. Copy No. Apper. III
Operation Order No. 55.

1. INFORMATION.
The 94th Machine Gun Company will be relieved in the line by the 93rd Machine Gun Company on the night of [illegible] February.

2. GUIDES.
None will be required.

3. TRANSPORT.
One limber for "B" Section at junction of [illegible] LINE and [illegible] SUGAR FACTORY ROAD at 7-0 p.m. - One limber for "A" Section at junction of [illegible]-SUGAR FACTORY ROAD and [illegible] LINE at 8-0 p.m. - One limber for "C" Section at [illegible] LOOP thence back to [illegible] LINE at 8-0 p.m. - One limber for "D" Section at [illegible] TRENCH thence to [illegible] LOOP at 7-30 p.m. - One limber for Company Headquarters at [illegible] as soon as possible.

4. HANDING-OVER.
Trench Stores and all lines and maps will be handed over, also belt boxes and tripods.

5. POSITIONS.
Positions will be handed over scrupulously clean. Water and firewood will be collected and handed-over at each position.

6. ON RELIEF.
Sections will move back under Section Officers to [illegible] where a hot meal will be provided.

7. CODE [illegible].
Completion of relief will be wired to Company Headquarters by the word "[illegible]".

8. ACKNOWLEDGE.

Lieut.
[illegible] O.C. 94th Machine Gun Company.

COPIES TO:-
1 - O.C. Company
2 - Transport Officer.
3 - O.C. "A" Section.
4 - O.C. "B" Section.
5 - O.C. "C" Section.
6 - O.C. "D" Section.
7 - O.C. 83rd M.G. Coy.
8 - D.H.Q.
9 - O.C.
10 - War Diary.
11 - War Diary.
12 - File.

Apex IV

MOVEMENT ORDER.

By :- LIEUT. J. S. WILSON M.C., Commanding 94th M. G. Coy.

28-2-18.

8-30.a.m. - A party of 8 men to report to C.Q.M.S. for loading S.A.A. etc., this party will march off at 2.p.m. under Sgt. Eaton.
Signaller to be detailed to guide the limber of S.A.A. to new Camp and remain there in charge, moving off at 8-30.a.m. from Transport Lines.
C.S.M. will make a list of Camp Stores by 10.a.m.
Lieut. Hood will proceed to Camp (B) at 10.a.m.
All blankets rolled and packed and be in Guard Room by 10-30.a.m.
Guard dismounted at 11-0.a.m.
All Officers valises loaded by 11-30.a.m.
Mess Cart to move off by 11-30.a.m.
Company Parade at 12-50.p.m., ready to move off by 1.p.m.
Dress :- Full Marching Order, Steel Helmets to be worn.
All Fighting Limbers to be ready to move off by XXXXXX 12-50.p.m.
Officers Chargers to be outside Officers Mess at 12-50.p.m.
S.A.A. Limbers to be in road outside Transport Lines by 1.p.m. ready to join column as Company moves out.
Camp will be visited by 2nd in command at 12-30.p.m.

JSWilson Lieut.,
Commdg. 94th Machine Gun Coy.

www.ingramcontent.com/pod-product-compliance
Lightning Source LLC
Chambersburg PA
CBHW080844010526
44114CB00017B/2367